Poverty

thefacts

4th edition

Marilyn Howard
Alison Garnham
Geoff Fimister and
John Veit-Wilson

CPAG • 94 White Lion Street • London N1 9PF

CPAG promotes action for the relief, directly or indirectly, of poverty among children and families with children. We work to ensure that those on low incomes get their full entitlements to welfare benefits. In our campaigning and information work we seek to improve benefits and policies for low-income families in order to eradicate the injustice of poverty. If you are not already supporting us, please consider making a donation, or ask for details of our membership schemes and publications.

Poverty Publication 103

Published by CPAG
94 White Lion Street, London N1 9PF

© CPAG 2001

ISBN 1 901698 23 8

The views expressed in this book are the authors' and do not necessarily express those of CPAG.

A CIP record for this book is available from the British Library

Cover and design by Devious Designs 0114 275 5634
Typeset by Boldface 020 7253 2014
Printed by Russell Press 0115 978 4505
Cover photos reproduced with permission of Format Photographers

CONTENTS

ACKNOWLEDGEMENTS

We are very grateful to all the people who contributed to this book. Special thanks must go to Fran Bennett for her invaluable comments on the draft manuscript. We would also like to thank Eileen Evason, Gill Scott, Eldin Fahmy and Tim Marsh for their time and help. We are grateful to Renee Carolan and William Pitt at the Department for Work and Pensions (DWP) for providing additional information from the HBAI series and to Bob Downes in the Analytical Services Division at the DWP. Thanks are also due to Alison Key for managing the production of this edition, Paula McDiarmid for proofreading the text and Sylvia Potter for compiling the index. Finally, a big thank you to our families and friends for their support.

ABOUT THE AUTHORS

Marilyn Howard is an independent social policy analyst, and has undertaken research and consultancy for a number of voluntary organisations, think tanks and universities, including government-commissioned evaluation. She has been an adviser to two select committees and is currently a member of the Disability Living Allowance Advisory Board. She has also worked as a probation officer, welfare rights adviser and community social worker.

Alison Garnham is Director of Policy, Research and Information at the National Council for One Parent Families and has worked there since 1997. Her long track record in the voluntary sector includes work for women's organisations and many years' experience as a welfare rights adviser before joining CPAG for seven years. At CPAG she co-authored a number of publications about the Child Support Act and has subsequently written about lone parenthood and child poverty. Before joining the National Council for One Parent Families she was Senior Lecturer in Social Policy at the University of North London.

Geoff Fimister currently combines his work as Research Officer for CPAG with freelance writing and consultancy on benefit policy issues. He was previously the manager and policy specialist of Newcastle City Council's Welfare Rights Service, which he set up in 1974. During this time he also worked as a welfare rights adviser to the Association of Metropolitan Authorities and subsequently the Local Government Association, on housing, social services, financial and anti-poverty issues, and has written and lectured extensively in these fields.

John Veit-Wilson is Emeritus Professor of Social Policy at the University of Northumbria and Visiting Professor in the Department of Sociology and Social Policy at the University of Newcastle upon Tyne. He has been engaged in research into poverty measures and their relationships with income maintenance systems since 1964, and was a founding member of CPAG in 1965.

Introduction

Many people associated with CPAG would say that one of the most frustrating aspects of arguing, lobbying and campaigning against poverty over the years has been the low political profile which this vital issue has too often suffered. We could not make this complaint today: after a discouraging start, implementing its predecessor's benefit cuts in the name of financial prudence, the Labour Government elected in 1997 subsequently changed its tune and has pushed poverty high up the political agenda.[1]

This Government has now been re-elected for a second term with a huge majority. What attitude should CPAG take, in the still fairly unfamiliar context of dealing with an administration which not only agrees that child poverty exists, but has said that it wants to end it and has indeed taken important steps along that road?

This is not to say that we are in an era when all news is good news. Yes, child poverty is being addressed, but other measures such as increased compulsion within the benefit system, the treatment of asylum seekers and the threat of further restriction of incapacity and housing benefits point in a different direction. Inequality also continues to grow – and does not seem to be regarded by the Government as a problem.

In many ways, lobbying and campaigning around poverty represents a more subtle and sophisticated challenge when policy is a mixture of welcome and unwelcome messages, than it does when bad news is generally the rule. CPAG has aimed to be a constructive critic, giving credit where it is due and challenge when it is required. We like to think that this approach will gain us more respect – and lead to our being taken more seriously – than the extremes of uncritical sycophancy or grumpy opposition.

But CPAG has a number of functions, and lobbying and campaigning for change is only part of the story. We also provide information, advice and training to a wide range of audiences and readerships. *Poverty: the facts* has its own place in that work. In a way, this book is something of a hybrid: it can be read through as a narrative, informing the reader and spreading awareness of the issues; or it can be used like a policy equivalent of our benefits guides – a ready source of indexed information. Given the current profile and pace of change of the poverty debate, a new edition is overdue.

WHAT POVERTY MEANS

Among the most frequent questions which CPAG is asked are 'what is the poverty line?' and 'how many children are in poverty?' The answers, of course, depend on what you mean by 'poverty'. The debate has been broadened out in recent times to embrace wider concepts of social exclusion, of which income poverty is one (albeit a major) aspect. However, even focusing specifically on income poverty is far from straightforward.

The idea that poverty means total destitution is now pretty much discredited. It seems these days to be generally accepted that a social context is necessary. What are the broad standards of social participation in a given society at a given time? It is in relation to these standards that we can start to identify and measure deprivations which can be said to constitute poverty.

Even accepting this approach, there are still alternative opinions and definitions. Recently, in the UK as elsewhere, the debate has tended to be conducted in terms of various percentages of different types of average income, the Government currently preferring to use incomes below 60 per cent of the median after housing costs as its poverty definition. This method, while preferable to some others, nevertheless has important weaknesses – notably the fact that, while it tells us about the distribution of incomes, it tells us nothing about the level of need represented by a particular percentage point or whether or not incomes at or above that point are sufficient for participation. To put it another way, we might say that percentages of averages are, strictly speaking, *proxies* for poverty lines, rather than measures of poverty as such.

This approach is, nevertheless, more socially relevant than notions of 'absolute' destitution. It is also much better than using the social assistance rates. For many years, it was conventional to cite the level of income support (and its predecessors) – or a percentage mark-up on that level – as the poverty line. The level of state minimum benefits and the numbers receiving them are interesting and very important matters, but they are problematic as definitions of poverty. They do not represent need, but simply what the state has decided to pay. If they are used as the basis of a poverty definition, then a real increase in their value will increase poverty correspondingly, while the easiest and cheapest way to bring down the numbers in poverty is to reduce the benefits.

It is because the issues around definitions of poverty need to be analysed and made explicit that we asked John Veit-Wilson, who has written and researched widely in this area, to contribute Chapter 1. In it, he unravels the various strands of the current debate and the different ways of defining and talking about poverty. He probes the merits or otherwise of a range of current definitions, including the United Nations-sponsored concepts of 'absolute' and 'overall' poverty. He favours approaches which enable us to explore needs in the context of contemporary standards, exemplified by the work of Peter Townsend and his colleagues and the original *Breadline Britain* team of Joanna Mack and Stewart Lansley. These are the lines of enquiry which need to be further developed. Although *Poverty: the facts* must of course take its content from the material available to the authors in the real world, Chapter 1 gives us the means of assessing both the value and the limitations of that material and of placing it in context.

Although the use, to define poverty, of percentages derived from the *Households Below Average Income* (HBAI) statistics has its problems, we can by no means ignore it. This is, after all, the measure which the Chancellor has used to justify diverting very significant additional resources to families with children. Moreover, if it is the measure which is going to be used by the UK and other governments, then we need to be familiar with it and with the figures which it produces, warts and all. Thus, in Chapter 2, Alison Garnham presents a range of material derived from this approach and explores what it tells us about the Government's achievements so far. There is no doubt that those achievements have been real, although the most recent HBAI figures are disappointing.

A selection of information from the Poverty and Social Exclusion Survey – the descendant of the *Breadline Britain* studies, whereby social science methods are used to find out what the general public perceives as acceptable minimum standards of living – is drawn out. This permits the construction of deprivation indicators and exploration of the numbers lacking these socially-defined necessities. This method has a robust political credibility. Who says these people are poor? Public opinion does.

Chapter 2 goes on to look at the Low Income Families method, which focuses on those living at, below or just above the level afforded by the social assistance scales. As noted above, these figures are important in themselves – and although it is problematic to regard derivatives of benefit levels as a definition, the continuing low level of income support enables us to say that those receiving it will certainly be among those living in poverty.

A number of other sources of information are summarised in Chapter 2, including the work of the Family Budget Unit in drawing up budget standards; evidence on family spending from the Centre for Research in Social Policy at Loughborough University; and work by David Piachaud and Holly Sutherland analysing the Government's performance. The Government's own poverty indicators, set out in its *Opportunity for All* reports, are also discussed. It is certainly a good thing that official indicators have been adopted, but there is much work to be done in improving them – not least to render them more specific.

The chapter also points to the need to find a way of connecting 'the voice of poor people themselves' to the Government's anti-poverty strategy. If this is to be more than a routine platitude, concrete mechanisms are needed. The involvement of local communities in national action plans which is being developed in Scotland, Wales, Northern Ireland and the Irish Republic could, it is argued, provide us with important lessons.

WHY PEOPLE ARE POOR

A number of groups within the population are particularly vulnerable to poverty. They vary both as a percentage of the total population and in terms of the degree of risk of poverty within the group. Their members have in common, though, an above-average probability of being poor.

Unemployment is much reduced, but far from beaten. Opinions differ as to how far economic management at the national level can keep unemployment under control on a sustained basis over a long period. Whatever the truth of the matter, it is hard to dispute that adverse economic developments internationally could potentially lead to a return to much higher levels of joblessness. This has considerable significance not only for the various New Deals in respect of those required to seek work as a condition of qualifying for benefit, but also for lone parents and others (see below) who are the subject of such policies, albeit so far without being compelled to look for a job. Up until now, these programmes have ridden the crest of a wave of high demand for labour: a change for the worse in this scenario would be a real test of the Government's anti-poverty credentials. Meanwhile, unemployed people and their families still have to live on plainly inadequate levels of benefit.

For those in work, *low pay* remains an issue. The Government has pursued a strategy here of establishing a statutory minimum wage and supplementing it with means-tested in-work benefits and tax credits. The tax credit strategy in particular is at the heart of Labour's plans. There is no doubt that the Government is serious about boosting the incomes of low-paid workers, although there are many criticisms which can be made of an approach which is cautious in respect of the minimum wage and entrenches means-testing ever more deeply for the 'working poor'.

Lone parents and their families are highly likely to be poor. Any family with children encounters additional risks, as needs increase while opportunities to earn become constrained. Lone parents, though, face particular barriers in juggling often conflicting responsibilities, frequently without anything like adequate support, materially or socially. For some, the Government's efforts to make it easier to work will be welcome and helpful. Others (for example, where childcare costs are high) may find them inadequate. Others still (for example, those who wish to stay at home and look after their children) may find them intimidating. Those who stay, willingly or otherwise, on income support will find it difficult to avoid financial hardship.

There is a growing diversity of income among *retired people*, as the effects of the past expansion of good occupational pensions and higher savings among some groups feed through. It cannot be guaranteed that this will remain the trend in future, as employment patterns become less secure and many employers retreat from 'defined benefit' schemes, substituting the more unpredictable 'money purchase' type of provision. However, for the present, there is a broad tendency for younger pensioners to be better off than their older counterparts. The Government has responded to the continuing problem of pensioner poverty with the promotion of 'stakeholder' money purchase pensions, increases in income support for pensioners, and a proposal for a means-tested 'pensioner credit' to reward those who have small savings and/or modest additional pensions. As in the case of low-paid workers, there is thus a controversial reliance on extended means-testing as the way to tackle poverty among this section of the population.

People who are ill are also very likely to be poor. There is a two-way relationship here: somebody may be ill because they are poor and suffering the stressful and health-damaging effects of their poverty. Or they may be poor because they are ill, finding their living expenses higher and their employment opportunities restricted or removed. They may well have fallen foul of both effects, caught in a vicious circle of poverty and ill-health. For those who can work, the likelihood of employment will depend on the buoyancy of the economy, which – along with the desire to make savings – explains the Government's current efforts to bear down on incapacity benefit claims and push claimants towards the job market.

Disabled people also tend to experience the double hazard of relatively high living expenses and reduced or zero earning capacity. For those with more severe disabilities, there are relatively high benefits, such as disability living allowance, which can compensate to a degree. However, although generous by social security standards, such payments are far from a guarantee against poverty. The Government's New Deal has a variant which is aimed at disabled people, although the degree to which the prospect of paid work is realistic will obviously vary from case to case. Moreover, as with lone parents, the line between constructive support and unwelcome pressure is likely to prove a fine one.

Carers are also vulnerable to poverty. We have mentioned those who care for children, but there are many also whose earning power is reduced or eliminated because they are caring for frail elderly, ill or disabled people, usually relatives. The modest invalid care allowance (and carer's premium within the means-tested benefits) could not seriously be described as adequate compensation, before or after the proposed limited improvements to these provisions. Again, the Government wishes to maximise carers' participation in the labour market and again there is a tension between support and pressure. In broad policy terms, it can be argued that society is playing a high-risk game in treating carers so badly. Especially when the economy is providing alternatives within the labour market, there is the prospect that many carers may be tempted to take paid work as an alternative to their caring role, rather than (as the Government wishes) in addition to it. This could lead to very expensive demands on public care provision, which is why carers' miserable benefits could prove to be a seriously false economy.

The great majority of lone parents are *women*, as are most poor pensioners, most low-paid workers and most carers. It is often said that poverty is a women's issue, which of course does not mean that there are no poor men and boys (there are lots of them) but rather that women are disproportionately likely to be poor, reflecting their still relatively disadvantaged position in the economy and society and their tendency to occupy poorly remunerated roles.

Young people can also be vulnerable in many ways. Those who have spent time within the public care system tend to fare especially badly, but hazards abound for the whole age group. Wages are often very low and even the statutory minimum has a lower level for young workers. The New Deal may lead to lasting employment opportunities, or merely provide a temporary respite – a problem which, as noted above, could assume much greater importance in less favourable economic circumstances. There are severe restrictions on means-tested benefits for 16/17-year-olds and lower rates for other single childless people aged under 25, including lower income thresholds at which housing benefit and council tax benefit begin to be withdrawn; and there are extra restrictions on the level of rent which housing benefit will meet for this age group. The previous Government set out deliberately to create an especially hostile benefit environment for young people, apparently in the belief that they should be at home with their parents. The current regime has done very little to correct this, putting almost all its policy effort into the New Deal.

Black and minority ethnic communities in the UK are diverse and have varying experiences in terms of their social and economic success or otherwise. Nevertheless, the pervasive influence of prejudice and discrimination, both at the individual and institutional levels, has created a disproportionate propensity for people from many of these communities to experience poverty. Historically, people from minority ethnic backgrounds have, moreover, been doubly exploited in Britain: economically, to meet labour shortages, often in low-paid public services; and too often politically, by unscrupulous politicians seeking a populist platform. Putting this right is surely a challenge which must be met by any society with aspirations to genuine civilisation.

Housing benefit recipients are also a diverse group, united by the need to rely on state support to meet their housing costs. Housing benefit, however, suffers from both structural and administrative problems. In theory, rents are covered in full for people living at the income support level, benefit tapering out as income rises. In reality, a variety of restrictions apply, especially in the private rented sector, which mean that many claimants have to meet their housing costs partly out of basic incomes meant for food, clothing, fuel and other non-housing necessities. This situation is compounded by widespread administrative problems, causing error, delay and sometimes consequent eviction. Housing benefit has been under review in one form or another ever since 1997, but the Government has been strikingly cautious, as any significant change will be expensive or will generate large numbers of losers. Analogous problems apply to a significant degree to council tax benefit, intended to help people on low incomes to pay their local taxes. Yet another set of difficulties applies to low-income owner-occupiers, who receive very restricted help with housing costs if out of work, losing even that if they take up a job (an area of the system which so far seems immune to the fashion for work incentives).

There is, of course, much overlap between these various groups: a low-paid lone mother with a disabled child; an unemployed black father with a partner who is ill; a disabled pensioner – any or all of them having trouble with their housing costs. Disadvantages combine and often exacerbate each other.

In Chapter 3, Marilyn Howard looks in detail at the evidence relating to most of the groups and themes referred to above. Additionally, in Chapter 5, she looks specifically at children and in Chapter 6 at ethnicity and poverty.

It should be stressed, however, that belonging to one of the above groups does not in itself cause poverty – the problem lies in the way in which they are treated, economically, socially and politically. Yes, unemployment, sickness, disability and caring responsibilities frequently result in poverty: but it is not *necessary* that this should be so. Income maintenance policies, the way in which black people are treated and even employment patterns are not natural disasters like earthquakes or floods: they are created in one way or another by human economic and social activity. Given the political will, problems can be solved and poverty can be prevented. We shall say more about this in the conclusion to this book.

THE IMPACT OF POVERTY

Chapter 4 looks at the effects, on individuals, families and children, of living on a low income. As ever, this sort of information makes depressing reading: going without basic household items which we ought all to be able to expect as part of ordinary modern living; not having enough food; not being able to afford nutritious food; not having enough money for fuel; struggling to afford clothing; grappling with housing costs; not being able to afford to travel; being excluded from social activities; living with stigma; struggling with malfunctioning but powerful bureaucracies; living with the stress of knife-edge budgeting; getting into debt – this is everyday life for millions. For some, very serious consequences such as ill-health, homelessness or premature death can follow.

Large numbers of people on low incomes respond to these conditions with resilience, creativity and a determination not to be defeated. But this does not render acceptable such a state of affairs.

Those of us who are not poor need reminding of all this. Nor should we be complacent: only the very affluent can insure themselves effectively against the economic consequences of all of life's possible but unexpected twists and turns – loss of a partner; disability caused by an accident; a serious illness; unexpected loss of a well-paid job. Poverty is not just about 'them' and even if we are not (as surely we should be) motivated by moral outrage and/or an inclusive concept of citizenship, then we would nevertheless do well to consider enlightened self-interest. A wider recognition of our common needs, a movement still further away from 1980s concepts of 'no such thing as society', could achieve much.

INEQUALITY

Inequality is a close relative of poverty. If we define income poverty in terms of resources which are insufficient to enable an individual to participate in the mainstream of her or his society, then inequality is built into our definition – there is an inherent concept of a hierarchy of incomes, the lower reaches of which take us into the condition of poverty. The complaint that 'you are not talking about poverty, you are talking about inequality' therefore posits something of a false dichotomy. Few people argue for absolutely equal incomes, but narrowing the range is a good way to address poverty, drawing both the rich and the poor closer to the mainstream. 'Taxing and spending' is a good way of doing this.

Moreover, inequalities of power and influence play a major part in sustaining the economic relationships which cause and characterise the condition of poverty.

Chapter 7 explores patterns of inequality in income, spending, earnings and wealth. It points out that social security and tax policies play an important role: as instruments of policy, they can be used either to reduce inequalities or to increase them. The picture, of course, is dynamic rather than static: tax and benefits go some way to smoothing out the unequal distribution of initial incomes, but if inequality in the latter is increasing, then the net result can be a continuing growth in inequality even when benefits for the poorest have improved.

Chapter 8 looks at geographical inequalities in the UK. This is an issue which can be over-simplified in the popular imagination – the deprived North and the affluent South. In fact, although there are certainly inequalities between regions, there are also striking disparities within them. The pattern is complex and the Government's various neighbourhood initiatives and patchwork of action zones of one kind and another represent an attempt to get to grips with it. An additional dimension, political as well as social and economic, is added by the devolutionary constitutional changes of recent years. Chapter 8 explores the issues at the levels of the UK, the devolved administrations, London, the regions, rural areas, constituencies, districts and wards. It concludes that no precise 'geography of poverty' can readily be drawn up, because of the amount of variation at all levels. It also points to the need for better information and hopes that the progress of devolution will help to stimulate it.

Chapter 9 examines poverty and inequality at the international level. General living standards of course vary greatly across the planet and many of us would want to argue for a convergence as the new century progresses, at the best level that is sustainable in environmental terms. Given the extreme deprivation that is widespread in some parts of the world, it may be thought that the poverty which manifests itself in the richer countries should perhaps have a lesser priority. However, there is no need for a competition of this sort. Whatever the case for reducing international inequalities, poverty, as noted above, has to be understood in the context of a given society at a particular time – and should be regarded as unacceptable anywhere, at any time. Perhaps the real difference in the case of the rich countries is that they have considerably less excuse. This chapter looks at the evidence as it relates to the European Union, to the more affluent countries in general and finally to the global picture.

THE FACTS

Why do we place such a lot of emphasis on assembling and disseminating the facts about poverty?

Partly, it is because information can influence the political process. It would be naïve to suppose that simply providing evidence will bring about change. But evidence helps, feeding into lobbying, campaigning and the processes of persuasion. This applies not only in relation to government, but across the political spectrum. We want to promote our policies as widely as possible.

We also need to raise public awareness about poverty. The more widely the issues are understood, the more fertile the soil for a healthy growth of support for change. We noted above that *Poverty: the facts* is designed either to be read through cover to cover, or dipped into like a handbook. Readers will have diverse reasons for using it – an MP or her or his researcher preparing for a debate; a journalist working on a story; a student preparing an essay or dissertation; anybody who just wants to know more about this vital question. As far as we are concerned, it all helps, one way or another, to spread the word.

We hope that the reader will find here useful information, ammunition and food for thought.

NOTES

1   For an assessment of the Government's record and the remaining tasks, see G Fimister (ed), *An End in Sight? Tackling child poverty in the UK*, CPAG, 2001

Concepts and measures

INTRODUCTION

What is *poverty*? How can it be conceptualised, defined or measured? What distinguishes poverty from *inequality* and when is inequality a problem? What are the similarities to and differences from the two related expressions which describe unsatisfactory conditions, *deprivation* and *social exclusion*? What do the statistics of poverty, deprivation and social exclusion within and between countries really tell us? What are the implications of these issues for government policies dealing both with the wider social evils and the adequacy of benefits under the income maintenance system?

These and similar questions generate enormous debate and literature, and often confuse rather than clarify the situation. An enormous amount has been written on these topics during the past century or more, but it has left the subject full of disagreements and contradictions. Some answers are argumentative rather than explanatory; some try to present ideological views as if they were the only possible ones; many answers deny the possibility of being objective and treat the whole matter as no more than the clash of subjective opinions. This is misleading, since social science allows us to discover what are reliable facts about societies and how they work. It is also evasive, since studying the facts about poverty is not a matter of playing word games but of confronting realities about the suffering of millions of people around the world.

This chapter aims to explain the language, and the ideas, values and ideologies behind it. It addresses these questions simply but more comprehensively than is generally the case where the findings of research by one method are being presented or a political argument is promoted. A short chapter cannot hope to explain everything about such a complicated subject or so many different approaches, so instead it summarises the key issues and the tools with which to make sense of the arguments about different approaches. As the subject is constantly developing, the current methods and data change, and government responses and initiatives rarely remain constant or focused on any one aspect. The references suggest further readings to expand on these matters.

TO START WITH

What are we talking about? We start with ideas, concepts, then we put them into words, definitions, and then we may want to study the scale of what they describe, and that is when we need measures. In the arguments about poverty all three of these are usually muddled with each other, but let us take each of them separately.

TWO BASIC IDEAS OF POVERTY

- Cultural difference.
- Lack of necessary resources.

One idea is about the *difference* between poor people and those who are not poor. The ways in which this is expressed vary greatly, but they always address the question, how can you distinguish a poor from a non-poor person or group? 'Social exclusion', being excluded from taking part in society in the same way as a non-poor person, is a common expression of this concept nowadays, but there are or have been many others referring to the appearance or behaviour of 'the poor' over the hundreds of years in which people have discussed poverty. Note that 'social exclusion' is also widely used to mean many other things apart from poverty, but this chapter uses only the poverty meanings.[1]

The other idea is about the *resources*, or rather the lack of them, needed not to be different, deprived or excluded. There is much argument about how far money is the most important of these resources in modern societies in which the usual way in which people meet needs is by spending money for goods and services. Again, the ways in which this idea is expressed usually answer the question, what resources, and how much of them, are needed not to be poor?

These two ideas of poverty are distinct but clearly connected to each other. What resources does a person need to avoid experiencing deprivation or exclusion, or being identified as such? Because of this the two ideas are often wrongly confused with each other. On the other hand, people sometimes argue that one idea excludes the other, that poverty is either a matter of not enough resources or a deprived lifestyle. That false distinction often comes before the prescription for action – either 'if poor people had enough money they wouldn't be deprived or excluded' or 'money is irrelevant – it's all a matter of behaviour'.

The common confusion gets worse when people muddle up what poverty is with the reasons why people become or stay poor. It is nonsense to say that being uneducated, unemployed, a lone parent, disabled or old are the *causes* of poverty or social exclusion. If they were, even the British Royal Family would be poor. The reason why people with these characteristics, or why women and some people from ethnic minorities, are more likely to be poor is simply that they are more likely than others to earn less or receive inadequate social security benefits.

HOW DO PEOPLE THINK AND TALK ABOUT POVERTY?

There are two underlying ideas about what poverty is, but in addition there are several distinct ways of thinking and talking about it. Choosing one of these ways then suggests what ought to be done about it. This is confusing, but it gets worse. When someone chooses one of these ways to think and talk about poverty, the choice makes it more difficult, even impossible, to use other ways in that debate. The result is that people who are poor by one way of thinking about it may be made invisible by another way. Policies to deal with one kind of poverty may fail to deal with the other kinds which have been 'closed off'.

Through their research, academics have tried to make sense of this confusing range of ideas and the ways in which they are discussed. One common name for the package of ideas, ways of discussion and prescriptions for action is a 'discourse'. John Veit-Wilson's research in ten countries[2] found seven distinct ways of thinking and talking about poverty in use, and perhaps there are more elsewhere. All of these are found in the UK – several of them even in this book – so we must try to understand them. Some are based on the idea that poor people are human beings in society (what in academic jargon he called 'humanistic discourses'), and some on the idea that being poor is a legal status or a position on a statistical distribution or an economic theory but not a matter of human beings in society (hence he called them 'asocial discourses'). Below are the seven kinds which have been described so far.

SEVEN KINDS OF TALK ABOUT POVERTY

HUMANISTIC DISCOURSES

'Poverty is a matter of behaviour'. People who are not poor identify people as poor by their way of living which deviates from what is conventionally 'decent'. 'Decency' here means a lifestyle free of shame and stigma, respected by others in society even if it is different. Examples of the use of this discourse are 'the underclass' or 'the culture of poverty'. Solutions implied by its use are adjustment of behaviour and re-education into conventional 'decency'; money incomes are often seen as unimportant for this process. It closes off the 'invisible poor' who lack resources for participation but try to live outwardly 'decent' lives.

'Poverty doesn't exist but some people are 'too unequal''. This is a version of the behavioural discourse, often found in the small-scale, culturally homogeneous Nordic countries, but also sometimes expressed in the UK. Assuming the effectiveness of egalitarian social policies and the adequacy of incomes and other resources, people who use this discourse denied the existence of poverty in their countries. If they identified a problem it was divergences from the average level of living in society. What was closed off was any discussion of how much divergence was intolerable, and to whom – what are the costs of participation and what is an inadequate income? If there were problems, the solutions lie in better access to services and perhaps behavioural readjustment.

'Social exclusion' discourse. Here[3] poverty is seen by non-poor people as the characteristics of individuals or groups who, they argue, are prevented or unable to take a 'decent' part in non-poor society because of these 'poor' characteristics. Examples of this discourse are the treatment of lone parents, unemployed people, ethnic minorities or people living in economically devastated areas as being 'socially excluded'. The solution to this problem is to alter these characteristics and enhance their integration into non-poor society. Income levels are seen as secondary or even irrelevant to this process. If they are seen as relevant at all, they are believed to follow the integration rather than precede it. What is closed off is the deprivation of members of groups which do not have these identifying characteristics or those who have low incomes but are 'integrated' into non-poor society, for instance deprived people in richer areas or those with intermittent employment. The discussion of how the exclusion comes about is also often closed off by this discourse – who is doing the excluding, and why are they doing it?

'Poverty is about how our society distributes resources through its structures and processes'. This takes the condition of poverty to be the lack of resources sufficient to take part in non-poor society according to the dominant social decency standards. It is structural because it sees both the setting of these standards and the distribution of those resources as caused by the ways in which the social, economic and political structures of society work. The question then is, whose are the decency standards and what resources, individual, collective and material, are needed to take a minimally decent part in society? Some researchers have used social science methods to find out what the whole population takes them to be, rather than relying on political prescription. The solutions implied by this discourse are the distribution of all the necessary resources to those who are deprived of them, which may be not only money incomes but other tangible and intangible resources such as political power. This discourse does not close off any aspect of poverty, but users tend to be sceptical about the capacity of the other discourses to deal adequately with understanding or acting on the total problem of poverty.

ASOCIAL DISCOURSES

'Poverty is a legal status'. This discourse treats poverty as the characteristics of those whom the state has defined as poor because they are claimants of means-tested social assistance benefits (income support in the UK) designed only for the poor. It has a long history in Europe and North America, where paupers, the recipients of Poor Law relief ('Welfare' in the USA), were a separate legal category from ordinary citizens. Its use persists, not only in the UK but across Europe, in the debates about 'official poverty' being defined as having an income at or below the current social assistance benefit levels. In the UK this was the basis of the Low Income Families (LIF) statistics, in which all households with incomes close to or below the benefit levels were counted as poor, a practice which led to complaints that whenever the Government raised the benefit rates it increased the numbers of the poor. In some countries, 'the poor' include those legally eligible to apply but not doing so, while having a low income but not being a claimant or legally eligible closes off identification as 'poor' within this discourse. The solution to this poverty lies in removing all the paupers: if there are no claimants there is no poverty, whatever one may call the situation of those with low incomes and suffering deprivations.

'Poverty is having an income below some statistical percentage of the national income distribution'. This is a very common discourse in the UK and in international use. It treats poverty simply as the condition of living in a household whose income (or sometimes expenditure) is below some specified percentage of the national mean or median household distribution, before or after housing costs and other deductions such as tax. Half of the average (mean) or 60 per cent of the median are both common among the many versions in use. In the UK the approach is called Households Below Average Income (HBAI) and the official measure has changed to 60 per cent of the median. The solution is to reduce household income inequality, but all discussion of the adequacy of incomes to avoid deprivations or ensure participation is excluded by this discourse, since it offers no evidence to test if the income percentile chosen is at, below or even above what is needed to allow a participatory lifestyle. Of course, not everyone who quotes UK official 'poverty' (that is, inequality) statistics agrees with their use in that way.

'Poverty is what economists say it is'. This is another common discourse, which treats people in a theoretical way, for instance as being purely physical beings whose minimal needs can be met by just sufficient nutritious food, clothing and housing – the 'minimum subsistence' approach. The solution to this poverty is income sufficient only for bodily health but ignoring the costs of social participation and psychological well-being. A version of this theoretical discourse also supposes that the sole motives for human action are 'rational' choices about maximising material rewards. All social values and psychological and altruistic motives for action (which in fact may be even more rational than self-interest), or the expenses of participation to society's own standards, are excluded by this discourse. Both experience and research show how unrealistic this discourse is.[4]

DEFINITIONS OF POVERTY

We can now look at the range of definitions of poverty and see how they relate to the different discourses, with all their limitations. They are not interchangeable at will, as some people treat them. Note that definitions of poverty are only descriptions of what the condition of being poor is about – they are not the measures by which lines can be drawn and numbers counted. All the discourses have an implicit definition but it is not always explicit, just as not every definition has a clear-cut measure.

A simple structural definition of poverty is that offered by the World Bank economist Martin Ravallion:

> 'Poverty' can be said to exist in a given society when one or more persons do not attain a level of material well-being deemed to constitute a reasonable minimum by the standards of that society.[5]

Elsewhere, the World Bank defines poverty as 'the inability to attain a minimal standard of living'.[6] This standard was based on the nationally conventional diets of the poor and the variable costs of participation, but the actual income measures used for counting the poor did not include the latter (see discussion of international measures below).[7] However, pre-eminent among structural definitions, which have led to measures usable in surveys, is the sociologist Peter Townsend's classic:

> People are relatively deprived if they cannot obtain, at all or sufficiently, the conditions of life – that is, the diets, amenities, standards and services – which allow them to play the roles, participate in the relationships and follow the customary behaviour which is expected of them by virtue of their membership of society. *If they lack or are denied resources to obtain access to these conditions of life and so fulfil membership of society they may be said to be in poverty.* People may be deprived in any or all of the major spheres of life – at work where the means largely determining position in other spheres are earned; at home, in neighbourhood and family; in travel; in a range of social and individual activities outside work and home or neighbourhood in performing a variety of roles in fulfilment of social obligations.[8]

A shorter structural definition is Joanna Mack and Stewart Lansley's: 'This study defines 'poverty' in terms of *an enforced lack of socially perceived necessities.*'[9] In each of these two cases, the definition's logic has been followed to devise measures with which to identify and count the poor, in the UK and increasingly in other countries, in terms of society's own standards.

There were nevertheless some differences between the Townsend and Mack and Lansley approaches in these early surveys, and these differences still arise in debate. Townsend was concerned that, when asked to specify what necessities were, people might not be aware of all the physical, social and psychological needs they really have, and so he tended to include items which social scientists identified as essential and which might not be purchasable.[10] By contrast, Mack and Lansley said they took simply what their sample of the population rightly or wrongly told them were necessities, and took account only of those which could be bought, so that they could find out how much money was needed not to be deprived and who had too little money to buy the necessities if they wanted to.[11]

An example of the social exclusion discourse's definition of poverty is that framed by the European Commission when the member governments demurred at definitions which used the word 'poverty' or referred to income levels. Note that this definition refers to the identification of the poor and not to the characteristics of poverty, and implies the research programme required to establish what the minimum acceptable way of life in each State is, and what resources are needed to meet this standard:

> For the purposes of this Decision 'the poor' shall be taken to mean persons, families and groups of persons *whose resources (material, cultural and social) are so limited as to exclude them* from the minimum acceptable way of life in the Member States in which they live.[12]

'ABSOLUTE' AND 'RELATIVE', 'PRIMARY' AND 'SECONDARY' POVERTY

Every textbook on the subject as well as most of the commentators includes definitions of these well-known terms. Why are they omitted here? The reason is simple – they do not really exist but are simply notions created for the purpose of arguing a case. They do not represent any real kind of poverty as it is experienced and can be studied, which the definitions above and to follow all do.

All the notions of 'absolute' definitions of poverty which suppose it to be a state of lacking all but a given list of physiological requirements ('minimum subsistence' measures) are impracticable in real human societies. No human lives like that, on physiological requirements alone, and even if they did, the variables are too immense for any one list to include them all. Human societies vary greatly over time and space. No conceivable definition of 'difference' or 'lack of resources' could encompass all the variables. By the same token, all approaches to definition must be relative to society, time, place and observer. Thus there can be no absolute definitions: they are all relative.

When the pioneer of empirical poverty research, Benjamin Seebohm Rowntree, devised the 'primary' poverty measure based on the cost of a basket of necessities for 'merely physical efficiency' a century ago, it was not because he thought this a viable definition of minimal adequacy (he did not) but because it was meant to show the non-poor classes that a large proportion of the poor (whom he identified and counted by appearance in a behaviourist way) had too little money even to meet physical, let alone social, requirements. 'Secondary' poverty was merely his name for the condition of those who had more income than 'primary' poverty but who still suffered poverty lifestyles.[13]

What, then, do people mean when they use these terms? Generally, the users of 'absolute' mean, asocially, a lack of physiological necessities, which they measure as the cost of 'minimum subsistence' shopping baskets. When asked to compose one, they fill it with what from their non-poor perspective are essential items relative to the society and time in which they live. Much economic theory assumes that this can be done reliably, an assertion which sociologists and psychologists would generally dispute.

On the other hand, relativity is a very broad notion. One must always ask 'relative to what?' Answers may include relative to society's present or past standards, relative to other people or groups in this country or in others, or other aspects of comparison. One meaning of relative poverty is the changing standards and the resources needed to achieve them which are relative to place, time and observer. A different but common one is the degree of inequality in society.

Neither absolute nor relative helps our understanding of poverty. Similarly, the distinction between primary and secondary poverty refers to a debate a century ago which presupposed the validity of minimum subsistence measures and middle-class judgements about working-class lifestyles. These words have no useful place in today's armoury.

POVERTY OVERALL AND ABSOLUTE POVERTY:
THE UN DEFINITIONS

In spite of the meaninglessness of the absolute/relative and primary/ secondary distinctions, the idea of 'an irreducible absolutist core in the idea of poverty' lives on, as the economist Amartya Sen put it. Using a narrow version of 'relative' he stressed that: 'If there is starvation and hunger then, no matter what the relative picture looks like, there clearly is poverty', admitting that this absolutist core is itself relativist in a wider sense.[14] The term thus continues to be used and we have to be clear about the meaning now attached to it, for instance by the United Nations' World Summit for Social Development in Copenhagen in 1995. Its Declaration defined what it meant by poverty in general, and within that, what it meant by absolute poverty.

The UN definition of poverty overall is very broad:

> Poverty has various manifestations, including lack of income and productive resources to ensure sustainable livelihoods; hunger and malnutrition; ill-health; limited or lack of access to education and other basic services; increased morbidity and mortality from illness; homelessness and inadequate housing; unsafe environments and social discrimination and exclusion. It is also characterised by lack of participation in decision making and in civil, social and cultural life. It occurs in all countries: as mass poverty in many developing countries, pockets of poverty amid wealth in developed countries, loss of livelihoods as a result of economic recession, sudden poverty as a result of disaster or conflict, the poverty of low-wage workers, and the utter destitution of people who fall outside family support systems, institutions and safety nets.[15]

It goes on to describe many of the groups who are especially vulnerable to poverty. Within this overall definition, absolute poverty has a more limited and extreme form:

> Absolute poverty is a condition characterised by severe deprivation of basic human needs, including food, safe drinking water, sanitation facilities, health, shelter, education and information. It depends not only on income but also on access to social services.[16]

As the research carried out at the University of Bristol has shown during the 1990s, if poverty is defined in this way then such 'absolute' poverty can be found even in the UK.[17] Similarly, the UN Administrative Committee on Co-ordination issued a statement of commitment for action to eradicate poverty in 1998 which defined poverty in terms which equally can apply to the most deprived people in the most deprived countries as well as to those in richer countries:

> Fundamentally, poverty is a denial of choices and opportunities, a violation of human dignity. It means lack of basic capacity to participate effectively in society. It means not having enough to feed and clothe a family, not having a school or clinic to go to, not having the land on which to grow one's food or a job to earn one's living, not having access to credit. It means insecurity, powerlessness and exclusion of individuals, households and communities. It means susceptibility to violence, and it often implies living on marginal and fragile environments, without access to clean water and sanitation.[18]

MEASURES OF POVERTY

SEVEN PURPOSES FOR POVERTY MEASURES

What do people want poverty measures for? There are at least seven different reasons[19] why they may want a method of distinguishing the poor from the non-poor population:

- Describing poverty and who is poor.
- Explaining why they are poor.
- Counting the poor.
- Comparing groups over place and time.
- Reporting what people describe as poverty.
- Discovering what a poverty income is and who is poor by it.
- Prescribing action to deal with the poor.

Each of these distinct purposes leads to a distinct kind of measure, and there is no point in arguing about measures without being clear what they are intended for. Historically, people developed the measures for the purposes they had in mind and within the different discourses they chose to use.

At the end of the nineteenth century, Seebohm Rowntree used the long-standing conventional middle-class visual measure of a squalid lifestyle to *identify* poor households and *count* them, but for the purposes of *explanation* he devised an asocial minimum subsistence cash measure (the 'primary poverty' budget) to show that at least one-third of those visibly poor had too little money even for physical necessities.

He observed that the remainder may have had enough money for their physical needs as he defined them, but they spent it on other social necessities, including the recreations of gambling and alcohol, and thus they did not have a non-poor appearance.[20]

Because Rowntree's 'primary poverty' tool seemed to be an objective measure, unlike the visual measure of domestic squalor which was interpreted subjectively, it became very popular as a means of counting and comparing the poor in the first half of the twentieth century. Indeed, the fact that it was deliberately chosen to be too little to live on socially was overlooked and instead it became used as a measure of what was minimally adequate for participation. Peter Townsend queried this; first, he proposed research to *discover* the income levels at which people *in practice* actually did not achieve the recommended nutritional intakes,[21] and when this was not carried out, he and colleagues carried out research to discover what the population itself defined as the characteristics of poverty, and the income levels at which such poor levels of living in fact occurred.[22] This involved surveying random samples of the population as a whole to discover what the majority thought were the necessities which nobody should be without, which has led it to be called the *deprivation indicator* approach, and then analysing the findings about incomes. The poverty measure which this produced is therefore derived from the survey findings and not from anyone's ideas of how much it should be.

A variant of this approach is the *focus group* method of discovering what people report, to ask much smaller groups, representative in type but not necessarily statistically, to discuss the issues surrounding the definitions of poverty, deprivation and exclusions and to come to conclusions about what these terms and experiences mean to them, and what income levels are needed to avoid them. Such groups may represent the population as a whole, or selected sections of it, such as families with children.[23]

Public opinion has also been used as the basis of measures designed by economists at the Universities of Leyden, Antwerp and elsewhere. These allow sample surveys of the population itself to *report* on the income levels which it felt were needed 'to make ends meet' or similar phrases suggesting minimal adequacy for participation.[24] Such reports were subject to complex statistical procedures to produce national average figures for households of varying size and composition. These reported cash sums are in effect proxies for the levels of living which they could support according to the varied conditions of what is marketed and what is 'free' (such as health or education) in each country in which they have been used. This makes comparison difficult.[25] Indeed, using this measure has produced poverty incomes so high that some economists have not liked to accept them as 'real' poverty, which they prefer, for whatever ideological reasons, to see as much greater hardship than the population's own definitions.[26]

The *budget* approach has been revived by Jonathan Bradshaw and colleagues in the Family Budget Unit, not as developed by Rowntree to create an impossibly low figure, but instead to use the evidence from many national surveys and databases of the British population's patterns of consumption of goods and services.[27] Also using the evidence from the deprivation indicator research findings of Gordon, Townsend *et al*,[28] they have calculated the total costs over time of what by these current British standards reflects a 'modest but adequate' or a 'low cost but acceptable' level of living. Each item in these measures is obvious and so can be adjusted to whatever open discussion suggests is the right standard to reflect minimally decent participation in society.

Here we have four kinds of objective, survey-based poverty measure – one derived from social survey statistics, one based on mass public opinion, one on small group discussion, and one calculated from national surveys of levels of living and social values. But these are not the only measures of poverty found in use. Two other types of 'poverty' measure are commonly used in other countries and internationally. These are prescriptive – that is, they state what poverty is to be taken as being, which may not be the same as what the population as a whole would say – and are usually based on political objectives.

One is the politically-set minimum income standards (MIS) which the governments of some countries have developed in order to carry out one or more of the functions of poverty measures:[29]

- Identifying individuals and groups 'in poverty' by this measure, counting them and calculating how far below the line they fall.
- Acting as criteria of the adequacy of the various income maintenance measures – minimum wage rates, tax thresholds, long and short-term social security and social assistance benefits.
- Acting as guidelines against which to calibrate the relations of the tiers of income maintenance.

A key difference between MIS and social science poverty measures is that MIS must be politically credible for use by governments for these purposes, while the findings of social science about the realities and extent of poverty may be unwelcome. The US National Academy of Sciences review of the MIS in USA in 1995 pointed out that political credibility involves public acceptability, methodological defensibility and administrative feasibility.[30] There is a contradiction between political measures – which have to be precise even if they are not reliable as reflections of poverty incomes – and research findings, which are reliable but rarely precise. Some commentators, therefore, do not treat these political measures as indicators of poverty in a country, but only of political reactions to it.

The other kind of international poverty standard is that used by agencies such as the World Bank and Organisation for Economic Co-operation and Development (OECD) for making global comparisons between countries. Some of these are statistical and refer to the degree of inequality in countries' measurable income distributions (as described above, or the Gini co-efficient which reflects income inequalities) or the gross domestic product per head of population. Others are based on some arbitrary notion of a given cash income, such as the World Bank's one or two US dollars per day per head, or variations on this approach. Measures of this kind are not based on the realities of each country's own society and domestic economy, and pay no attention to differences between and within countries in people's need for cash among the various resources to meet human needs.

International measures like these do not allow who is poor in a country to be identified reliably, nor show what should be done to relieve that poverty. The problem of who is poor, where, and which distinct elements of their deprivations need policy attention, each have to be studied with appropriate measures separately. That is too large and contentious a subject to touch on here.

CONCLUSION: WHAT ANTI-POVERTY POLICY NEEDS

What deprived and excluded people need is enough of the resources (whether tangible and intangible, personal and collective) to meet their needs, over time, and allow them to take part in society to the extent that – according to its standards – they are no longer deprived or excluded. Money is only one of these resources, though it is of crucial importance in modern industrial societies.

But what is meant by such words as 'human needs' or 'adequacy'? Here again we face an enormous body of argument and literature. The questions we must pose in dealing with it are always the same – *needed or adequate for what? for how long? for whom? and who says?*[31] The social science approaches to poverty research try to answer the questions from the perspective of representative samples of the population as a whole, or from more intensive small-group survey methods which focus on the currently poor as well as the non-poor population. Similarly, long-term studies of the dynamics of poverty reveal different aspects of it from cross-sectional studies at one point in time, but in each case the aim is to illuminate what being able to take part in society or being prevented from it by poverty really mean. These dynamic studies have also revealed how many more people are affected by poverty over time than are counted at one time.[32]

On the other hand, the prescriptive approaches answer these questions on the basis of the interests of one section or another of the elites who hold power, whether social, political or economic. If one reckons that human needs are everything which is required over time to enable the adult human to play a full part in her or his society, one can see how broad the issues really are. We are not talking about the miserable evasions of the 'minimum subsistence' shopping basket for short-term emergency use. It is easy to get lost in the thicket of what all these definitions and measures refer to. Amartya Sen tried to clarify the issue by pointing out that the objective was not a list of resources (means) but of what people ought to be able to do to participate in society decently (ends), what he called *capabilities*.[33] The UN definitions embody both kinds of element, resources needed for capabilities and measures of capabilities being achieved.

We must continue to demand better ideas and research tools with which to study poverty so that we can abolish the human suffering it causes. We must not allow the situation to continue in which politicians promise to abolish poverty, deprivation and exclusion but make little or no attempt to find out what causes poverty or what resources are needed to overcome it, fearing what it might cost to raise incomes sufficiently. So whichever idea of poverty you hold, lifestyle or resources, you still have to make sure that everyone has the resources to avoid poverty before you condemn the lifestyle. As Mack and Lansley noted in their research, 'the rich do not choose the lifestyles associated with the lack of necessities'.[34] Can you be confident that everyone has enough money not to be poor?

NOTES

1 For a wider discussion see for example, D Byrne, *Social Exclusion*, Open University Press, 1999 and R Levitas, *The Inclusive Society? Social Exclusion and New Labour*, Macmillan, 1998

2 J Veit-Wilson, *Setting Adequacy Standards: how governments define minimum incomes*, The Policy Press, 1998

3 See note 1

4 See for example, P Taylor-Gooby (ed), *Choice and Public Policy: the limits to welfare markets*, Macmillan, 1998

5 M Ravallion, *Poverty Comparison: a guide to concepts and methods*, Living Standards Measurement Study Working Paper No 88, The World Bank, 1992

6 As quoted in D Gordon and P Townsend (eds), *Breadline Europe: the measurement of poverty*, The Policy Press, 2000, p83

7 See the discussion of these issues in D Gordon and P Townsend (eds), *Breadline Europe: the measurement of poverty*, The Policy Press, 2000, pp83-85

8 P Townsend, *The International Analysis of Poverty*, Harvester Wheatsheaf, 1993, p36 (emphasis added)

9 J Mack and S Lansley, *Poor Britain*, Allen and Unwin, 1985, p39 (emphasis added)

10 P Townsend, *Poverty in the United Kingdom*, Penguin, 1979

11 See note 9 and also J Veit-Wilson, 'Consensual Approaches to Poverty Lines and Social Security', *Journal of Social Policy*, 16(2), 1987, pp183-211

12 EEC, 'On Specific Community Action to Combat Poverty' (Council Decision 19 December 1984), 85/8/EEC, *Official Journal of the EEC*, 2/24, 1985 (emphasis added)

13 B S Rowntree, *Poverty: a study of town life*, Macmillan, 1901; see also J Veit-Wilson, 'Paradigms of Poverty: a rehabilitation of B S Rowntree', *Journal of Social Policy*, 15(1), 1986, pp69-99 and 'Paradigms of Poverty: a reply to Peter Townsend and Hugh McLachlan', *Journal of Social Policy*, 15(4), 1986, pp503-507

14 A Sen, 'Poor, Relatively Speaking', *Oxford Economic Papers*, 35, 1983, pp153-169; P Townsend, 'A Sociological Approach to the Measurement of Poverty: a rejoinder to Professor Amartya Sen', *Oxford Economic Papers*, 37, 1985, pp659-668

15 United Nations, *Report of the World Summit for Social Development, Copenhagen 6–12 March 1995; Annex II: Program of Action of the World Summit for Social Development; Chapter II: Eradication of Poverty*, United Nations, 1995, para 19

16 See note 15

17 P Townsend, D Gordon, J Bradshaw and B Gosschalk, *Absolute and Overall Poverty in Britain in 1997: what the population themselves say: Bristol Poverty Line Survey, Report of the Second MORI Survey*, Bristol Statistical Monitoring Unit, University of Bristol, 1997; D Gordon and P Townsend (eds),

Breadline Europe: the measurement of poverty, The Policy Press, 2000

18 See note 6, p37

19 J Veit-Wilson, 'Horses for Discourses: poverty, purpose and closure in minimum income standards policy' in D Gordon and P Townsend (eds), *Breadline Europe: the measurement of poverty,* The Policy Press, 2000, pp142-146

20 For a discussion of this point, see J Veit-Wilson, 'Paradigms of Poverty: a rehabilitation of B S Rowntree', *Journal of Social Policy,* 15(1), 1986, pp69-99 and 'Paradigms of Poverty: a reply to Peter Townsend and Hugh McLachlan', *Journal of Social Policy,* 15(4), 1986, pp503-507

21 P Townsend, 'Measuring Poverty', *British Journal of Sociology,* 5(2), 1954, pp130-137

22 See note 10

23 D Gordon, A Adelman, K Ashworth, J Bradshaw, R Levitas, S Middleton, C Pantazis, D Patsios, S Payne, P Townsend and J Williams, *Poverty and Social Exclusion in Britain,* Joseph Rowntree Foundation, 2000

24 K Van den Bosch, 'Poverty Measures in Comparative Research', in J Berghman and B Cantillon (eds), *The European Face of Social Security,* Avebury, 1993, pp3-23

25 See J Veit-Wilson, 'Consensual Approaches to Poverty Lines and Social Security', *Journal of Social Policy,* 16(2), 1987, pp183-211

26 H Deleeck, K Van den Bosch and L De Lathouwer, *Poverty and the Adequacy of Social Security in the EC,* Avebury, 1992, pp37-38

27 J Bradshaw (ed), *Budget Standards for the United Kingdom,* Avebury, 1993; H Parker (ed), *Low Cost but Acceptable: a minimum income standard for the UK,* Family Budget Unit, The Policy Press, 1998

28 D Gordon and C Pantazis (eds), *Breadline Britain in the 1990s,* Avebury, 1997

29 See note 2

30 C F Citro and R T Michael (eds), *Measuring Poverty: a new approach,* US National Research Council Panel on Poverty and Family Assistance Report, National Academy Press, 1995

31 S Dubnoff, 'How Much Income is Enough? Measuring public judgements', *Public Opinion Quarterly,* 49(3), 1985, pp285-299 and J Veit-Wilson, 'Poverty and the Adequacy of Social Security,' in J Ditch (ed), *Introduction to Social Security: policies, benefits and poverty,* Routledge, 1999, pp78-109

32 L Leisering and S Leibfried, *Time and Poverty in Western Welfare States,* Cambridge University Press, 1999

33 See note 14

34 See note 9, p96

2 Poverty: the facts

Measuring poverty is an exercise in demarcation. Lines have to be drawn where none may be visible and they have to be made bold. Where one draws the line is itself a battlefield.

(Meghnad Desai, *Excluding the Poor*)[1]

INTRODUCTION

CPAG is in no doubt about the existence, nature and growth in poverty in Britain. At its heart, poverty is about exclusion from social participation. At the end of the twentieth century, the British Government began for the first time in many years to admit the existence of poverty and to sanction the use of official measures – attaching these to public targets for the elimination of child poverty. However, there is still no one, official, poverty line – no government-sanctioned marker as there is in, for example, the United States. Instead, a basket of measures or indicators has been adopted – we examine these in more detail on p65. Nevertheless, since our task is to estimate the extent of poverty, we need to establish a line – one which divides those who are poor from those who are not poor. We have chosen to look first at a possible income poverty line and second at a broader measure of poverty and social exclusion. See Chapter 1 for a detailed discussion of the limitations of each approach.

The first poverty line is based on the *Households Below Average Income* (HBAI) statistics. We use 50 per cent of average (mean) income after housing costs and including the self-employed, adjusted for family size, as a proxy for the poverty line. It is an explicitly 'relative' measure which looks at how people at the bottom of the income distribution have fared in relation to the mean. Most recently the Government has favoured using a poverty line of 60 per cent of median income and this is shown here for comparison (also after housing costs and including the self-employed).

A second poverty line, based on the Poverty and Social Exclusion (PSE) Survey, is not an income poverty line but adds an independent measure of deprivation showing items people lack or cannot afford despite the fact that they are considered to be necessities by the majority.

Each approach has its strengths and weaknesses and by examining each side by side we are able to present a more comprehensive picture of poverty.

KEY RESULTS

Despite their different approaches, the figures reveal:

- In 1999/2000, 14 million people (25 per cent of the population) were living below 50 per cent of mean income after housing costs. In 1979, 5 million people (9 per cent of the population) were living below 50 per cent of mean income after housing costs.[2]
- In 1999/2000, 13.3 million people (23 per cent of the population) were living below 60 per cent of median income after housing costs. In 1979, 7.1 million (13 per cent of the population) were living below 60 per cent of median income after housing costs.[3]
- At the end of 1999, 14.5 million people (26 per cent) were living in poverty (defined as lacking two or more socially perceived necessities) according to the PSE Survey. A comparison with earlier *Breadline Britain* surveys shows that in 1983, 14 per cent of households lacked three or more socially perceived necessities rising by 1990 to 21 per cent and by 1999 to over 24 per cent – roughly one in four households.[4]

So, whatever generally accepted method you use to measure it, poverty has grown significantly over recent years and by 1999/2000, between 13 and 14.5 million people in the United Kingdom (UK) – around a quarter of our society – were living in poverty.

CONTEXT

What is the context in which we are looking at these changes in poverty? The HBAI figures cover the period 1979 to 1999/2000.

During that time there were major economic and social changes. As a result, poverty levels rose in the 1980s, fell, and then rose again in the 1990s. Between 1979 and 1999/2000, such changes included:[5]

- a rise in the Gross Domestic Product (GDP) of 55 per cent in real (ie, after inflation) terms, although the rise was not consistent over this period and real GDP fell by over 3 per cent between 1979 and 1981 and by more than 1 per cent between 1990 and 1991 because of recession;
- very substantial rises in mean incomes – a rise of around 80 per cent in real personal disposable income between 1979 and 1999/2000;[6]
- a rise in average earnings of nearly 50 per cent in real terms between 1990 and 2000, although the earnings of the rich and poor became more dispersed;
- an increase in prices of 213 per cent;
- a very sharp rise in the number of people unemployed and seeking work, which rose from just over one million in 1979 to more than three million in 1986. Levels fell in the late 1980s to peak again at just under three million in 1993. By 1999/2000 the claimant count had again fallen almost to 1979 levels at just over one million. In February 2001 the number of people unemployed and claiming benefits fell below one million for the first time in over twenty years;
- according to the International Labour Organisation (ILO) definition of unemployment there were more than three million unemployed in the 1980s and again in 1993. By 1999 there were around 1.7 million unemployed by this definition.
- the weakening of some contributory parts of the social security system, such as sickness, incapacity and unemployment benefits, leaving many more people to fall back on means-tested benefits;
- increases in the proportion of the population receiving means-tested benefits, from 17 per cent in 1979 to 25 per cent in 1999;
- a change in employment patterns, with the growth of part-time, temporary and self-employed work;
- an increase in employment in service industries and a decline in manufacturing jobs;
- a downward trend in male employment rates and slower recovery after the two recessions, whereas female employment rates have risen and recovered more quickly – both are now rising at similar rates;
- a rise in the proportion of households with no one in paid work from below 10 per cent in the mid-1970s to nearly 19 per cent in 1996. The fastest rises took place in the mid-1970s and early 1980s –

today, around 16 per cent of working-age households have no one in paid work;

- bonuses for the average earner and windfalls for the rich through reductions in income tax. However, national insurance contributions and indirect taxes were increased;
- increases in the number of single adults below pension age without children, pensioners and lone-parent families – all these groups tend to have lower than average incomes;
- decreases in the number of couples with children and of children in general.

In short, the persistence of high unemployment coupled with increased average incomes for most of these two decades have forged a much wider gap between the people who were dependent solely on benefits (which generally rise by the level of inflation only) or reliant on low wages, and those on average earnings and above.

WHAT THE FIGURES MISS OUT

The HBAI figures up to 1994/95 are derived from UK-wide data from the Family Expenditure Survey (FES) and from 1994/95 onwards from the larger Family Resources Survey (FRS), an annual government survey of nearly 25,000 private households in Britain. Overlapping figures are available for the years 1994/95 to 1996/97. The FRS only covers Great Britain (not the UK) and due to the nature of the FRS, the following people are also excluded from the figures:

- people living in residential institutions – eg, hospitals, nursing homes, barracks, student accommodation, residential homes and prisons;
- homeless people or those in bed and breakfast accommodation.

The exclusion of homeless people and people living in institutions means that all the figures we present below are likely to be an underestimate. This is because homeless people and people living in institutions often have very little money.

HOUSEHOLDS BELOW AVERAGE INCOME STATISTICS

WHAT ARE THE HOUSEHOLDS BELOW AVERAGE INCOME STATISTICS?

Households Below Average Income (HBAI) was published for the first time in 1988. It is now the major source of official information about people living on a low income. The latest edition, *Households Below Average Income 1994/5-1999/00,* was issued in July 2001. For comparisons dating back to 1979, the earlier *Households Below Average Income, a statistical analysis, 1979-1996/97* is used.[7] HBAI replaced the previous Low Income Families (LIF) Statistics – see p55. It examines the living standards of people in the lower half of the income distribution. The series shows:

- the number of individuals in households with incomes below various thresholds of the mean, from 40 per cent up to the mean household income;
- the number of individuals in households with incomes below various thresholds of the median, from 40 per cent up to the median household income;
- the number of individuals living in households in the bottom 10 per cent, 20 per cent, 30 per cent, 40 per cent and 50 per cent of the income distribution (these are known as decile groups), and the rises in real income for each of these groups;
- the number of individuals ranked into five equal-sized groups (or quintiles) where the lowest quintile is the bottom 20 per cent of the income distribution; *and*
- the number of dependent children below various thresholds and within certain income distributions.

WHAT IS THE POVERTY LINE IN THE HOUSEHOLDS BELOW AVERAGE INCOME STATISTICS?

HBAI does not contain an obvious poverty line. We have chosen 50 per cent of average (mean) disposable income[8] as the poverty line, a definition which is widely used by commentators and in international studies. For comparison, 60 per cent of median income is sometimes shown, as it is used by the British government. It is argued that, in times of rising prosperity, the mean can be inflated and affected by small numbers of rich people at the top of the income distribution. Comparing people at the bottom to the median (or mid-point) of the income scale is less vulnerable to this effect (although results would be skewed if a large proportion of the population were predominantly either rich or poor).

HBAI presents figures both before and after housing costs. There are arguments for using both measures.[9] We have chosen in most cases here to use figures which show numbers and income after housing costs for the following reasons. First, the figures are more comparable with income support which does not include housing costs. Second, housing expenditure is different from other kinds of expenditure, varying widely between geographical areas and different stages of life. Third, it is also a fixed cost for many families, particularly those on low incomes, who have little choice about the amount they spend on their housing and therefore about the money they have left, for example, to meet their children's needs.

We show in Table 2.1 a poverty line defined as 50 per cent of mean income after housing costs and including the self-employed. In

---

TABLE 2.1: **The poverty line in 1994/95 and 1999/2000 and expressed in December 2000 prices: defined as 50 per cent mean income (after housing costs), £ per week**

	1994/95 £	1999/2000 £
Single person	72	83
Lone parent with child aged 3	96	110
Lone parent with two children (aged 3 and 8)	126	145
Lone parent with two children (aged 8 and 11)	136	157
Couple	131	151
Couple with one child aged 3	155	178
Couple with two children (aged 3 and 8)	185	213
Couple with two children (aged 8 and 11)	195	225
Couple with three children (aged 3, 8 and 11)	219	252
All (equivalised income value)[10]	£131	£151

Source: Derived from Department of Social Security, *Households Below Average Income 1994/95-1999/00*, Corporate Document Services, 2001

1999/2000 (the date of the latest set of figures) a two-parent family with two children aged three and eight were living in poverty if they had an income (after paying for their housing costs) of less than £213 a week in December 2000 prices. Figures that include the self-employed are used throughout this chapter unless otherwise stated.

WHAT DO THE HOUSEHOLDS BELOW AVERAGE INCOME FIGURES SHOW?

HBAI presents the official figures on low income. HBAI shows that in the UK in 1999/2000:

- 14 million people were living in poverty (below 50 per cent of mean income after housing costs) – one quarter of the population. This is almost three times the number in 1979 – five million, or 9 per cent of the population; *or*
- 13.3 million people were living in poverty (below 60 per cent of median income after housing costs) – 23 per cent. Nearly twice the number in 1979 – 7.1 million, or 13 per cent of the population.[11]

WHO IS IN POVERTY?

The figure of 14 million hides within it important patterns. We can look at the composition of poor people – which groups make up the bulk of those in poverty; we can also assess the risk of poverty – which groups are most likely to be poor. These two things are different – eg, lone parents make up only a small proportion of the total number of people in poverty as they are a small group; however, they have a high risk of poverty.

First we look at the composition of people in poverty, by economic status and family status. A family here is taken to be a single adult or couple together with any dependent children. Figure 2.1 illustrates how poverty is distributed among different groups.

Looking at economic status first, unemployment is a crucial cause of poverty, accounting for one in eight of those in poverty. Couples where both partners are working full time and single people in full-time work make up only 4 per cent of those in poverty. The growing importance of two wages coming in to protect couples and families against poverty is illustrated by the figures, which show that couples where only one

FIGURE 2.1: **The composition of people in poverty (defined as living below 50 per cent of mean income after housing costs) in 1999/2000**

By family type

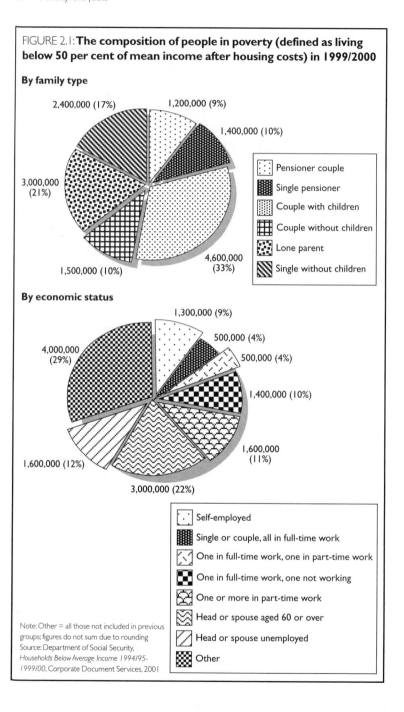

2,400,000 (17%)   1,200,000 (9%)

1,400,000 (10%)

3,000,000 (21%)

4,600,000 (33%)

1,500,000 (10%)

Pensioner couple

Single pensioner

Couple with children

Couple without children

Lone parent

Single without children

By economic status

1,300,000 (9%)

500,000 (4%)

4,000,000 (29%)

500,000 (4%)

1,400,000 (10%)

1,600,000 (11%)

1,600,000 (12%)

3,000,000 (22%)

Self-employed

Single or couple, all in full-time work

One in full-time work, one in part-time work

One in full-time work, one not working

One or more in part-time work

Head or spouse aged 60 or over

Head or spouse unemployed

Other

Note: Other = all those not included in previous groups; figures do not sum due to rounding
Source: Department of Social Security,
Households Below Average Income 1994/95-1999/00, Corporate Document Services, 2001

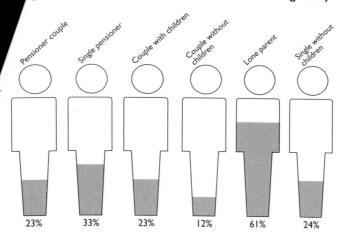

FIGURE 2.3: The risk of poverty by family status in 1999/2000 (defined ...g below 50 per cent of mean income after housing costs)

Pensioner couple — 23%
Single pensioner — 33%
Couple with children — 23%
Couple without children — 12%
Lone parent — 61%
Single without children — 24%

Proportion living in poverty

Source: Department of Social Security, *Households Below Average Income 1994/95-1999/00*, Corporate Document Services, 2001

FIGURE 2.4: **The risk of poverty for men, women and children in 1990/2000 (defined as living below 50 per cent of mean income after housing costs)**

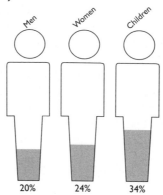

Men — 20%
Women — 24%
Children — 34%

Proportion living in poverty

Source: Department of Social Security, *Households Below Average Income 1994/95-1999/00*, Corporate Document Services, 2001

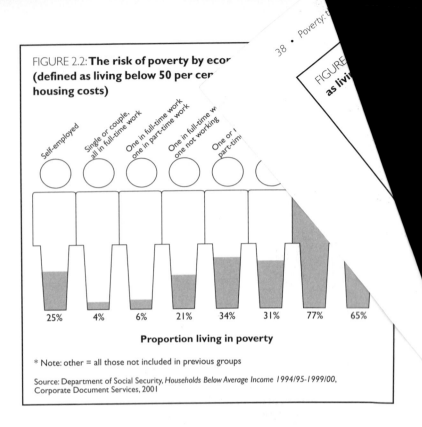

FIGURE 2.2: **The risk of poverty by ecor
(defined as living below 50 per cer
housing costs)**

Self-employed

Single or couple,
all in full-time work

One in full-time work
one in part-time work

One in full-time w
one not working

One or
part-time

25%   4%   6%   21%   34%   31%   77%   65%

Proportion living in poverty

* Note: other = all those not included in previous groups

Source: Department of Social Security, *Households Below Average Income 1994/95-1999/00,*
Corporate Document Services, 2001

member is working full time and one not at all make up 10 per cent of
those in poverty. People in families where one or more is in part-time
work constitute a similar proportion of those in poverty – 11 per cent.[12]

Turning to family status, couples with children account for the
largest group in poverty – 33 per cent. The next largest group is lone
parents who make up 21 per cent of those in poverty.[13] Poverty among
lone-parent families has increased dramatically in recent years. Nearly
half (45 per cent) of all poor children now live with a lone parent and
nearly 43 per cent of all poor children live with a lone parent who is
not working full time.

The risk of poverty for different groups is illustrated clearly in
Figures 2.2 and 2.3.

The group with the highest risk is the unemployed – nearly four-
fifths of them are in poverty. People in families where there is only part-
time work also carry a high risk of poverty – more than one in three.[14]
Looking at risk by family status shows that 61 per cent of individuals in

lone-parent families are in poverty.[15] The next most vulnerable group is single pensioners where 33 per cent are in poverty. Both the lone parent and the single pensioner group are dominated by women, showing their vulnerability to poverty. Figure 2.4 shows the risk of poverty for men, women and children.

HOW MANY CHILDREN?

Poverty that afflicts children is perhaps the most shocking. Figures 2.5 and 2.6 show that children have been more vulnerable to poverty than society as a whole throughout the period from 1979 to 1999/2000.

In 1999/2000, a higher proportion of children was living in poverty than the population as a whole. This was true on either definition of poverty:[16]

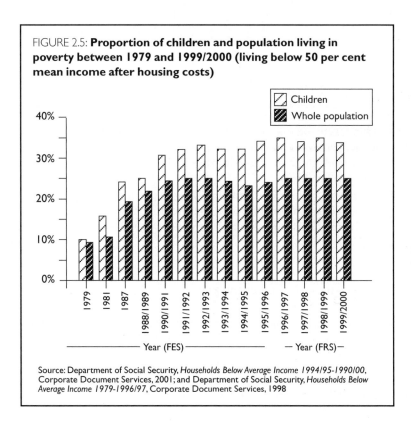

FIGURE 2.5: **Proportion of children and population living in poverty between 1979 and 1999/2000 (living below 50 per cent mean income after housing costs)**

Source: Department of Social Security, *Households Below Average Income 1994/95-1990/00*, Corporate Document Services, 2001; and Department of Social Security, *Households Below Average Income 1979-1996/97*, Corporate Document Services, 1998

FIGURE 2.6: **Proportion of children and population living in poverty between 1979 and 1999/2000 (living below 60 per cent median income after housing costs)**

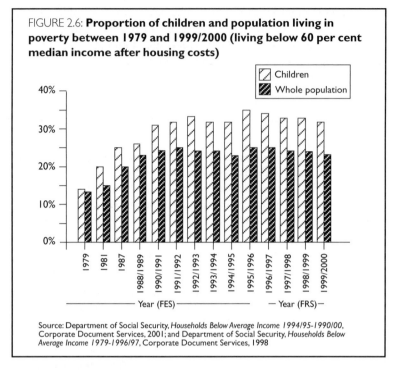

Source: Department of Social Security, *Households Below Average Income 1994/95-1990/00,* Corporate Document Services, 2001; and Department of Social Security, *Households Below Average Income 1979-1996/97,* Corporate Document Services, 1998

- There were 4.3 million children living in poverty (defined as below 50 per cent of mean income after housing costs) – one third (34 per cent) of all children. This compares to 1.4 million in 1979 – 10 per cent of all children.
- There were 4.1 million children living in poverty (defined as below 60 per cent of median income after housing costs) – 32 per cent of all children. This compares to 1.9 million in 1979 – 14 per cent of all children.

WHICH CHILDREN ARE IN POVERTY?

Of the 4.3 million children living in poverty (defined as below 50 per cent of mean income after housing costs) in 1999/2000:[17]

- 1,438,000 were living in families where there was one or more full-time workers – 33 per cent of all children living in poverty;
- 2,967,000 were living in families where there was no full-time

worker – 67 per cent of all children living in poverty. Within this group three in five were living with lone-parent families (about 37 per cent of these children lived in two-parent families, and about 63 per cent in lone-parent families).

Children at greatest risk of poverty were those living in families where there was no full-time worker, particularly in large families:

- 73 per cent of children in couples with no full-time worker were living in poverty.
- 72 per cent of children in lone-parent families with no full-time worker were living in poverty.
- The risk of poverty was much lower for children in families where there was a full-time worker; however, there was still an increased risk of poverty for large families.
- 9 per cent of children in families with one or more full-time workers and one or two children were in poverty.
- 23 per cent of children in families with one or more full-time workers and with three or more children were in poverty.

WHAT HAS HAPPENED SINCE 1979?

HBAI only provides comparative data as far back as 1979, so we cannot make comparisons over a longer time span.[18] Poverty increased dramatically between 1979 and 1999/2000 whether measured before or after housing costs (see Tables 2.2 and 2.3).

Although presented as a continuous series, the HBAI figures suffer from a degree of discontinuity due to the change in methodology in 1994/95.[19] However, it is still possible to draw broad conclusions about changes in the poverty figures over time.

The HBAI statistics used above are based on the contemporary mean which changes as average incomes rise. But HBAI also uses a range of fixed or constant thresholds that do not change as mean income rises. We pick out 50 per cent of mean income after housing costs in 1979, which is only increased to allow for inflation rather than in line with any growth in real average incomes. The comparison with 1979 using the FES is only available up to 1995/96. On this measure, poverty increased from 5 million to 5.3 million, an increase of 6 per cent.[20] But the figure disguises two periods of rapid poverty growth within this period – one in the early 1980s and again in the early 1990s.[21] The same measure also shows an increased risk of poverty over

TABLE 2.2: **Numbers and proportions of individuals living below 50 per cent of mean income before and after housing costs**

Year	Before housing costs		After housing costs	
	Number (millions)	%	Number (millions)	%
1979	4.4	8	5.0	9
1981	4.7	9	6.2	11
1987	8.7	16	10.5	19
1988/89	10.4	19	12.0	22
1990/91	11.6	21	13.5	24
1991/92	11.7	21	13.9	25
1992/93	11.4	20	14.1	25
1993/94	10.7	19	13.7	24
1994/95	10.3	18	13.4	23
1995/96	10.7	18	14.1	24
1996/97	10.5	19	14.1	25
1997/98	10.7	19	14.0	25
1998/99	11.0	19	14.3	25
1999/2000	10.7	19	14.0	25

Note: figures for individuals include children
Source: Department of Security, Households Below Average Income 1994/95-1999/00, Corporate Document Services, 2001

this period for certain groups – eg, couples with children and single people without children. Between 1979 and 1995/96, on this measure, the number of children in poverty increased from 1.4 to 1.7 million – a rise of 21 per cent.[22]

The same constant or fixed measure can be used to look at the most recent period. Based on the FRS, we use a fixed threshold of 50 per cent of mean income after housing costs in 1994/95.[23] Using this measure, poverty has decreased from 13.3 million to 10.3 million – nearly a 23 per cent decrease. The most rapid fall occurred between 1996/97 and 1998/99 – a fall from 12.9 to 11.5 million (11 per cent) on this constant measure. The number of children in poverty fell from 4 to 3.7 million – a fall of 7 per cent.[24] However, as outlined earlier (see p20), we do not believe that this constant measure is the right approach to looking at changes in poverty over time, as it fails to take into account how the poorest have fared in relation to the rest of the population.

TABLE 2.3: **Numbers and proportions of individuals living below 60 per cent of median income before and after housing costs**

Year	Before housing costs		After housing costs	
	Number (millions)	%	Number (millions)	%
1979	6.5	12	7.1	13
1981	6.9	13	8.1	15
1987	9.3	17	11.1	20
1988/89	10.9	19	12.6	23
1990/91	11.4	20	13.5	24
1991/92	11.7	21	13.9	25
1992/93	11.4	20	13.9	24
1993/94	10.5	18	13.5	24
1994/95	10.2	18	13.4	23
1995/96	10.8	19	14.2	25
1996/97	10.4	18	13.9	25
1997/98	10.3	18	13.5	24
1998/99	10.2	18	13.4	24
1999/2000	10.0	18	13.3	23

Note: figures for individuals include children
Source: Department of Social Security, *Households Below Average Income* team

By considering the poorest 10 per cent of the population in 1979 and 1999/2000 (after housing costs), we can see how the *composition* of the poorest groups has changed.[25] Figure 2.7 shows how pensioners made up a much smaller proportion of the poorest 10 per cent in 1999/2000 than in 1979 (down from 20 per cent to 5 per cent of the bottom 10 per cent); couples with children made up a slightly smaller proportion (down from 41 per cent to 37 per cent); couples without children made up made up a larger proportion (up from 9 to 14 per cent); lone parents made up a significantly larger proportion of the poorest (up from 9 per cent to 15 per cent); and the proportion of single people without children in the bottom 10 per cent more than doubled between 1979 and 1999/2000 (from 10 per cent to 24 per cent) a fact rarely commented on in the recent debate. Looking at *economic status*, the effect of unemployment for much of these two decades is evident – in 1979 only 16 per cent of the bottom 10 per cent were unemployed – by 1999/2000 the figure had risen to 19 per cent. Also, the proportion of self-employed and households with one or

FIGURE 2.7: **The changing composition of the poorest 10 per cent between 1979 and 1999/2000 (income after housing costs)**

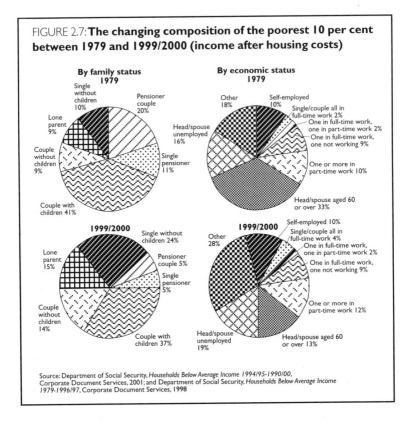

Source: Department of Social Security, *Households Below Average Income 1994/95-1990/00,* Corporate Document Services, 2001; and Department of Social Security, *Households Below Average Income 1979-1996/97,* Corporate Document Services, 1998

more part-time workers in the poorest 10 per cent had also increased substantially (from 10 per cent to 14 and 12 per cent respectively).

GROWING DIVISIONS

The figures also show a stark picture of poor people falling further and further behind the rest of society since 1979 (see Chapter 7 for more detail). Over the 20-year period from 1979 to 1999/2000, the real incomes of the poorest 10 per cent saw a real rise after housing costs of only 6 per cent compared to a rise of 80 per cent for the mean.[26] The richest 10 per cent saw a staggering rise in real income after housing costs of 86 per cent. These figures include the self-employed. If the self-employed are excluded, the real income of the poorest 10 per cent shows a slightly higher real rise of 9 per cent.[27] Before housing costs, the real incomes of the poorest 10 per cent (including the self-employed) saw a rise of 21 per cent. This compares with a rise of 55 per cent for the mean.

If we look over a slightly earlier period and compare the poorest 10 per cent in 1979 with the poorest 10 per cent in 1995/96, there was a *fall* in real income after housing costs of 9 per cent, while there was a rise of 44 per cent for the mean. The richest 10 per cent saw a real increase of 70 per cent over the same period. These figures include the self-employed. If the self-employed are excluded, the real income of the poorest 10 per cent shows a fall of 5 per cent.[28] Incomes before housing costs also show a very large gap between the poorest and the mean – the real incomes of the poorest 10 per cent (including the self-employed) rose by 12 per cent compared with a rise of 42 per cent for the mean between 1979 and 1995/96.[29]

Between 1994/95 and 1999/2000 the poorest 10 per cent saw an increase in real income after housing costs of between 6 and 32 per cent, while the rise for the mean was 15 per cent. If we look at incomes before housing costs, the range of increase for the poorest 10 per cent falls to between zero and 12 per cent compared with 12 per cent for the mean. This fall may be accounted for by changes in housing benefit income as a proportion of all income due to rising housing costs. If the self-employed are excluded, the increase in real income for the poorest 10 per cent falls to between zero and 8 per cent before housing costs and zero and 20 per cent after housing costs – while mean real increases for the whole population stay at 12 per cent and 15 per cent respectively.

Some caution is needed in interpreting these signs of improvement, as other official data shows that between 1997 and 1999/2000 the incomes of the richest and poorest deciles continued to move apart[30] and child poverty remained little changed. However, there is evidence from income modeling that by 2001 there may have been a significant reduction in child poverty (see p63).[31]

It is the rise in unemployment and to a lesser extent, self-employment, which largely explains the sharp fall in real income after housing costs for the poorest 10 per cent between 1979 and 1999/2000. However, the picture is not a straightforward one: over the same period (1979–1999/2000) the *expenditure* of the poorest 10 per cent increased.

Poor people's share of total income after housing costs fell between 1979 and 1995/96. The share of the bottom 10 per cent fell from 4 per cent to 2.2 per cent, and the share of the bottom 50 per cent fell from nearly a third (32 per cent) to one quarter (25 per cent).[32] Between 1994/95 and 1999/2000 the income share of the poorest 10 per cent rose slightly from 1.8 to 1.9 per cent although the poorest 20 per cent saw a slight fall from 6 to 5.9 per cent.[33] The bottom half of the population retained a quarter share of total income (25 per cent). The share of the top ten per cent rose from 27 to 29 per cent. (See Chapter 7 for more detail.)

DO PEOPLE STAY POOR?

> Time is not simply the medium in which poverty occurs, it forges its very nature...While poverty in childhood may not always be a significant problem, poverty throughout childhood most definitely is.
> (Robert Walker, *Lifetime Poverty Dynamics*)[34]

The length of time in poverty and the frequency of spells in poverty are key to explaining the intensity of the experience of poverty and its long-term effects. Short-term poverty occurs in households that still have resources to fall back on, whereas longer periods in poverty are characterised by debt, difficulty in replacing worn items, uncertainty, and increasing powerlessness, exclusion and disadvantage (see Chapter 4). It is therefore important to look in more detail at the frequency and persistence of poverty.

HBAI looks at what has happened to the incomes of the poorest 10 per cent. But, it is important to remember that the people who were in the bottom 10 per cent in 1998/99 are not necessarily the same people who were in the bottom 10 per cent in 1979. The figures do not mean that any one person has stayed in the bottom tenth since 1979 with the same real income.[35] But if the person at this point in 1979 has moved up, then someone else has had a *fall* in real income. Researchers working on the British Household Panel Survey[36] and others have begun to look at poverty over a longer period looking at the dynamics of movement in and out of poverty and in some cases over a lifetime.

Recent evidence on income dynamics shows considerable mobility from one year to the next although the change in income is not always great. Based on analysis of the British Household Panel Survey, Stephen Jenkins concludes: 'of those who are poor in one year, almost one half are not poor the following year – but those who escape poverty often remain on low incomes and have a high risk of returning to poverty in future years. Income mobility also means that the proportion of the population that is touched by poverty over a six-year period is twice as large as the proportion that is poor in any one year.'[37] These findings challenge policy makers to adopt a more dynamic approach to tackling frequent or chronic spells in poverty. New evidence is bringing to light the different life 'events' likely to give rise to movements in and out of poverty. These can be related to income, such as gaining or losing a job, or family and demographic change such as gaining or losing a partner. For some groups, such as lone parents, the main reason for moving into poverty is loss of a partner. But more than four-fifths of movements out of poverty and three-fifths of movements into poverty are linked to income changes[38] (see Chapter 3 for more detail).

WHO IS AT RISK OF PERSISTENT POVERTY?

As well as looking at movements in and out of poverty it is also important to look at the experience of poverty, particularly for those people who experience persistent or prolonged spells in poverty. Certain groups are systematically more at risk of falling into poverty and being in it for longer. These include:[39] large families, lone parents, single people, households with a very young or old family head, those with low levels of educational attainment, people from minority ethnic groups, those living in areas of high unemployment or who are themselves unemployed, retired, disabled or on maternity leave.

Very young children are at particular risk of being poor for long periods, even when income is averaged over six years to take account of temporary spells of low income.[40] A study for UNICEF has shown that some children were poor in every year (1.4 per cent), while 14 per cent were poor at least three times compared with 9.7 per cent of adults. On average, 15 per cent of children were poor and 9 per cent chronically poor[41] over the six-year period compared with rates of 11 and 7 per cent respectively for adults.

Recent government indicators acknowledge the damaging effects of prolonged or repeated poverty by setting as a target the reduction of persistent poverty in addition to reducing the extent of poverty.[42] The measure is the proportion of children and working-age adults with incomes below 60 per cent median income (before housing costs) in at least three out of four years.[43] On this measure, persistent child poverty fell by as little as 19 per cent during 1991-1994 to 16 per cent during

1996–1999. For adults of working age, the proportion fell from 8 to 7 per cent over the same period.

THE POVERTY AND SOCIAL EXCLUSION SURVEY 1999

The Poverty and Social Exclusion (PSE) Survey 1999 was based on research from a team of academics and published by the Joseph Rowntree Foundation.[44] It extends the approach used in previous *Breadline Britain* surveys and attempts to measure both the scale and severity of poverty and the relationship between poverty and social exclusion. It also attempts to put into operation the definition of poverty agreed at the World Summit for Social Development in 1995 (see Chapter 1) and establish an objective basis for deciding on the levels of 'absolute' and 'overall' poverty in Britain today.

The PSE Survey uses a consensual definition of poverty derived from public assessment of a range of items deemed to be necessities. Someone is considered to be poor if they lack two or more of these socially perceived necessities – this is its strength. The HBAI measure is a convenient but essentially arbitrary cut-off point in deciding who is and who is not poor. Some below the line may have a relatively high standard of living, while some above it may be severely deprived of essentials. The PSE Survey attempts to measure this deprivation more objectively, in order to capture the reality of poverty.

The weakness of the PSE approach is that not everyone will agree about what counts as a necessity; leaving the results, as with other definitions of poverty, open to public debate. Also it is not part of a continually updated or internationally comparable series like the HBAI – although it could become so. However, this evidence adds significantly to income measures such as the HBAI series because it tells us more about what poverty and social exclusion mean in people's lives.

- At the end of 1999, 14.5 million people (26 per cent) were living in poverty (defined as lacking two or more socially perceived necessities) according to the PSE Survey.
- A comparison with earlier *Breadline Britain* surveys shows that in 1983, 14 per cent of households lacked three or more socially perceived necessities rising by 1990 to 21 per cent and by 1999 to over 24 per cent – roughly one in four households.[45] (In order to

make comparisons over time, the poverty line used here is households lacking three or more socially perceived necessities taken from the 1983 *Breadline Britain* survey.)

WHAT IS THE POVERTY AND SOCIAL EXCLUSION SURVEY?

[The PSE] measures poverty by looking at both deprivation and income level: whether people lack items that the majority of the population perceive to be necessities, and whether they have incomes too low to afford them...its main data are derived from the investigation of socially perceived necessities.

(D Gordon et al, *Poverty and Social Exclusion in Britain,*
Joseph Rowntree Foundation, 2000)

A nationally representative sample was asked which household goods and activities no one should be without in Britain. Those who could not afford the items defined as essential by a majority (more than 50 per cent) were deemed deprived (see Table 2.4).[46] A poverty threshold was then established by charting the incomes and living standards of the sample and finding the optimum poverty threshold between those with high incomes and living standards and those with low incomes and living standards. In addition, social exclusion was analysed along four dimensions – impoverishment, labour market exclusion, service exclusion and exclusion from social relations. The analysis is based unapologetically on contemporary perceptions of conditions and requirements.

WHAT IS THE POVERTY LINE IN THE PSE SURVEY?

In the PSE Survey 1999, the poverty line is set at the point where an individual is unable to afford at least two socially defined necessities.[47] The researchers further defined some people as having recently 'risen out of poverty' – eg, by getting a job, or as being 'vulnerable to poverty' – eg, having recently lost a job but still retaining certain necessary items. This provides helpful additional evidence on the nature of chronic and persistent poverty, see p47.

- 27.7 per cent of individuals lacked at least two socially perceived necessities.

TABLE 2.4: **Number of items respondents 'don't have' and 'can't afford'**

Items lacking	Number	%
0	891	58.1
1	218	14.2
2	87	5.7
3	73	4.8
4	50	3.2
5	34	2.2
6	32	2.1
7	22	1.4
8	19	1.3
9	22	1.4
10	18	1.2
11	13	0.8
12	11	0.7
13	17	1.1
14	10	0.6
15	7	0.5
16	2	0.1
17	2	0.2
18	2	0.1
19	1	0.1
21	1	0.0
Total	**1,534**	**100.0**

Figures do not sum due to rounding
Source: D Gordon et al, *Poverty and Social Exclusion in Britain*, Joseph Rowntree Foundation, 2000

TABLE 2.5: **PSE poverty classifications**

	Number	%
Poor	393	25.6
Vulnerable to poverty	158	10.3
Risen out of poverty	28	1.8
Not poor	955	62.2
Total	**1,534**	**100.0**

Figures do not sum due to rounding
Source: D Gordon et al, *Poverty and Social Exclusion in Britain*, Joseph Rowntree Foundation, 2000

• 72.3 per cent of individuals did not.

Once account is taken of those who are vulnerable to or rising out of poverty, the classifications in Table 2.5 emerge.

There was also a very close association between actually being poor and a person's own subjective assessment of the adequacy of their income – 85 per cent of those who said their income was a lot below what they needed to stay out of poverty were found to be poor in the survey.

THE RISK OF POVERTY

Although the proportion of people who are poor is around 26 per cent, some groups have a greater risk of poverty – for example, unemployed people (77 per cent), those on income support (70 per cent), lone parents (62 per cent), local authority tenants (61 per cent), sick or disabled people not in work (61 per cent) and housing association tenants (57 per cent). Men have a 22 per cent chance of being poor compared with 29 per cent for women. Young people and those with younger children were also more likely to be poor. Although there are some differences, these proportions bear close comparison with the risk of poverty shown in the HBAI results (see pp35-39). Table 2.6 and Table 2.7 show the risk of poverty by employment status and household composition.

TABLE 2.6: **The risk of poverty in the PSE Survey 1999 by employment status**

	Poverty rate (% in poverty)	Poverty proportion (% of all in poverty)	Number
One worker	28	26	361
Two workers	14	19	520
Three workers	23	8	141
No workers – retired	23	21	354
No workers – sick/disabled	61	10	62
No workers – unemployed	77	10	48
No workers – other	76	8	38

Source: D Gordon et al, *Poverty and Social Exclusion in Britain*, Joseph Rowntree Foundation, 2000

TABLE 2.7: **The risk of poverty in the PSE Survey 1999 by household composition**

	Poverty rate (% in poverty)	Poverty proportion (% of all in poverty)	Number
Single adult	32	22	274
Lone parent with 1 child	66	5	29
Lone parent with 2 children	62	3	21
Lone parent with 3+ children*	89	2	9
Couple	15	18	485
Couple with 1 child	24	7	108
Couple with 2 children	26	11	172
Couple with 3 children	39	6	57
Couple with 4+ children	29	2	21
Two or more adults no children	34	6	71
Two or more adults with children	52	4	33
Couple with one or more adults no children	21	9	159
Couple with one or more adults and 1 child	13	2	56
Couple with one or more adults and 2+ children	37	4	41

* Based on 20 cases or fewer and not reliable

Source: D Gordon et al, *Poverty and Social Exclusion in Britain*, Joseph Rowntree Foundation, 2000

WHAT DO THE RESULTS OF THE PSE SURVEY SHOW?

From the PSE Survey it is possible to tell who is poor because they are deprived of socially perceived necessities. This information, together with income data, can be used to formulate a poverty threshold (see p49). In addition, the extent of social exclusion and the subjective experience of poverty are assessed.

Certain items were regarded as necessities by a high proportion of respondents. For example, 'beds and bedding for everyone', 'heating to warm living areas of the home', 'a damp-free home', 'visiting friends or family in hospital' and 'medicines prescribed by doctor' were deemed essential by over 90 per cent of people. Fewer than 10 per cent regarded a dishwasher, a mobile phone, internet access or satellite television as necessities.

From the results, it is neither possible to tell which combination of items were lacked by any given deprived individual nor which items are most commonly lacked by those defined as poor – it is safe, therefore, to assume that the effects of poverty are different from one individual to the next. However, a higher proportion lacked certain items than others. For example, over 10 per cent lacked 'regular savings (of £10 per month) for rainy days or retirement', 'a holiday away from home once a year (not with relatives)', 'money to keep home in a decent state of decoration', 'a small amount of money to spend on self weekly not on family', 'replace or repair broken electrical goods and replace worn out furniture'.

Poor people were also able to comment on the degree to which they felt socially excluded by answering questions about their experience of poverty, their perception of poverty in Britain, their sense of security in their own neighbourhood, participation in civic life and the effect of money on well-being. Eighty-six per cent of those who felt poor 'all the time' were also poor by the definition used in the survey (lacking two or more socially perceived necessities). Those feeling most dissatisfied with their neighbourhood or very unsafe in their own home tended to be poor (48 per cent and 45 per cent respectively). The people most likely to say that they did not participate in civic life tended to be the poorest group (43 per cent).

HOW MANY CHILDREN ARE POOR IN THE PSE SURVEY?

Twenty-seven items were thought to be necessities by over half the parents in an Omnibus survey. A child was considered poor in the PSE Survey if they lacked one or more of the items on the list. By this definition, 34 per cent of children are poor. If defined by lacking two or more items, then 18 per cent were poor. The item lacked by the highest proportion of children was 'a holiday away from home at least one week a year'.

WHICH CHILDREN ARE AFFECTED?

Children were more or less deprived depending on the household they lived in (see Table 2.8). A higher proportion were deprived of items in

TABLE 2.8: **Children deprived of socially perceived necessities by employment status, household type, age and number of children, tenure and benefit receipt**

	% lacking one or more item	% lacking two or more items
Employment status of household:		
Two full-time/more than two workers	32	15
One full-time, one part-time	19	6
One full-time	37	19
One or more part-time	52	30
No workers	63	42
Household type:		
Couple	29	11
Lone parent	52	33
Other	39	13
Age of child:		
0 to 1	36	16
2 to 4	37	23
5 to 10	37	17
11 to 16	29	15
Number of children in household:		
1	29	13
2	25	11
3	42	25
4+	68	39
Tenure:		
Own	24	11
Local authority	69	41
Other rented	57	34
Member of household gets income support/ jobseeker's allowance:		
No	28	12
Yes	66	43

Source: D Gordon et al, *Poverty and Social Exclusion in Britain*, Joseph Rowntree Foundation, 2000

households with only part-time workers or no paid worker (52 per cent and 63 per cent lacking at least one item respectively). Children in lone-parent households were deprived to the same extent as 'workless' households (52 per cent). Thirty-seven per cent of children aged two to four were deprived with a significantly higher chance of lacking two or more items than other age groups. Larger families, those in local authority or other rented property and those in receipt of income support or jobseeker's allowance were also more likely to be deprived.

LIVING ON THE POVERTY LINE

The PSE Survey highlights the deprivation of families living in poverty. This, together with the HBAI thresholds, presents a more comprehensive picture of poverty. Other indicators can also shed light on the type of income and expenditure that gives rise to such high levels of deprivation. Here, we look first at benefit levels for out-of-work families and second at family budgets and spending as indicators of need.

CLAIMING INCOME SUPPORT

Prior to 1995, although not an official poverty line, the Government produced figures based on income support/supplementary benefit levels. These Low Income Families (LIF) figures were originally published by the Department of Social Security (for the years 1972-85), subsequently by the independent Institute for Fiscal Studies and then under the auspices of the House of Commons Social Security Committee until 1995.[48] They were replaced by HBAI in 1988. The figures showed the numbers of people living on, below or just above the supplementary benefit/income support level. Researchers also looked at those people living between 100 per cent and 140 per cent of the supplementary benefit/income support level and described them as living on the *margins* of poverty. This approach followed the pioneering work of Peter Townsend and others.[49] A 'constant' or 'fixed' threshold was also used in the LIF figures to scale down the income support threshold to its real 1979 level.

Income support replaced supplementary benefit as part of the 1988 social security changes. Like its predecessor, supplementary benefit, it is a means-tested benefit for people who are not in 'full-time' work. However, it has a different structure from supplementary benefit. Instead of scale rates and extra weekly additions for certain needs such as heating and diet, income support consists of personal allowances and premiums for certain groups such as families with children, pensioners,

TABLE 2.9: **Supplementary benefit, income support and income-based jobseeker's allowance, children, adults and all individuals, 1979-2001***

Year	Number of dependent children (000's)	Number of adults (000's)	Number of individuals (000's)
1979	955	3416	4370
1980	1125	3739	4863
1981	1550	4571	6122
1982	1793	5277	7070
1983	1868	5370	7238
1984	2033	5696	7729
1985	2033	5696	7729
1986	2227	6064	8291
1987	2236	5969	8205
1988**	2196	5193	7388
1989	2139	4885	7023
1990	2151	4871	7022
1991	2497	5250	7747
1992	2874	5979	8853
1993	3163	6659	9822
1994	3185	6667	9852
1995	3158	6616	9774
1996	3123	6465	9587
1997***	2919	6005	8924
1998	2727	5629	8356
1999	2660	5482	8141
2000	2577	5326	7904
2001	2530	5358	7887

* All estimates relate to a point in time. In 1979 the month was November, from 1980-84 the month was December, for 1986 the month was February, from 1987-2000 it was May and for 2001 the month was February
** Income support replaced supplementary benefit in 1988
*** Income support for the unemployed was replaced by jobseeker's allowance in October 1996

Source: Figures supplied by the Department for Work and Pensions, Analytical Services Division, rounded to the nearest thousand

lone parents, disabled people and carers. This change in the social security system created some difficulties in looking at the LIF figures over time — income support statistics are unable to reflect the detrimental effect of these changes on some groups.

The LIF figures were used until 1995 by CPAG and others as a proxy for the poverty line and defined all those living on and below supplementary benefit/income support as living in poverty. It allowed us to assess how many people were on or below what the state deems a minimum level of income for people who are not in 'full-time' work. Income support and supplementary benefit act as a 'safety net'; but these benefit rates rise year on year, in most cases by price inflation only, and thus do not completely reflect rising living standards. Also, if over time this minimum standard increases, the number of families deemed to be living on minimum income will also rise. Thus, raising benefit rates increases the number of people deemed to be poor. For this reason these figures are no longer produced or used as the basis for poverty estimates. Here we use benefit statistics simply to add another dimension to the picture of poverty detailed in the HBAI and PSE Survey evidence above.

WHAT DO THE INCOME SUPPORT FIGURES SHOW?

Today, 7.8 million people live on income support/income-based job-seeker's allowance (see Table 2.9). Jobseeker's allowance replaced income support for unemployed claimants in October 1996. The proportion of the population relying on supplementary benefit/income support/jobseeker's allowance has risen from 8 per cent in 1979 to a peak in 1993 of 15 per cent. In 2000, the proportion living on income support/ jobseeker's allowance remained at 13 per cent. As well as telling us the number and proportion of people living on the state minimum, it tells us that reliance on income support increased for certain groups and family types – most notably children in general and lone-parent families. Both the number and proportion of children in families on income support has been falling since a peak year in 1993/94. For lone parents too, after a peak year in 1995, the number and proportion on income support have been falling.

To a large extent, the rise and fall in claimant numbers coincide with periods of recession, falls in GNP and rises in unemployment (see p31). Jonathan Bradshaw argues that the relationship between official unemployment and the proportion of households without a full-time worker has been diverging over the past two decades and he links this to the rising number of lone-parent families.[50] Regional and local variation is also significant and figures are now available to show how many people live on income support at a local authority or ward level

TABLE 2.10: **Income support levels (after housing costs)**

Family type	Income support rates*				
	Apr 1997- Mar1998	Apr 1998- Mar 1999	Apr 1999- Mar 2000	Apr 2000- Mar 2001	Apr 2001- Mar 2002
Non-pensioners					
Single person aged 18-24	38.90	39.85	40.70	41.35	42.00
Aged 25+	49.15	50.35	51.40	52.20	53.05
Lone parent with one child (aged under 11)**	81.80	78.70 From Nov '98: 81.20	85.50 From Oct '99: 90.20	93.05 From Oct '00: 97.40	99.00 From Oct '01: 100.50
Couple***	77.15	79.00	80.65	81.95	83.25
Couple with two children (aged under 11)	121.75	124.65 From Nov '98: 129.65	134.95 From Oct '99: 144.35	149.25 From Oct '00: 158.10	160.65 From Oct '01: 163.65
Pensioners (aged 60-74)					
Single person	68.80	70.45	75.00	78.45	92.15
Couple	106.80	109.35	116.60	121.95	140.55

Notes
* These figures were the levels of income support paid at the time and are cash figures not adjusted for inflation.
** Lone parent is aged 18 or over and is a new claimant.
   The enhanced lone parent rate of family premium was abolished for new claimants in April 1998 – these
   figures are based on the rate for new claimants.
***At least one member of the couple is aged 18 or over.

Source: *National Welfare Benefits Handbook*, 1997/98, 1998/99, and *Welfare Benefits Handbook*, 1999/2000,
2000/01, 2001/02, CPAG

which combined with other indicators gives a guide to local levels of deprivation[51] – see Chapter 8 for more on small area data.

The figures in Table 2.10 show that for most people, benefit levels have risen substantially over the past five years. But one group, lone parents, saw a real terms cut in income support in 1998 through the abolition of the lone parent rate of the family premium. Benefit increases for children in subsequent years have compensated for this although the premium has not been restored. Most of the benefit increases took place after 1999/2000 – the last available year of the HBAI figures and after the PSE Survey in 1999. As a result, it will be some time before the effects of these increases will show up in the official poverty figures – but see below for an analysis of the effects of these changes on child poverty after 1997.

HOW MANY CHILDREN?

Around 2.4 million children under 16 rely on income support today. In 1979, only 7.3 per cent of children in Great Britain lived on income support but this proportion rose to 25.7 per cent by 1993.[52] By 2000, it continued to stand at more than one in five children, at 20.4 per cent – a fall of about one-fifth in seven years compared with a two and a half-fold increase in the 14 years from 1979. The fact that this fall has been less steep than the rapid rise in the 1980s perhaps reflects a rise in the number and proportion of workless households (see Chapter 3).

LIVING BELOW INCOME SUPPORT LEVELS

Entitlement to benefits does not always guarantee a minimum standard of income and many live below these levels. One of the principal reasons why people are living below the income support level is that they are not taking up the means-tested benefits to which they are entitled. Table 2.11 shows the latest take-up figures for the main means-tested benefits, produced by the Department for Work and Pensions.[53]

TABLE 2.11: **Estimates of take-up of means-tested benefits by caseload and expenditure in 1999/2000**

	% take-up by caseload Range	% take-up by expenditure Range	Total unclaimed (millions)* Range
Income support	77-87	87-94	720-1,620
Housing benefit	89-95	92-97	290-840
Council tax benefit	73-80	76-83	460-710
Jobseeker's allowance (income-based)	67-78	74-84	490-900

* Rounded to the nearest ten million
Source: Department of Social Security, *Income-related Benefits: estimates of take-up in 1999/2000*, The Stationery Office, 2001

It reveals that at the lowest estimate, around £2 billion of means-tested benefits went unclaimed in 1999/2000.

This poverty gap highlights the problems inherent in targeting help on poor households. It also provides a warning against relying too heavily on assumptions about the actual income received by many families. For many it is not safe to assume that they receive all they are entitled to.

LIVING ON THE POVERTY LINE

We have looked at what each poverty line represents in cash terms. Comparing the poverty lines represented by both the HBAI and PSE side by side we have shown that the income level represented by each measure cannot provide an adequate standard of living in today's society. Some suggest that the vast numbers in poverty are due to over-generous poverty lines. The evidence suggests that the level of income measured by both poverty lines is unquestionably meagre in an affluent society.

The Family Budget Unit has drawn up a 'low cost but acceptable' budget (LCA) standard for different family types, drawing on a panel of experts and consumer groups and using expenditure data.[54] The budget standard estimates the income needed by a particular family type or household to reach a benchmark living standard. This is achieved by identifying a basket of key goods and services and estimating the quality, quantity and cost of each over a given lifetime. The LCA budget standard can be seen as representing a level of income that allows people to reach only a minimum income standard or poverty threshold. No childcare costs or costs of seeking work are included. Housing costs include rent, council tax and water charges in council property. Gas central heating is assumed for the lower floor only – costs may in fact be higher in poor standard accommodation without central heating. Travel costs include bus fares, two emergency taxi journeys a year, the purchase of second-hand bikes for each adult and a journey by coach to a holiday destination (about 40 miles away) and a theme park twice in three years. Pocket money, Christmas and birthday presents are incorporated into the leisure budget for each child.

In Table 2.12 we compare the living standard represented by income support with the LCA budget standard in 1998. It shows that in 1998, both poverty lines still fell below this standard for families with children. For example, income support for a couple with two children

TABLE 2.12: **Value of the income support (IS) scales over time and comparison with the Family Budget Unit (FBU) low cost but acceptable budget**

	Lone parent plus two children under 11			Couple plus two children under 11		
	IS per week	FBU low cost but acceptable budget per week*	Shortfall per week	IS per week	FBU low cost but acceptable budget per week*	Shortfall per week
Jan 1998	£98.70	£122.21	-£23.51	£121.75	£154.04	-£32.29
Uprated by RPI** Jan 1998 to Sept 2000	£108.46	£134.30	–	£133.79	£169.27	–
Actual Oct 2000	£128.35	–	-£5.95	£158.10	–	-£11.17

*FBU low cost but acceptable budget for families with a boy aged 10 years old and a girl age 4. It excludes alcohol expenditure and the value of milk tokens and free school meals
** Index less housing costs
Source: J Bradshaw, 'Child Poverty Under Labour', in *An End in Sight? Tackling child poverty in the UK*, CPAG, 2001

represented 79 per cent of the low cost but acceptable budget. By 2001, the shortfall had been much reduced due to increases in income support for children. Income support for a couple with two children now represents 93 per cent of the LCA budget. However, this budget represents a very basic standard of living in the twenty-first century.

The Family Budget Unit also produces a 'modest but adequate' (MBA) budget. This represents a level of income that allows people to participate fully in society rather than merely exist. According to the Family Budget Unit: 'Households at MBA level can afford to live comfortably, run a car, avoid debt problems and take an annual holiday. In the Netherlands, Scandinavia and Finland, a similar standard, called 'reasonable', is widely used.'[55] It is set well below an affluent standard of living. Income support levels and the 50 per cent of mean income poverty line would fall well short of this standard.

The examples in Table 2.12 look at families not in paid work. The LCA standard of living would arguably be much lower than that required for a working family. At this level, families on mean earnings are still caught in the poverty trap facing high marginal 'tax' rates of around 70 per cent.[56] The MBA is perhaps a better tool for comparison for working families. This is significant as 45 per cent of working-age adults in households with incomes below 50 per cent of the mean after housing costs (excluding the self-employed) contain one or more workers.[57] The same proportion fall below 60 per cent of median income after housing costs and excluding the self-employed. In terms of the risk of poverty, where adults in a family are working full time then 6 per cent of the working-age population are likely to be poor and 31 per cent are poor if adults are working part time.[58] Again, the results are the same whether poverty is defined as below half mean income or 60 per cent of median income after housing costs.

EVIDENCE ON FAMILY SPENDING

Important evidence on family spending also comes from the Centre for Research in Social Policy at Loughborough University. This evidence shows that, on average, food accounts for 63 per cent of spending on children and that parents spend far more on their children than is allowed in income support allowances for children.[59] In fact, income support provided only 70 per cent of the actual spending on children at the time of this study, with younger children costing only slightly less than older children. Clearly, this evidence has influenced subsequent government thinking on benefit levels for children (see Table 2.10, p58). Besides confirming these benefit shortfalls, this study also revealed the efforts made by parents to protect their children from the effects of poverty. For example, economic circumstances and family type were a poor predictor of spending on children, although the most significant chance of lower spending occurred in families with no one in paid work. Children in lone-parent families were more likely to go without regardless of whether the parent was in paid work, although lone parents and families on income support spent almost as much at Christmas as other parents. But most revealing was the evidence of the practical consequences of managing on such an inadequate income. Significantly, mothers reported going without clothes, shoes and entertainment to provide for their children. One in twenty mothers went without food to meet a child's needs and lone mothers on income support were 14 times more likely to go without food than mothers in non-claimant, two-parent families.

The 13 – 14.5 million people who are living in poverty (whether poverty is defined as below half mean income or below 60 per cent median income after housing costs) are forgoing many of the things that more than half of our society take for granted, whether it is a varied and healthy diet, enough money for transport, new but basic clothing, or treats such as going to the pantomime once every two years.

PROGRESS SINCE 1997

Our historic aim will be for ours to be the first generation to end child poverty, and it will take a generation. It is a 20-year mission, but I believe it can be done.

(Tony Blair, *Beveridge Revisited: a welfare state for the 21st century*, Speech at Toynbee Hall, 18 March 1999)

The historic commitment by Tony Blair, the Prime Minister, to end child poverty in a generation makes it important to assess any progress made to date. This commitment relates only to ending child poverty so, in this section, we concentrate solely on this aspect of the evidence. Since 1997 a number of policy changes have been made with the aim of reducing child poverty and encouraging the move from 'welfare to work'. The policies include, the working families' tax credit introduced in 1999, increases in benefit rates for children under 11 in means-tested benefits, increases in child benefit, a £5 increase in the income support earnings disregard, certain income tax changes and the introduction of the children's tax credit. David Piachaud and Holly Sutherland have assessed how successful these policies have been since 1997 in reducing child poverty using a range of measures.[60] This analysis updates the official statistics used in the rest of this chapter – these are available only after a two-year delay.

Using a micro-simulation model, Piachaud and Sutherland systematically assessed the impact of post-1997 policies. Taking into account policy changes announced up to and including the 2001 Budget and using DSS estimates of benefit take-up, they conclude that: 'Overall about one million children have been brought out of poverty, equally divided between one and two-parent families. In addition, of all those brought out of poverty, half are children.'[61] The poverty threshold used here is the one often used by the Government – 60 per cent of equivalised median income before housing costs. The results are sensitive to the poverty definition used. Using a threshold of 70 per cent median adds another 650,000 children to the total and if 50 per cent median is used it results in only 720,000 children being lifted out of poverty. If a constant threshold is used, then 1.33 million children have been lifted out of poverty; a 39 per cent reduction in child poverty. Actual figures will not be known until the HBAI figures for 2001/02 are published.

Some caution is needed. Sutherland and Piachaud warn that child poverty remains extremely high by post-war standards and is vulnerable to the state of the economy. So far, those children closest to the poverty line have simply been pushed just above that line. Raising the incomes of those in the deepest and most persistent poverty will be more difficult and will require the transfer of further resources to families. There is much left to do. Even if the ten-year target of halving child poverty is reached, levels will still be higher than in 1979.

Using a different poverty threshold of half mean income before housing costs,[62] the model shows that one in five children in households in the bottom income decile (300,000) are worse off under the post-1997 reforms (this time only up to and including the 2000 Budget). In terms of family type, the figures also illustrate graphically the results of lone parent benefit cuts in 1998. Some lone parents earning around £100 a week actually see a lower return from work as a result of the reforms announced since 1997.[63] Sixty-six per cent of lone parents working 16 hours a week on the minimum wage gain less from entering work under the modeled policy changes than under pre-1997 policies (by contrast, 58 per cent of those working for 30 hours a week gain more as a result of post-1997 policies). Although large numbers of children are moved out of poverty as a result of the reforms, some 10,000 children in lone-parent families see income reductions such that they move into poverty. These figures leave little room for doubt that lone parents and particularly working lone parents lost out through benefit cuts. These are likely to be households that lost MIRAS or are in receipt of income support with children over 11 who lost the lone-parent rate of child benefit and premiums. The fall in income is small but would be, for this group, significant. However, in the model, all lone parents are assumed to be new claimants who have suffered benefit cuts, when in fact many lone parents will be existing claimants whose benefits were frozen but not reduced. No account is taken either of child maintenance changes or the introduction of the childcare tax credit. We await official figures to see what the actual effect of the cuts has been.

TABLE 2.13: **Income support and poverty levels (defined as half mean income after housing costs) 2001/02***

	Income support (IS)	Poverty level (PL)	IS as % of PL
Couple with one child aged 6	129.95	192.06	67.7%
Couple with two children aged 4, 8	162.15	223.81	72.4%
Couple with three children aged 3, 8 11	194.35	265.08	73.3%
Lone parent with one child aged 6	101.15	120.63	83.9%

*Income support level is mean of rates applying April – September 2001 and October 2001 – March 2002; HBAI figures for 1998/99 are used, adjusted for the actual and forecast rise in real household disposable income and the Retail Price Index
Source: D Piachaud and H Sutherland, 'Child Poverty: aims, achievements and prospects for the future', *New Economy*, Volume 8, Issue 2, IPPR/Blackwell, 2001

Table 2.13 shows that benefit rates still fall short of a poverty level set at half mean income after housing costs, uprated to take account of rises in real income and prices. Here, income support for a couple with two children provides only 72 per cent of the poverty level. The researchers estimate that benefits would need to increase by £62 or 38 per cent in order to reach this level.

The authors conclude that: 'If child poverty is to be abolished in a generation then it will not be enough to roll forward the policy initiatives taken so far. It will be necessary for poor families to earn more – which will require skills, childcare and jobs – and to receive more transfers from the state either in subsidies to low pay or social benefits – which will require more redistribution.'[64]

GOVERNMENT INDICATORS – OPPORTUNITY FOR ALL

In order to monitor progress towards its 20-year target, the Labour Government has published three annual reports that include a range of criteria against which progress is to be judged.[65] The most recent report, *Opportunity for All: making progress*, was published in September 2001. The report incorporates four sets of indicators to monitor the impact of government policy on a range of outcomes, covering: children and young people, people of working age, and older people and communities. The latest results are reproduced in Table 2.14.

Jonathan Bradshaw argues that some of the indicators are too narrow in scope and that some are not, strictly speaking, indicators of poverty.[67] Some concentrate on inputs or causes of poverty (such as worklessness) rather than outcomes, some are based on departmental and service activities rather than outcomes (such as rates of admission to hospital or proportion of 16–18-year-olds in education), and others (such as Sure Start data) have no regular or national data source. For some indicators there are still only baseline figures and no way to assess any improvement or deterioration. The New Policy Institute has also published three reports containing a range of similar indicators, shadowing, and in some cases pre-dating, those included in *Opportunity for All*.[68] In view of the wide range of measures, there is a certain lack of clarity about what this combination of indicators actually tells us. And the wide range of indicators leaves it open for the Government to highlight the indicators that show the most favourable results. Nevertheless, an important start has been made in evaluating national progress to eliminate child poverty.

An important element missing from the Government's anti-poverty strategy is the voice of poor people and their representatives.[69] In Scotland, Wales and Northern and Southern Ireland a more inclusive process has been developed involving communities in the development of national action plans. Further action is needed if this important opportunity is not to be lost in England.

TABLE 2.14: **Summary of indicators in *Opportunity for All*** [66]

Children and young people:

1. Reduction in the proportion of children living in workless households (GB)*

1996	1997	1998	1999	2000	2001
19.3%	17.9%	17.8%	17.3%	15.7%	15.3%

2. a) Reduction in the proportion of children living in households below 60% of median income (GB)

	1996/97	1997/98	1998/99	1999/2000
Before housing costs:	26%	25%	24%	23%
After housing costs:	34%	33%	33%	32%

2. b) Reduction in proportion of children living in households below 60% of 1996/97 median held constant in real terms (GB)

	1996/97	1997/98	1998/99	1999/2000
Before housing costs:	26%	24%	22%	19%
After housing costs:	34%	32%	31%	28%

2. c) Reduction in proportion of children living in households with persistently low income (below 60% and 70% median before housing costs in at least three out of four years) (GB)

Below 60% median in at least three out of four years:

1991-1994	1992-1995	1993-1996	1994-1997	1995-1998	1996-1999
19%	17%	16%	16%	17%	16%

Below 70% median in at least three out of four years:

1991-1994	1992-1995	1993-1996	1994-1997	1995-1998	1996-1999
28%	28%	26%	25%	26%	26%

3. Increase in proportion of seven-year-olds in Sure Start areas achieving level 1 or above in Key Stage 1 English and Maths tests (England)

Awaiting baseline data

4. Increase in proportion of 11-year-olds achieving level 4 or above in Key Stage 2 tests for literacy and numeracy (England)

	1996	1997	1998	1999	2000	2001
English	57%	63%	65%	71%	75%	75%
Maths	54%	62%	59%	69%	72%	71%

5. Increase in proportion of 16-year-olds with at least one GCSE at grade A*-G (England)

1996	1997	1998	1999	2000
92.2%	92.3%	93.4%	94.0%	94.4%

6. Increase in proportion of 19-year-olds with at least a level 2 qualification or equivalent (England)

1996	1997	1998	1999	2000
69.7%	72.3%	73.9%	74.9%	75.3%

7. Reduction in the proportion of truancies and exclusions from school (England)

1996/97	1997/98	1998/99	1999/2000
0.17%	0.16%	0.14%	0.11%

8. Increase in proportion of young people leaving care with one or more GCSEs at grade A*-G 1999/2000

31%

9. Reduction in proportion of children who live in a home which falls below the set standard of decency (England)

1996

23%

10. Reduction in the infant mortality rate (per thousand live births) between manual groups and the population as a whole (England and Wales)

	1996	1997	1998
All social classes:			
(married & joint-registrations only)	5.79	5.66	5.53
Manual groups:	6.29	6.08	6.02
Non-manual groups:	4.75	4.62	4.46
Sole registrations:	7.50	7.41	7.58

11.a) Reduction in smoking rates during pregnancy (England)

1995	2000 (data source changed)
23%	18%

11.b) Reduction in smoking rates among children aged 11–15 (England)

1996	1998	1999	2000
13%	11%	9%	10%

12. Reduction in admission rates (per thousand) to hospital of children under 16 as a result of unintentional injury resulting in a hospital stay of longer than three days (England)

1996/97	1997/98	1998/99	1999/2000
1.20	1.12	1.02	1.02

13. Reduction in proportion of children registered on child protection register who have been previously registered (England)

1997/98	1998/99	1999/2000
19%	15%	14%

14. a) Reduction in under-18 conception rate (per thousand) aged 15–17 (England)

Under-18 conception rates

1996	1997	1998	1999
45.9%	45.5%	46.5%	44.7%

14. b) Reduction in proportion of teenage parents not in education, employment or training (GB)

1996	1997	1998	1999	2000	2001
83.5%	82.1%	72.6%	72.9%	68.4%	71.0%

15. Increase in proportion of 16–18-year-olds in learning (England)

1996	1997	1998	1999	2000
76.3%	74.9%	74.9%	75%	75.8%

Working-age people:

16. Increase in the proportion of working-age people in employment, over the economic cycle (GB)

	1996	1997	1998	1999	2000	2001
All:	71.9	72.7	73.3	73.8	74.5	74.8
Men:	76.6	77.6	78.2	78.6	79.3	79.5
Women:	66.7	67.4	67.8	68.5	69.2	69.6

17. Reduction in proportion of working-age people living in workless households, for households of a given size (GB)

1996	1997	1998	1999	2000	2001
13.7%	13.1%	12.8%	12.3%	11.8%	11.7%

18. Reduction in number (millions) of working-age people under 60 living in families claiming income support or income-based jobseeker's allowance who have been claiming for long periods of time (GB)

1996	1997	1998	1999	2000	2001
2.29	2.00	1.84	1.76	1.75	1.75

19. a) Increase in employment rates of disadvantaged groups – people with disabilities, lone parents, ethnic minorities and the over-50s (GB)

	1997	1998	1999	2000	2001
Lone parents:	45.6%	46.9%	48.6%	51.4%	51.5%
Over 50:	64.7%	65.7%	66.3%	66.9%	68.3%
People with disabilities:	-	43.5%	46.2%	46.8%	47.4%
Minority ethnic people:	55.1%	56.6%	57.1%	58.2%	–
All:	72.7%	73.3%	73.8%	74.5%	74.8%

19. b) Reduction in the employment rate gap between disadvantaged groups and the overall rate (GB)

	1997	1998	1999	2000	2001
Lone parents	27.2	26.4	25.2	23.1	23.3
Over 50	8.0	7.6	7.5	7.6	6.5
People with disabilities:		29.8	27.6	27.7	27.4
Minority ethnic people:	17.7	16.7	16.8	16.4	–

20. a) Reduction in the proportion of working-age people living in households below 60% of median income (GB)

	1996/97	1997/98	1998/99	1999/2000
Before housing costs:	15%	15%	14%	15%
After housing costs:	20%	20%	19%	20%

20. b) Reduction in proportion of working-age people living in households below 60% of 1996/97 median held constant in real terms (GB)

	1996/97	1997/98	1998/99	1999/2000
Before housing costs:	15%	14%	13%	12%
After housing costs:	20%	19%	18%	17%

20. c) Reduction in proportion of working-age people living in households with persistently low incomes (below 60% and 70% median before housing costs in at least three out of four years) (GB)

Below 60% median in at least three out of four years:

1991-1994	1992-1995	1993-1996	1994-1997	1995-1998	1996-1999
8%	7%	7%	7%	7%	7%

Below 70% median in at least three out of four years:

1991-1994	1992-1995	1993-1996	1994-1997	1995-1998	1996-1999
12%	13%	13%	12%	12%	12%

21. Reduction in proportion of working-age people without a qualification (England)

1996	1997	1998	1999	2000	2001
21.3%	18%	17.4%	16.5%	15.7%	15.6%

22. Reduction in number of people sleeping rough (England)

	1998	1999	2000	2001
	1,850	1,633	1,180	703

23. Reduction in proportion of young people aged 16-24 using illegal drugs in last month and previous year and reduction in use of most harmful class A drugs – eg, heroin, cocaine ecstasy and LSD (England and Wales)

	1998
Use of any class A drug last month:	3%
Use of any class A drug last year:	8%

24. Reduction in smoking rates for adults 16 and over in all social classes and in manual socio-economic groups (England)

	1996	1998
All:	28%	27%
Manual:	34%	32%

25. Reduction in death rates (per hundred thousand) from suicide and undetermined injury for 16–64-year-olds (England)

	1996	1997	1998
	11.9	12.1	12.5

Older people:

26. a) Reduction in the proportion of older people living in households below 60% of median income (GB)

	1996/97	1997/98	1998/99	1999/2000
Before housing costs:	21%	22%	23%	22%
After housing costs:	27%	27%	27%	26%

26. b) Reduction in proportion of older people living in households below 60% of 1996/97 median held constant in real terms (GB)

	1996/97	1997/98	1998/99	1999/2000
Before housing costs:	21%	21%	20%	17%
After housing costs:	27%	25%	24%	19%

26. c) Reduction in proportion of older people living in households with persistently low incomes (below 60% and 70% median before housing costs in at least three out of four years) (GB)

Below 60% median in at least three out of four years:

1991-1994	1992-1995	1993-1996	1994-1997	1995-1998	1996-1999
16%	14%	15%	15%	16%	18%

Below 70% median in at least three out of four years:

1991-1994	1992-1995	1993-1996	1994-1997	1995-1998	1996-1999
32%	31%	30%	32%	32%	34%

27. Increase in proportion of working-age people contributing to a non-state pension (GB)

	1996/97	1997/98	1998/99	1999/2000 (re-based)
Men:	56%	55%	54%	50%
Women:	38%	38%	39%	38%
All:	47%	47%	47%	45%

28. Increase in the amount contributed (billions) to non-state pensions (UK)

	1996	1997	1998	1999	2000
	£45	£50	£65	£60	£69

29. Increase in proportion of working-age people who have contributed to a non-state pension in at least three out of the last four years (GB)

	1994-1997	1995-1998	1996-1999
Men:	55%	58%	58%
Women:	36%	39%	40%
All:	46%	49%	50%

30. Reduction in proportion of older people who live in a home which falls below the set standard of decency (England)

	1996
	38%

31. Increase in healthy life expectancy in years at age 65 (England)

	1995	1997
Male:	11.4	11.9
Female:	13.2	13.3

32. Increase in the proportion of older people aged 65 and over being helped to live independently (England)

Helped to live at home through community-based services (people per thousand head of population):

	1996/97	1997/98	1998/99 (re-based)	1999/2000
	83%	81%	82%	85%

Intensive home care (more than ten contact hours and six or more visits a week per thousand head of population):

	1998/99	1999/2000
	7.8	8.8

33. Reduction in proportion of older people whose lives are affected by fear of crime (England and Wales)

1998	2000
10%	10%

Communities:

34. Reduction in the difference between the employment rate for the most deprived local authority areas and the overall employment rate, over the economic cycle (GB)

	2000	2001
30 most deprived areas:	62.1%	63.1%
All working-age people:	74.5%	74.8%
Employment rate gap:	12.4	11.7

35. Reduction in the overall rate of domestic burglary per thousand households and reduction between the areas with the highest rates and the overall rate (England and Wales)

1998/99	1999/2000	2000/01
22.0	20.7	18.4

The rate in Crime and Disorder Partnerships was between two and three times the overall rate in 2000/01.

36. Reduction in the proportion of households living in a home that falls below the set standard of decency (England)

1996
32%

37. Reduction in the gap between the fifth of health authorities with the lowest life expectancy at birth and the population as a whole (England)

		1996	1997	1998
Men:	lowest fifth	72.5	72.8	73.0
	whole population	74.6	74.9	75.1
	difference	2.1	2.1	2.1
Women:	lowest fifth	78.2	78.2	78.3
	whole population	79.7	79.9	80.0
	difference	1.5	1.7	1.7

*Indicates which parts of the UK are covered by each data source

Source: Department for Work and Pensions, *Opportunity for All: making progress*, Third Annual Report 2001, Cm 5260, 2001
Department of Social Security, *Households Below Average Income 1994/95-1999/00*, Corporate Document Services, 2001 and G Fimister (ed), *An End in Sight? Tackling child poverty in the UK*, CPAG, 2001

THE NEED FOR A NATIONAL INDEX OR COMBINED MEASURE

Income, regularity and persistence of poverty as well as ownership of assets, spending and deprivation all need to be taken into account in any reliable poverty indicators. It is possible to conceive of a composite index (like the United Nations Development Programme's Human Development Index (HDI)) producing an aggregate poverty measure based on the different data sources, or a core measure supplemented by additional indicators and trends.[70] See also Chapter 8 for a discussion of another index – the United Nations Human Poverty Index.

An index based on a single number could increase public awareness of poverty by making it easier to tell, on balance, whether poverty had risen or fallen over any given period. It would provide both clarity and an entry point to the individual indicators thus drawing people into an understanding of the multi-dimensional nature of poverty and social exclusion. Both national and local level figures could be provided. An important consideration would be what weight to give the individual elements. Alternatively, John Hills has proposed a measure based on income and living standards that could be made up of a core or headline measure – such as the HBAI figures and the PSE Survey (to provide a measure of deprivation).[71] Around this core would be supplementary detail of leading trends and indicators such as economic indicators (for example, the Retail Price Index and unemployment figures), evidence on the depth and persistence of poverty and a range of technical assumptions such as housing costs. A second set of indicators would be needed to capture other aspects of participation and well-being (including the subjective assessments of poor people themselves). Development of such a national measure could provide the key to a more inclusive and accountable public debate around the crucial issues of poverty and social exclusion.

CONCLUSION

This chapter has looked at facts and figures about poverty in the UK. In the past, the task of estimating the extent of poverty was made much more difficult because governments of all political colours neither established an official poverty line, nor attempted to relate rates of benefit to research into people's basic needs. There is still no one official measure or yardstick. (But see Chapter 1 for a discussion of the potential for a minimum income standard.)

There is no single answer to the question of how many people are poor in Britain today. The answer is multi-faceted and multi-dimensional.[72] Here, we have relied on a number of sources to estimate the extent of poverty while drawing attention to the pitfalls of each. In future, it may be possible to construct an agreed constellation of indicators as a national index that would facilitate greater public understanding of the debate (see p73).

Recently, however, the Government has made improvements in how it produces information on low income. The Family Resources Survey now provides material about the household incomes of families with children, unemployed people, elderly people and sick/disabled people. And a breakdown of some of the data by ethnic origin is also given (see Chapter 6). The Department for Work and Pensions is committed to producing HBAI each year along with the results of its own indicators in *Opportunity for All*. It also now provides more extensive material modeling the effects of different assumptions.

Poverty grew rapidly between 1979 and 1999/2000. Whichever poverty line is used, around a quarter of our society was living in poverty in Britain in 1999/2000. The poverty encountered by children is even greater than for society as a whole – around a third of children in Great Britain were living in poverty in 1999/2000. Over 7.8 million people were living on the 'safety net' benefit of income support/jobseeker's allowance in February 2001. By the mid-1990s, the UK had child poverty rates higher than any other industrialised nation with the exception of the USA and Russia.[73] Rates rose more dramatically here than in most other countries, rising most steeply in the early 1980s and then again in the early to mid-1990s. Clearly, there have been important changes since 1979, with a decline in the proportion of pensioners in the poorest 10 per cent and a rise in the proportion of single people without children and families with children. While the average person found their income growing very comfortably by 44 per cent between 1979 and 1995/96, the poorest 10 per cent saw a fall of 9 per cent in their real income (after housing costs).[74] The latest figures show that between 1979 and 1999/2000 the growth in real income for the poorest 10 per cent grew by a mere 6 per cent compared to 80 for the mean and by a massive 86 per cent for the richest 10 per cent.[75]

The figures we have looked at stop in 2000. Since then despite continued economic recovery, recent events indicate an economic slow down may be on the horizon. Since 1997 new policies targeted at poor families have been introduced – increases in child benefit, higher benefits for children in income support and tax credits, changes to income disregards, the introduction of the working families' tax credit and the childcare tax credit. New tax credits are planned for 2003. Other government policies attempt to recognise that the risk and persistence of poverty for certain groups requires a more dynamic approach. Policies such as the New Deals and the National Childcare Strategy are in part a response to this. However, earnings inequalities have continued to increase and when the next official figures are produced, whichever poverty line we choose, we fear that poverty is likely to be only a little different from what it was in 2000.

NOTES

1 M Desai, 'Drawing the line', in P Golding (ed), *Excluding the Poor*, CPAG, 1986
2 Department of Social Security, *Households Below Average Income 1994/95-1999/00*, Corporate Document Services, 2001; and Department of Social Security, *Households Below Average Income 1979-1996/97*, Corporate Document Services, 1998. Results prior to 1996/97 derive from the smaller Family Expenditure Survey; since 1994/95 the larger Family Resources Survey has been used – with two overlapping years 1994/95-1996/97. Although some discontinuities result from this change in methodology a continuous series is shown in this volume wherever possible.
3 Information provided by HBAI team at the Department for Work and Pensions.
4 In order to make comparisons over time, the poverty line used here is households lacking three or more socially perceived necessities taken from the 1983 *Breadline Britain* survey. The 1999 PSE Survey uses households lacking two or more items as a poverty line. D Gordon, L Adelman, K Ashworth, J Bradshaw, R Levitas, S Middleton, C Pantazis, D Patsios, S Payne, P Townsend and J Williams, *Poverty and Social Exclusion in Britain*, Joseph Rowntree Foundation, 2000
5 Office for National Statistics, and Office for National Statistics, *Economic Trends Annual Supplement*, No. 26, The Stationery Office, 2000; see note 2; and Office for National Statistics, *Social Trends*, 31, The Stationery Office, 2000
6 See note 3
7 See note 2
8 In order to make comparisons between households, HBAI measures are also adjusted or 'equivalised' to take into account family size and the composition of households. Equivalisation is based on the assumption that a large family needs a higher income than a single person in order to enjoy the same standard of living. Thus, equivalence scales take a couple as the

reference point with a value of one. It is a matter for debate whether the current equivalence scales (the McClement's scales) over-or under-estimate the incomes of certain groups.

9 See note 2

10 See note 8

11 See note 3

12 See note 2

13 See note 2

14 See note 2

15 See note 2

16 See note 2, Table F3 (AHC)

17 See note 16

18 However, the Joseph Rowntree Foundation Inquiry looked at changes over a longer period – *Inquiry into Income and Wealth*, Volumes 1 and 2, Joseph Rowntree Foundation, 1995

19 See note 2

20 See note 2 – *Households Below Average Income 1979-1996/97*, Table H2

21 The most rapid rise to 6.2 million (a 24 per cent increase) took place between 1979 and 1981, falling by 1988/89 to 5.3 million. Poverty rose again in the early 1990s – in all a rise of 21 per cent between 1979 and 1992/93, when poverty grew from 5 to 6.1 million on this constant measure. Each period of rapid increase coincided with a major economic recession.

22 See note 2 – *Households Below Average Income 1979-1996/97*, Table E3

23 See note 2 – *Households Below Average Income 1994/95-1999/00*

24 See note 2 – *Households Below Average Income 1994/95-1998/99*, Table E3

25 See note 2, Tables D1 and D2 (AHC)

26 See note 3

27 See note 2 – *Households Below Average Income 1979-1996/97*, Table A1, HMSO, 1998. As HBAI has stated: 'a significant proportion of the self-employed report very low incomes; this can be for a variety of reasons. Some are genuine causes of low income, such as a new business, a failing business or because the income from the business fluctuates substantially from year to year.' So excluding the self-employed may understate the growth in the number of people with low incomes. But, there is also evidence that 'survey questions prior to 1996/97 collected information inadequately from some self-employed people, leading to an under-estimation of household income... The very low incomes do not necessarily reflect the living standard or lifestyle of these households.' CPAG thinks that on balance, it is difficult to be confident whether the results including the self-employed, or those excluding them, give the better indication of the growth in numbers of people with low reported incomes and low living standards.

28 See note 27

29 See note 2 – *Households Below Average Income*, Table A1. The changes in real

income of the bottom decile are less certain in accuracy due to sampling error and the choice of equivalence scales.

30 C Lakin, 'The Effects of Taxes and Benefits on Household Income, 1999-2000', *Economic Trends*, No. 569, April 2001, The Stationery Office, 2001

31 J Bradshaw, 'Child Poverty under Labour', in G Fimister (ed), *An End in Sight? Tackling child poverty in the UK*, CPAG, 2001

32 See note 2 – *Households Below Average Income 1979-1996/97*, Table A3

33 See note 2 – *Households Below Average Income 1994/95-1999/00*, Table A3

34 R Walker, 'Lifetime Poverty Dynamics', in *Persistent Poverty and Lifetime Inequality: the evidence*, CASE/HM Treasury, 1999

35 A B Atkinson, *DSS Report on Households Below Average Income 1981-1987*, paper for the Social Services Select Committee, 1990

36 M S Hill and S P Jenkins, 'Poverty Among British Children: chronic or transitory?' in B Bradbury, Micklewright and Jenkins, *Falling In, Climbing Out: the dynamics of child poverty in industrialised countries*, UNICEF, 1999; and see notes 23 and 26

37 S P Jenkins, 'Dynamics of Household Incomes', in R Berthoud and J Gershuny, *Seven Years in the Lives of British Families: evidence on the dynamics of social change from the British Household Panel Survey*, The Policy Press/ISER, 2000

38 S P Jenkins, 'Income Dynamics in Britain 1991-96', in *Persistent Poverty and Lifetime Inequality: the evidence*, CASE/HM Treasury, 1999

39 F Devicienti, *Poverty Persistence in Britain: a multivariate analysis using the BHPS, 1991-1997*, Working Paper 2001-02, ISER, University of Essex, 2001

40 See note 36

41 Someone is defined as chronically poor if 'smoothed' income falls below the poverty line. Income is smoothed when income for each year is averaged over a six-year period removing variation between each year.

42 See note 34 and most recently Department for Work and Pensions, *Opportunity for All: making progress*, Cm 5260, The Stationery Office, 2001; see note 2

43 Department for Work and Pensions, *Opportunity for All: making progress*, Cm 5260, The Stationery Office, 2001; and see note 2

44 D Gordon et al, *Poverty and Social Exclusion in Britain*, Joseph Rowntree Foundation, 2000; and see note 4

45 See note 4

46 See note 44

47 Lacking two or more socially perceived necessities is used as a poverty line in the 1999 PSE Survey. In order to compare findings with the earlier *Breadline Britain* surveys in 1983 and 1990, the PSE team define poverty as lacking three or more socially perceived necessities. See note 4

48 Department of Health and Social Security, *Low Income Families 1985*, HMSO, 1988; Social Security Committee, *Second Report, Low Income*

Statistics: Low Income Families (LIF) 1979-1989, HMSO, 1993; and Social Security Committee, *First Report, Low Income Statistics: Low Income Families (LIF), 1989-1992*, HMSO, 1995

49 P Townsend, *Poverty in the United Kingdom*, Penguin, 1979

50 See note 31

51 Department of the Environment, Transport and the Regions, *Indices of Deprivation 2000*, Regeneration Research Summary No. 31, 2000

52 House of Commons, *Hansard*, Written Answers, January 2001, Col 607W

53 Department of Social Security, *Income-related Benefits: estimates of take-up in 1999/2000*, The Stationery Office, 2001

54 H Parker (ed), *Low Cost but Acceptable, A Minimum Income Standard for the UK: families with young children*, The Policy Press/Zacchaeus 2000 Trust, 1998 and Family Budget Unit, Memorandum submitted to the Social Security Committee, House of Commons, Session 2000-2001; Social Security Committee: Second Report, *Integrated Child Credit*, The Stationery Office, 14 March 2001

55 Memorandum to the Social Security Committee, see note 54

56 See note 54

57 See note 2 – *Households Below Average Income*, Table 6.8

58 See note 2 – *Households Below Average Income*, Table 6.9

59 S Middleton, K Ashworth and I Braithwaite, *Small Fortunes: spending on children, childhood poverty and parental sacrifice*, Joseph Rowntree Foundation, 1997

60 D Piachaud and H Sutherland, 'Child Poverty: aims, achievements and prospects for the future', *New Economy*, Volume 8, Issue 2, IPPR/Blackwell, 2001; H Sutherland and D Piachaud, 'Reducing Child Poverty in Britain: an assessment of government policy 1997-2001', *The Economic Journal*, 111 (February), F85-F101, Royal Economic Society, Blackwell, 2001; D Piachaud and H Sutherland, *How Effective is the British Government's Attempt to Reduce Child Poverty?* CASE Paper 38, CASE/LSE/STICERD, 2001; and H Sutherland, *The British Government's Attempt to Reduce Child Poverty: a Budget 2000 postscript*, Microsimulation Unit Research Note No. 36, Microsimulation Unit, 2000

61 D Piachaud and H Sutherland, 'Child Poverty: aims, achievements and prospects for the future', *New Economy*, Volume 8, Issue 2, IPPR/Blackwell, 2001

62 H Sutherland and D Piachaud, 'Reducing Child Poverty in Britain: an assessment of government policy 1997-2001', *The Economic Journal*, 111 (February), F85-F101, Royal Economic Society, Blackwell, 2001

63 D Piachaud and H Sutherland, *How Effective is the British Government's Attempt to Reduce Child Poverty?* CASE Paper 38, CASE/LSE/STICERD, 2001; and H Sutherland, *The British Government's Attempt to Reduce Child Poverty: a Budget 2000 postscript*, Microsimulation Unit Research Note No. 36, Microsimulation Unit, 2000

64 See note 62

65 Department of Social Security, *Opportunity for All: tackling poverty and social exclusion*, First Annual Report 1999, Cm 4445, The Stationery Office, 1999; and Department of Social Security, *Opportunity for All, One Year On: making a difference*, Second Annual Report 2000, Cm 4865, The Stationery Office, 2000; Department for Work and Pensions, *Opportunity for All: making progress*, Third Annual Report 2001, Cm 5260, The Stationary Office, 2001

66 Department for Work and Pensions, *Opportunity for All: making progress*, Third Annual Report 2001, Cm 5260, The Stationary Office, 2001; Department of Social Security, *Households Below Average Income 1994/95- 1999/00*, Corporate Document Services; G Fimister (ed) *An End in Sight? Tackling child poverty in the UK*, CPAG, 2001; strategies for Scotland, Wales and Northern Ireland are set out in *Social Justice Annual Report*, 2000 (Scotland), *Plan for Wales 2001* and *New Targeting Social Need* (NI)

67 J Bradshaw, 'Poverty: the outcomes for children', in DSS/CASE, *Indicators of Progress: a discussion of approaches to monitor the Government's strategy to tackle poverty and social exclusion*, CASE Report 13, 2001

68 C Howarth, P Kenway, G Palmer and C Street, *Monitoring Poverty and Social Exclusion: Labour's inheritance*, Joseph Rowntree Foundation, 1998; C Howarth, P Kenway, G Palmer and R Miorelli, *Monitoring Poverty and Social Exclusion 1999*, Joseph Rowntree Foundation, 1999; M Rahman, G Palmer, P Kenway and C Howarth, *Monitoring Poverty and Social Exclusion 2000*, Joseph Rowntree Foundation, 2000

69 F Bennett and C Roche, 'Developing Indicators: the scope for participatory approaches', *New Economy*, March 2000, Volume 8, Issue 1, pp4-28(5); Blackwell, *Listen Hear: the right to be heard*, Report of the Commission on Poverty, Participation and Power, The Policy Press/UK Coalition Against Poverty, 2000

70 J Micklewright, 'Should the UK Government measure poverty and social exclusion with a composite Index?' in DSS/CASE, *Indicators of Progress: a discussion of approaches to monitor the Government's strategy to tackle poverty and social exclusion*, CASE Report 13, 2001

71 J Hills, 'Measurement of income poverty and deprivation: the British approach', in DSS/CASE, *Indicators of Progress: a discussion of approaches to monitor the Government's strategy to tackle poverty and social exclusion*, CASE Report 13, 2001

72 For a useful discussion of this, see A Goodman, P Johnson and S Webb, *Inequality in the UK*, Oxford University Press, 1997

73 B Bradbury and M Jantti, *Child Poverty Across Industrialised Nations*, Innocenti Occasional Papers, Economic and Social Policy Series No. 71, UNICEF International Child Development Centre, 1999; UNICEF, *A League Table of Child Poverty in Rich Nations*, Innocenti Report Card, Issue No.1, June 2000, UNICEF, 2000

74 See note 2 – *Households Below Average Income 1979-1996/97*

75 Information provided by the HBAI team at the Department for Work and Pensions – see note 3

3 Circumstances leading to poverty

Over the past two decades, inequality and its visible impact in the UK have increased dramatically. Major economic and social changes have contributed to this process and to escalating problems in the most deprived communities. In the past, policies have been slow to react, and uncoordinated in the solutions they sought to offer. The result: too many people are poorer than they should be.

(Department of Social Security, *Opportunity for All: tackling poverty and social exclusion*)[1]

As noted in Chapter 1, some people are poor not because of their characteristics (like lone parenthood) but because they lack resources, often from earnings. This chapter highlights how people can become poor because of social and economic processes, such as unemployment and changing family structures. Those who do not have access to paid employment, or who face additional costs (perhaps because of disability) can be poor. Both factors combined can make the experience of poverty particularly acute, and a poor working life can lead to further poverty in old age. Government policies can also perpetuate or contribute to poverty.[2]

As noted in Chapter 2, the recent *Poverty and Social Exclusion in Britain* report found that, while one in four of the population was poor (defined as being unable to afford two or more necessities), some groups were particularly at risk:

- Working-age unemployed (77 per cent of whom were poor).
- Working-age sick or disabled (61 per cent).
- People on income support (70 per cent).
- Lone parents (62 per cent).

- Local authority tenants (61 per cent) and housing association tenants (57 per cent).[3]

LABOUR MARKET CHANGES

Changes in the labour market can influence the scale of unemployment, in turn affecting poverty. During times of economic downturn, more people are likely to be without work; the number of workless households (whether counted as unemployed or 'inactive', such as sick or with caring responsibilities) increased from 9 per cent in 1979 to 20 per cent in 1995/96, reducing to 16 per cent by early 2001.[4] Around 10.6 million people experienced a spell of unemployment between 1991 and 1995.[5]

People without work are more likely to have low incomes over long periods. During the 1990s, nearly a half of workless households spent three years in the bottom three-tenths of the income distribution, compared with around one in thirteen households in work.[6] The majority of people in households with an unemployed person were in the lowest fifth of the income distribution (72 per cent on the 'after housing costs' (AHC) measure) in 1999/2000.[7] In 1999/2000, 42 per cent of unemployed households had at least half of their income from means-tested benefits.[8]

MACRO RISKS OF UNEMPLOYMENT – THE ECONOMY

Unemployment can be dictated by the rate at which people are recruited into jobs or made redundant – 'the business cycle'.[9] The UK economy contracted in the early 1980s and early 1990s; this increased unemployment, especially from redundancies in industries like shipbuilding, mining and steel manufacturing. The proportion of skilled manual workers dropped from 40 per cent in 1971 to 33 per cent in 1996.[10] Collapsing demand for unskilled workers in the 1970s and 1980s accounted for 20 per cent of unemployment over that period.[11]

Longer periods of unemployment accounted for some of the growth in unemployment between the 1970s and 1990s, together with increasing numbers becoming unemployed during the recessions.[12]

Rising unemployment was accompanied by efforts to reduce the head-count of unemployed people; between 1979 and 1995 the counting method was changed 33 times.[13] The claimant count – those classed as unemployed – is susceptible to changes in benefit rules and administration. The International Labour Office measure – those looking for work and available to start, irrespective of benefit status – is more relevant to a focus on worklessness and has also been adopted by the Labour Government.

MICRO RISKS OF UNEMPLOYMENT – THE INDIVIDUAL

Some individual characteristics can also be associated with unemployment. Around half of unemployed people were in work before they became unemployed, mainly because of redundancy or a temporary job ending. Figure 3.1 shows the routes into unemployment.

The reason for someone's last job ending seems to affect the duration of unemployment. For instance, nearly half (46 per cent) of unemployed men who were made redundant stayed unemployed for a year or more, compared with 31 per cent of those whose temporary job had come to an end.[14]

Some *occupations* have a higher unemployment rate, such as plant and

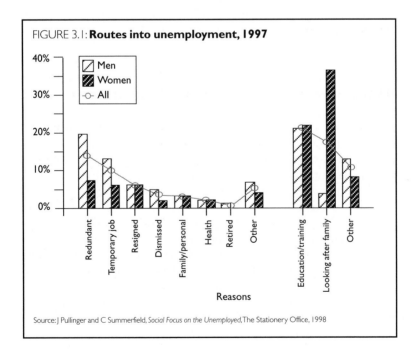

FIGURE 3.1: **Routes into unemployment, 1997**

Source: J Pullinger and C Summerfield, *Social Focus on the Unemployed*, The Stationery Office, 1998

machine operatives and low-skilled manual work; in contrast, professional occupations have the lowest unemployment rate.[15] Unemployment for semi- or unskilled workers is four times higher than for professional/managerial workers.[16]

Individual factors associated with a higher risk of unemployment include lacking qualifications, being male, older, from some minority ethnic groups, being single, having dependent children and living in rented accommodation – skills and qualifications perhaps being one of the most important.[17] In the mid-1990s, long-term unemployed people tended to have characteristics similar to other unemployed people – eg, male, over 55, or with children (especially pre-school) or health problems; younger people tended to move off benefit more quickly, but two-fifths returned to benefit within six months.[18]

Where people live can also influence the likelihood of unemployment (see Chapter 8). In 1998, 37 per cent of long-term unemployment (over six months) was concentrated in just 10 per cent (37) of local authority districts; in 24 districts more than half of all unemployed people were long-term unemployed, when the national average was 43 per cent.[19]

POLICIES TO TACKLE UNEMPLOYMENT

Over the past 20 years, many policies have been intended to reduce the number of claimants, either by placing people on work schemes or by restricting eligibility.[20] In October 1996, jobseeker's allowance replaced unemployment benefit with tougher eligibility rules and reduced amounts (the period of contributory benefit was reduced from 12 months to six).[21] Evaluation found the following:

- Although more people moved off the claimant count in the first year of jobseeker's allowance, thereafter the effects were smaller, and mainly in areas of low unemployment and among longer-term claimants.
- People made more regular job applications, even in areas of high unemployment, though this did not seem to help people obtain work.
- Partners' withdrawal from the labour market tended to occur earlier, at six months instead of twelve – possibly reflecting the reduced period of contributory benefit. Perceived benefit disincentives seemed to influence partners' economic activity, but to a lesser extent than domestic commitments.[22] It has been estimated that

only a fifth of the difference in the employment rate of partners of unemployed claimants could be attributed to the benefits system.[23]

Time spent unemployed seems to be more affected by being male, having limited educational qualifications, ill-health, limited recent work experience, lack of a driving licence or access to personal transport, than by jobseeker's allowance.[24] Robert Walker concludes that people tend to become long-term unemployed not because they receive benefit but because they lack the attributes that would help them gain work.[25]

The Labour Government has adopted a series of policies and targets to reduce workless households. New Deal programmes have been set up for specific groups, such as young people, those over the age of 50, and long-term unemployed people. 1.2 million more people were in jobs by 2001 than in 1997, and the proportion of working-age households without work dropped from 13.1 per cent to 11.7 per cent.[26] The Government's third annual poverty report included further intentions to make the New Deals permanent and launching a new agency for people of working age (Jobcentre Plus) in 2001.[27]

IN-WORK POVERTY

The structure of the labour market, and levels of pay, can affect the risk of poverty for children whose parents are in work, especially families with young children, large families, certain minority ethnic groups and lone-parent families.[28] By 1995/96 there were twice as many poor children in working families than in 1979,[29] as a result of greater

TABLE 3.1: **Children in working families in the bottom fifth of incomes (including self-employed), 1999/2000, AHC**

Per cent in bottom fifth	Couple families	Lone-parent families
With a full-time worker	12	12
With a part-time worker only	58	30
With two adults working	7	–
With one adult working	31	22

Source: Department of Social Security, *Households Below Average Income 1994/95–1999/2000*, 2001, Table 5.1

wage inequality (see Chapter 7) and growing part-time work.[30] Part-time incomes are insufficient to lift a family out of poverty, with almost a third of households with one (or more) of its members working part time being in the bottom fifth of incomes, as Table 3.1 shows.[31]

'FLEXIBLE' WORK AND LOW PAY

Part-time and temporary work has increased (by 8 per cent between 1981 and 1993), with a quarter of men and a half of women in non-standard employment by the mid-1990s.[32] People entering employment after a period out of work tend to be more likely to get a low-paid, insecure job:

• Approximately half of people leaving unemployment for work took temporary jobs at a time when only 8 per cent of all working-age adults were in this type of work.[33]

'Entry jobs'– those taken by the previously unemployed – tend to be in high turnover sectors such as retail, and in less skilled manual and non-manual occupations, often part time or temporary.[34] In one study, three-quarters of the jobs obtained by people out of work were 'flexible' jobs, resulting in little upward mobility during the course of four years.[35]

THE LOW PAY, NO PAY CYCLE

People who are low paid can also be vulnerable to unemployment, and are often lower paid if subsequently returning to work hence they get into a 'low pay, no pay' cycle.[36] A worker re-entering work after involuntary job loss will earn on average 9 per cent less than in her/his previous job.[37] The longer someone stays in work once they have left benefit, the better their chances of keeping off benefit.[38] Similarly, the more often someone claims benefit, and the longer they do so, the shorter the time subsequently spent in work.[39]

WHO ARE THE LOW PAID?

Low pay has been more common for less skilled, poorly educated workers, women and part-timers, often in wholesale, retail and catering.[40] Women, and older and less educated workers, are more likely to remain low paid than younger workers, and the longer someone has been low paid, the more likely they are to remain so:

- About a half of people who are low paid will increase their earnings over two years, but three-quarters of those who have been low paid for two years will be low paid in the third year.[41]

Young people are disproportionately affected by low wages, particularly those with limited education; in the early 1990s, men without any formal qualifications were almost twice as likely to be in the bottom fifth of income distribution.[42] This may have been exacerbated by the abolition of wages councils in 1993, covering young people, and which subsequently led to a fall in wages across the industries covered.[43]

IN-WORK SUPPORT

The Low Pay Commission estimates that the introduction of a national minimum wage in April 1999 has raised the earnings of 1.3 million low-paid workers; reforms to national insurance contributions and a lower starting rate of income tax should also increase take-home pay.[44] Tax credits complement the minimum wage in tackling in-work poverty for particular groups.[45] In-work benefits for families with children (family credit) and disabled people (disability working allowance) were replaced by tax credits (working families' tax credit and disabled person's tax credit respectively) in October 1999. By 2000, more people were receiving tax credits than the former in-work benefits.[46]

Family credit was a safety net for families already in work, acting as a 'parachute' for two-earner couples when one lost their job, helping couples with pre-school children and lone parents with children of school age.[47] Lone parents tended to stay on family credit for longer, perhaps having less opportunity to increase their earnings.[48] However, some lone parents have climbed out of poverty through family credit; over a three-year period, over half who started on family credit had moved off it onto housing benefit/council tax benefit only, or had moved above the income thresholds for in-work benefits altogether.[49] Lone parents now represent more than half (51 per cent) of working families' tax credit recipients,[50] an increase from only 28 per cent of the family credit caseload in 1988 as the 'hours' threshold has been progressively reduced.

Other in-work benefits can be payable (such as housing benefit and council tax benefit), though gains in tax credits can sometimes be offset by losses in housing benefit. This 'poverty trap' arises where a modest increase in gross earnings rarely leads to significantly higher net disposable income as only very low levels of earnings above income support level are permitted before entitlement to housing benefit is reduced. The overlap of the rates at which housing benefit and working families' tax credit are withdrawn can mean families are left with as little as five pence from each additional £1 gross earnings; although with a lower taper than the former family credit, the working families' tax credit was estimated to cut by a third the numbers of families with marginal tax rates of 70 per cent or more.[51] While estimated numbers facing marginal tax rates above 70 per cent dropped by 490,000 between 1997 and 2000 as a result of measures in the Budget 2000, 950,000 people faced marginal tax rates of 60 per cent or more, mainly in the 60–70 per cent band.[52] A further issue for many families is the lack of entitlement to free school meals once the parent leaves income support or income-based jobseeker's allowance, though the tax credit rates take this into account to some extent.

CHANGES IN FAMILY LIFE

Changes in family structure have increased the risk of poverty for some families. Divorce increased by 42 per cent between 1973 and 1997, and births outside marriage grew from 8 per cent to 38 per cent.[53] Some families, such as lone parents, are particularly at risk of poverty (Chapter 5), and poverty itself can place strains on family roles and relationships (see Chapter 4).[54] Families with children can also incur additional costs (Chapter 5).

Labour market changes have also affected families; the proportion of women in employment rose from 59 per cent in 1979 to 67 per cent in 1996,[55] with more mothers returning to work within a year of the birth.[56] However, the employment position of lone parents has deteriorated relative to that of married mothers.[57]

Childbirth, as well as other family changes like divorce, can precipitate poverty:

- For one in three people, the birth of a child results in a drop down the income distribution by a fifth or more, and for 10–15 per cent, it results in poverty.

TABLE 3.2: **Main events leading into or out of a low income**

Per cent	Into low income	Out of low income
Demographic event	37.7	17.7
Household head earnings change	31.0	33.6
Spouse or other earnings change	15.9	28.5
Non-labour income change	15.5	20.2

Source: S Jenkins, *The Distribution of Income by Sectors of the Population*, ISER working paper, 2000-18, 2000

- A tenth of all entries into low income are associated with separation or divorce, the chances of poverty being four times higher if the mother does not subsequently work.[58]

Each year about one in ten individuals change family type, and about a quarter change economic status. But *demographic* events (changes in household composition, such as childbirth) are more important in accounting for movements into low income than movements out, compared with *income* events (such as a drop in wages, job loss or gain), as shown in Table 3.2.[59]

LONE PARENTS

The number of lone parents tripled to 1.7 million between 1971 and 1998.[60] By 1998, a quarter of families with dependent children were headed by a lone parent, compared with only 8 per cent in 1971, with fewer and younger children (40 per cent of lone parents have a child under five).[61]

The majority of lone parents are women. Half of women separating from their partners experience a drop in income, while men are more likely to have an increased income, often being the main earner.[62] On separation or divorce, mothers with children find their income falls by an average of £20 a week.[63]

The fastest growing component of lone parenthood since the 1980s has been *single never-married lone parents*. This has been thought by Steve McKay to reflect disadvantages among the family of origin, such as having lived in the social rented sector, and changing employment opportunities.[64] McKay argues that family change can be analysed as an effect of labour market change rather than only as a cause.

Some studies indicate a strong correlation between lone parenthood and male unemployment.[65] One analysis of the British Household Panel Survey with unemployment data for 300 areas suggested that worse employment opportunities locally were associated with more childbearing outside marriage:

- A 1 per cent increase in the area unemployment rate could represent a 10 per cent increase in the rate of first births before marriage.[66]

This may reflect the reduced chances of working for both young men and women in those areas, as well as lower 'opportunity costs' of having children – ie, there are no 'wages' to give up when having a child (Chapter 5).

Couples at greatest risk of *marital breakdown* tended to be those who had conceived before marriage and were younger when they married.[67] Signs of affluence, such as marrying later and owner-occupation, were associated with marriage stability, whereas early marriage, living in rented accommodation or remaining in the parental home were linked to breakdown.[68] Relationship breakdown seems to be more important than job loss as a route into non-working lone parenthood (46 per cent compared with 27 per cent), though as many workless lone parents left this situation by finding a job as finding a partner.[69]

An increasing number of lone parents have relied on income support, rising from 213,000 in 1971 to 972,000 in 1998 (mainly attributable to younger never-married lone parents, with younger children).[70] In 1998/99, 55 per cent of lone parent families relied on income support compared with only 4 per cent of two-parent families.[71] Numbers of lone-parents receiving income support have stopped rising since 1996, though during 1998 and 1999 this was only partly attributable to the New Deal for lone parents.[72]

POLICIES FOR FAMILY SUPPORT

Child benefit was introduced in the late 1970s as a means of offsetting some of the costs of a child (see Chapter 5). An addition for lone parents was payable with child benefit (one parent benefit), though concerns about the growing numbers of lone parents led to plans for its abolition and the corresponding premium in 1996, subsequently carried out in 1998 for new lone parents. However, a 26 per cent increase in child benefit between 1997 and 2000, together with a 45 per cent rise in means-tested payments for children, has largely compensated for the reduction. This, together with the children's tax credit which replaced the married couple's tax allowance, will form the basis for an 'integrated child credit' in 2003.[73]

A government target is to reduce by at least a quarter the proportion of children living in households with incomes of less than 60 per cent of the median by 2004. Government policies announced between 1997 and the 2000 Budget are estimated to reduce poverty according to this measure by more than 40 per cent in lone-parent families and just under a third in two-parent families.[74] Another target to reduce the proportion of children living in workless households, which fell from 17.9 per cent to 15.3 per cent between 1997 and 2001, may reduce poverty further.[75]

SICKNESS AND DISABILITY

Sick and disabled people experience disadvantage in the labour market, and greater reliance on benefits. Although there are questions of how to define 'disability', the trends show that, for example, between 1984 and 1996, there was a doubling of households containing at least one sick or disabled person.[76] Disabled people are more likely to be out of work than non-disabled people, facing negative attitudes or discrimination from employers.[77]

In 1996/97, a disability survey estimated that a fifth of the adult population in Britain – 8.5 million – were disabled.[78] The risks of becoming disabled were higher for older people and for those on low incomes, in social rented housing and in particular areas (highest in Wales, the North West and North East). Using a ten-point 'severity scale',[79] the survey classified a third as scoring 1 and 2 (relatively mild), 45 per cent in the middle-range categories of 3-6, and 21 per cent scoring 7 or over (severely disabled).

SICKNESS

Sickness differs from disability, though there are sometimes overlaps; disabled people are not necessarily sick, and ill-health may not lead to disability.[80] However, there is an association between poor health and poverty, explored in the next chapter. The Acheson inquiry into inequalities in health indicated that, while some people in poor health may become unemployed, this does not fully explain the links between unemployment and ill-health.[81] It does, however, illustrate that ill-health can increase the risk of unemployment, and unemployment can in turn damage health.

Labour market change may also affect illness; for instance, to be in work, men aged 20-59 had to be in better health in 1993 than 20 years earlier:

- In 1979, 72 per cent of men in the lowest socio-economic group were in work despite long-term health problems, but by 1993 only 43 per cent in the same category were employed.[82]

DSS studies of lone parents have also shown that, between 1991 and 1996, households with at least one member with a longstanding illness doubled from a quarter to a half. Illness seems to be associated with factors such as age, employment status, smoking, severe hardship and a history of marital violence.[83]

DISABILITY

Disabled people can be at risk of poverty because of additional disability-related costs and lower incomes.

HIGHER COSTS

The additional costs faced by disabled people can be considered as two types:

- personal support – ie, the goods and services needed to help with tasks that non-disabled people can do by themselves, like housework and intimate tasks such as dressing and bathing; *and*
- higher spending on everyday items like heating, laundry and transport.[84]

Although not a precise fit, those with the most severe impairments tend to be more likely to have additional costs. When asked about extra spending, a third of disabled people in the 1996/97 disability survey said they spent more on transport, 45 per cent spent more on heating and electricity; those with the highest severity scores were twice as likely to spend more.[85]

However, the amount people *actually spend* may be constrained by income, making it difficult to make comparisons with non-disabled people. Richard Berthoud has summarised the different approaches adopted in research:

- An official disability survey in 1985 asked people how much they actually spent, arriving at an average of £20 a week (updated to 1998 prices).
- Detailed interviews with disabled people suggested that the actual costs could be six times higher (£120 a week at 1998 prices).
- A mid-point estimate was reached in a comparison of the living standards of disabled and non-disabled people, using measures of ownership of seven consumer durables, questions about budgeting, and participation in social activities (£50 a week at 1998 prices).[86]

Disablement Income Group research with severely disabled people found that actual spending underestimated what someone *needs* to spend.[87] This research cautions that there is no simple correlation between the severity of impairment and spending; for instance, transport costs may be lower if someone goes out less frequently because of their impairment (rather than because of the cost).

Comparing disabled and non-disabled people's perceptions of their financial situation, disabled people who were not poor were three times more likely than 'non-poor, non-disabled' people to report financial difficulty, which could mean that the extra costs reduced living standards.[88]

TABLE 3.3: **Perception of financial situation by poverty and disability**

	'Poor' disabled %	'Poor' non-disabled %	'Non-poor' disabled %	'Non-poor' non-disabled %
Very difficult	18.3	14.0	9.1	3.0
Quite difficult	24.1	20.1	13.5	6.9
Getting by	42.9	37.8	36.1	27.6
Doing alright	7.9	19.2	20.0	33.1
Comfortable	6.8	8.8	21.3	29.4

Source: H Barnes, *Working for a Living? Employment, benefits and the living standards of disabled people*, The Policy Press, 2000

Extra costs have been rising because of the expanding numbers of local authorities charging for their community care services. An Audit Commission survey found that most authorities charged for items like personal care and mobile meals, with increasing maximum weekly amounts (half of those surveyed charged some users over £50 a week).[89] The numbers of people claiming benefits for extra disability-related costs (such as disability living allowance) have grown considerably since their introduction (see below).

LOWER INCOMES

- Household incomes tend to be 20 – 30 per cent lower for disabled than non-disabled adults.[90]
- Working-age disabled people are seven times more likely to be out of work and claiming benefits than non-disabled people.[91]
- People receiving disability and carer benefits tend to be just above the bottom of the income distribution; in 1999/2000, 19 per cent were in the bottom fifth of incomes (AHC) and 32 per cent were in second fifth.[92] Households containing one or more diabled children are more likely to be in the bottom two-fifths of the income distribution; during 1999/2000, 57 per cent of households with one or more disabled children and 73 per cent of households with a disabled child and adult were in the bottom two-fifths. Households containing one or more disabled children were more likely to be in the bottom two-fifths of income; during 1999/2000, 57 per cent of households with one or more disabled children and 73 per cent of households with a disabled child and adult were in the bottom two-fifths.[93]

However, given additional costs, incomes alone may not be a good reflection of living standards. A further analysis comparing working-age disabled people between 1985 and 1996/97 found that, when adjusting for additional costs, the numbers of disabled people below half average incomes in both years rose to about half; almost two-thirds of those considered the most severely disabled (in categories 9 and 10) were below this threshold in 1996/97.[94]

Labour market changes described above, such as the increase in workless households, have had a significant impact on disabled people:

- In 1985, 48 per cent of working-age disabled people were living in workless families, rising to 59 per cent in 1996/97.

- Fewer disabled people are in two-earner households (from 16 per cent in 1985 to 12 per cent in 1996/97).
- Disabled people are less likely to have work experience and qualifications than non-disabled people, and are *six times less likely* to get work.
- Disabled people comprise half of those who are not employed but would like a job, and one-third of those available to start in a fortnight.
- A third of disabled people who move into work have lost their job by the following year, compared with a fifth of non-disabled people.[95]

When in work, disabled people are more likely to be in manual occupations than non-disabled people (50 per cent compared with 39 per cent), and more likely to be lower paid (hourly earnings of £6.50 compared with £8.10 in 1996/97).[96]

Within a year of becoming disabled, one in six people lose their jobs.

POLICIES FOR SICK AND DISABLED PEOPLE

Benefits for disabled people were introduced in the 1970s for income maintenance (for inability to work, such as invalidity benefit), or as a contribution towards extra costs (such as attendance allowance). During the 1980s and 1990s, some entitlement was restricted, including earnings-related additions. In response to the tripling of invalidity benefit awards, tighter eligibility criteria and reduced payments were introduced in 1995, and a change of name (now incapacity benefit). However, few who were disallowed benefit returned to work, and a significant proportion (35 per cent) subsequently re-claimed incapacity benefit.[97] At the same time, the caseload of people on income support with a disability premium has continued to rise.[98]

Despite a ten-fold increase in recipients since the 1970s, and the introduction of an additional lower tier of benefit rates, take-up of the extra costs benefits remains low, with half or more entitled to benefit not claiming it.[99] Even among the most severely disabled people, a fifth of those entitled have not claimed.[100]

On taking office the Labour Government set up a Disability Rights Task Force to recommend action on discrimination against disabled people, and a Disability Rights Commission was established in April 2000. Pilot projects and a personal adviser service tested out ways to help people on incapacity benefits return to work. As well as further limits on eligibility for incapacity benefits and a more active approach to disability benefits generally, the Government has announced an enhanced premium, payable to severely disabled people aged under 60 with income support (the 'disability income guarantee'), introduced in 2001.[101]

PROVIDING CARE

People who provide unpaid care to an elderly or disabled person can themselves be vulnerable to poverty, often as a result of giving up work or through incurring additional expense (for caring for children see Chapter 5).

In 1998, an estimated 5.7 million people in Britain were carers.[102] Three in ten lived with the cared-for person, and one in five spent 20 hours or more each week in caring activities.[103] The proportion spending long hours caring increased after 1993, apparently coinciding with the implementation of community care.

LOW INCOMES AND HIGHER COSTS

Carers tend to have low incomes. In 1997/98, half of carers spending more than 35 hours a week caring received less than £50 a week before benefits.[104]

A Carers UK (previously the Carers National Association) survey found that many carers were unable to afford necessities like fuel bills, one in five cut back on food, and one in three were in debt.[105] The longer the time spent caring, the greater the financial difficulties encountered. One reason for carers having low incomes is that they are less likely to undertake paid work; only 37 per cent of male carers and 22 per cent of female carers worked full time, compared with 52 per cent of all men and 28 per cent of all women.[106] A Women's Unit study showed that caring may have a greater impact on men's employment, as men who were unemployed when caring began were twice as likely to remain unemployed; women seemed more likely to reduce their hours.[107] The Carers UK survey showed that over seven in ten carers had given up work, and believed they were worse off since caring began.[108] A third of carers surveyed received income support, notably younger carers and those from minority ethnic groups.[109] They were also more likely to have given up work to care (70 per cent compared with 55 per cent of non-recipients of income support). Both groups faced financial hardship, especially those receiving income support. When employed, carers tend to work for fewer hours and lower pay:

- In one survey, almost three-quarters of carers had suffered an average annual loss of £5,000.[110]
- Caring can reduce wages by an estimated 12 per cent.[111]

As well as low incomes, carers often have extra outgoings; over two-thirds of carers in the above survey incurred costs because of the additional expense associated with disability, such as transport to the disabled person's home.[112]

POLICIES FOR CARERS

Since the late 1970s, invalid care allowance has been payable to carers who do not undertake any substantial paid employment. Invalid care allowance has tended to go to people on low incomes, largely because of the lower likelihood of employment.[113] Entitlement has been tied to the disabled person's benefit, so that only those looking after someone receiving the highest rates of disability living allowance or attendance allowance were eligible for invalid care allowance. In 1990, a carer premium was added to means-tested benefits.

The Labour Government launched a National Carers Strategy in 1999 and has subsequently extended respite care, increased the carer premium and extended and improved invalid care allowance.

GROWING OLD

Numbers of pensioners have risen over the last 30 years, mainly due to extended life expectancy; in 1971, men at age 60 were expected to live another 15.3 years, rising to 18.5 years in 1996; for women, life expectancy at 60 was 19.8 years in 1971 and 22.4 years in 1996.[114] In 1999, there were almost 11 million people in the UK over pension age (60 for women, 65 for men).[115]

INEQUALITY IN PENSIONER INCOMES

Inequality of incomes in retirement reflects the growing numbers receiving an occupational pension, together with uprating of the basic state retirement pension with prices rather than earnings from 1979.[116] The growth in incomes has been greatest among better-off pensioners and least among poorer pensioners:

- The median income of the top fifth increased by 80 per cent in real terms between 1979 and 1996/97, but only by 34 per cent for the bottom fifth.[117]
- 40 per cent of pensioners had some occupational pension in 1979, increasing to 57 per cent by 1996/97.[118]
- Half of those in the bottom fifth did not receive any occupational pension, representing a quarter of all pensioner couples and half of all single pensioners.[119]

Income from occupational pensions increased by 162 per cent in real terms between 1979 and 1996/97; couples tending to have higher incomes than single pensioners, and newly retired pensioners higher incomes than older (over 75) ones.[120] However, receipt of occupational pensions by men may have peaked; the proportion in occupational schemes has fallen by 10 per cent, reflecting the decline in large and public sector employers, and changes to regulations for occupational schemes.[121] In contrast, the proportion of women with occupational pensions continues to grow, but still falls short of the proportion of men with such pensions.

PENSIONER POVERTY

Pensioners are more likely to be persistently poor than working-age people. Between 1991 and 1994, 22 per cent of pensioner couples and 42 per cent of single pensioners spent at least three years in the bottom three-tenths of incomes, and between 1995 and 1998, 29 per cent of couples and 38 per cent of singles, compared with 14 per cent of the working-age population in both periods. Between 1996 and 1999 28 per cent of pensioner couples and 38 per cent of single pensioners were in the bottom 30 per cent of incomes in three years out of four.[122]

The poorest pensioners now tend to be:

- older;
- women;
- carers;
- from minority ethnic groups;
- self-employed workers;
- in workless households;

- persistent low earners;
- people with a long-term illness or disability.[123]

These groups are poorer because of being low paid during working life (and so have limited second-tier pensions) or because of reduced benefit entitlement. As an example of the latter, carers may only have home responsibilities protection, which may reduce entitlement to the full basic pension or the additional State Earnings Related Pension (SERPS).

Older pensioners have lower incomes than the more recently retired; twice as many people aged over 80 were in the bottom fifth of pensioner incomes than people in their 60s.[124] This may be due to more newly retired people having occupational pensions, more women in the older age groups, and the more generous indexing of pensions and earnings-related second tier pensions of the newly retired. Minority ethnic pensioners may have arrived in the UK in the middle of their working lives and therefore be less likely to have basic entitlement or if unemployed or low paid, missing out on occupational pensions (see Chapter 6).[125] The number of disabled pensioners rose by a quarter between the 1970s and 1990s;[126] they have lower incomes than those without a disability, are more likely to have worked in manual trades, have few qualifications, and live in local authority accommodation. [127]

The *process* of becoming retired seems to be associated with a low income. Retirement represents a marked change for someone formerly in full-time work, but less so for someone previously unemployed, disabled, or a carer:

- For men, being in full-time work reduces the chances of being in the poorest third on retirement.
- For women, work status is less relevant. Factors associated with a greater likelihood of being poor include living in social housing, not being in an occupational pension scheme, and retiring before state pension age.
- People with a working partner are less likely to be poor; those without a partner at all were the poorest.[128]

POLICIES FOR PENSIONERS

Until 1980 the retirement pension was increased along with increases in earnings; since then it has been uprated by prices only. Successive governments have encouraged second-tier provision rather than increasing the basic pension. The Labour Government is introducing the state second pension to replace SERPS, designed to help modest earners, and widening coverage to include carers and some disabled people.[129]

The minimum income guarantee was introduced in April 1999 as an additional element in income support for pensioners. It has been uprated with earnings since April 2000, and 1.6 million have claimed, though more are entitled.[130] The Government has also introduced a winter fuel allowance for pensioner households and free TV licences for the over-75s. Even so, between 1996/97 and 1999/2000, the proportions of pensioners on incomes below 60 per cent of the median increased from 21 to 22 per cent on the 'before housing costs' measure, though decreased on the 'after housing costs' measure.[131] A further 'pension credit' is planned to assist those with modest incomes or savings from 2003.

CONCLUSION

Factors influencing poverty during the past 20 years include labour market change, reflecting trends in the wider economy and pushing up unemployment during recessions. Flexible and low-paid work has grown, resulting in a 'low pay, no pay cycle' for some people on low incomes. At the same time, changes in family life have contributed to the growth in lone parenthood. Rising numbers of people with a sickness or disability, often facing additional costs, have been excluded from work. Increasing life expectancy and the growth in second-tier pensions have reinforced pensioner inequality and poverty.

Policies during the 1980s and early 1990s tended to exacerbate poverty by restricting benefit entitlement. More recently, the Labour Government has sought to reduce the proportion of households without work through policies such as New Deal, together with a national minimum wage and tax credits. Additional financial support has been targeted at those who are not expected to work, largely through increases in means-tested support. At the time of writing it is too early to tell if these changes will have influenced the circumstances which lead people into poverty.

NOTES

1   Department of Social Security, *Opportunity for All: tackling poverty and social exclusion*, First Annual Report 1999, Cm 4445, The Stationery Office, 1999

2   See for example, Social Exclusion Unit, *Bringing Britain Together: a national strategy for neighbourhood renewal*, Cabinet Office, 1998

3   D Gordon et al, *Poverty and Social Exclusion in Britain*, Joseph Rowntree Foundation, 2000

4   HM Treasury, *Tackling Poverty and Extending Opportunity: the modernisation of Britain's tax and benefit system*, Number 4, March 1999 and National Statistics, *Work and Workless Households Spring 2001*, 2001

5   HM Treasury, *Employment Opportunity in a Changing Labour Market: the modernisation of Britain's tax and benefit system*, Number 1, 1997

6   Department of Social Security, *Households Below Average Income, 1994/95-1999/2000*, 2001

7   See note 6

8   Department of Social Security, *Family Resources Survey 1999/2000*, 2001

9   J Pullinger and C Summerfield, *Social Focus on the Unemployed*, The Stationery Office, 1998

10 R Walker with M Howard, *The Making of a Welfare Class? Benefit receipt in Britain*, The Policy Press, 2000

11 M Campbell with I Sanderson and F Walton, *Local Responses to Long-Term Unemployment*, Joseph Rowntree Foundation, 1998

12 See note 5

13 Personal communication, Unemployment Unit, February 1995

14 See note 9

15 See note 9

16 See note 11

17 See note 11

18 H Trickey et al, *Unemployment and Jobseeking: two years on*, DSS Research Report 87, 1998

19 See note 11

20 See note 10

21 I Murray, *Desperately Seeking...A Job: a critical guide to the 1996 jobseeker's allowance*, Unemployment Unit, 1995

22 E Raynor et al, *Evaluating Jobseeker's Allowance: a summary of the research findings*, DSS Research Report 116, Corporate Document Services, 2000

23 See note 10

24 A Smith et al, *Understanding the Impact of Jobseeker's Allowance*, DSS Research Report 111, Corporate Document Services, 2000

25 See note 10

26 Department of Social Security, *Opportunity for All: making progress,* Third Annual Report 2001, Cm 5260, 2001

27 See note 26

28 HM Treasury, *Tackling Poverty and Making Work Pay – Tax Credits for the 21st Century: the modernisation of Britain's tax and benefit system*, Number 6, March 2000

29 P Gregg, S Harkness and S Machin, *Child Development and Family Income*, Joseph Rowntree Foundation, 1999

30 HM Treasury, *Supporting Children Through the Tax and Benefit System: the modernisation of Britain's tax and benefit system*, Number 5, November 1999

31 See note 6

32 A Rix et al, *The Training and Development of Flexible workers*, DfEE Research Brief 118, 1999

33 See note 24

34 P Gregg and J Wadsworth, 'The Changing Nature of Entry Jobs in Britain', in P Gregg (ed) *Jobs, Wages and Poverty: patterns of persistence and mobility in the new flexible labour market*, London Centre for Economic Performance, 1997

35 M White, and J Forth, *Pathways Through Unemployment: the effects of a flexible labour market*, Joseph Rowntree Foundation, 1998

36 M Stewart, 'Low Pay, No Pay Dynamics', in *Persistent Poverty and Lifetime Inequality: the evidence*, HM Treasury Occasional Paper No. 10, 1999

37 P Gregg, 'Scarring Effects of Unemployment', in *Persistent Poverty and Lifetime Inequality: the evidence*, HM Treasury Occasional Paper No. 10, 1999

38 A Shaw et al, *Moving off Income Support: barriers and bridges*, DSS Research Report 53, Corporate Document Services, 1996

39 See note 18

40 J Seymour (ed), *Poverty in Plenty: a human development report for the UK*, UNED-UK, 2000

41 See note 36

42 A Gosling et al, *The Dynamics of Low Pay and Unemployment in Early 1990s Britain*, Joseph Rowntree Foundation, 1997

43 R Dickens and A Manning, 'After Wages Councils', *New Economy*, Volume 2, Issue 4, 1995

44 See note 28 and Low Pay Commission, *The National Minimum Wage: making a difference*, Third Report, Volume 1, Cm 5075, 2001

45 See note 28

46 See note 26

47 A Marsh and S McKay, *Families, Work and Benefits*, Policy Studies Institute, 1993

48 A Bryson and A Marsh, *Leaving Family Credit*, DSS Research Report 48, 1996

49 M Noble et al, *Lone Mothers Moving In and Out of Benefits*, Joseph Rowntree Foundation, 1998

50 Inland Revenue, *Working Families' Tax Credit Statistics*, Quarterly Enquiry, May 2000, National Statistics, 2000

51 See note 28 and the House of Commons Social Security Select Committee, Housing Benefit, Volume 1, Annex 2, HC 385-I, July 2000

52 HM Treasury, *Budget 2000: Prudent for a Purpose: working for a stronger and fairer Britain*, HC 346, March 2000

53 See note 10

54 See note 30

55 J Pullinger and C Summerfield, *Social Focus on Families*, National Statistics, 1997

56 See note 55

57 For example, J Bradshaw et al, *The Employment of Lone Parents: a comparison of policy in 20 countries*, Family Policy Studies Centre, 1996

58 See note 4

59 S Jenkins, *The Distribution of Income by Sectors of the Population*, ISER working paper, 2000–18, 2000

60 See note 10

61 A Bridgewood et al, *Living in Britain: results from the 1998 General Household Survey*, National Statistics, 2000

62 See note 55

63 S Jarvis and S Jenkins, 'Marital Dissolution and Income Change: evidence for Britain', in R Ford and J Millar (eds), *Private Lives and Public Responses: lone parenthood and future policy in the UK*, Policy Studies Institute, 1998

64 S McKay, 'Exploring the Dynamics of Family Change: lone parenthood in Britain', in L Leisering and R Walker (eds), *The Dynamics of Modern Society*, The Policy Press, 1998

65 D Webster, 'Promoting Jobs Could Reduce Lone Parenthood', *Working Brief*, Unemployment Unit, October 1997

66 J Ermisch, *Employment Opportunities and Pre-Marital Births in Britain*, ISER working paper 2000-26

67 See note 64

68 See note 64

69 M Iacovou and R Berthoud, *Parents and Employment*, DSS Research Report 107, 2000

70 See note 10

71 See note 8

72 See note 10

73 See note 26

74 H Sutherland, *The British Government's Attempt to Reduce Child Poverty: a Budget 2000 postscript*, Microsimulation Unit Research Note No. 36, Cambridge University, June 2000

75 See note 26

76 For a discussion of definitions, see R Walker with M Howard, *The Making of a Welfare Class: benefit receipt in Britain*, The Policy Press, 2000; T Burchardt, *Enduring Economic Exclusion: disabled people, income and work*, Joseph Rowntree Foundation, 2000; I Bell et al, 'Workless Households, Unemployment and Economic Inactivity', *Labour Market Trends*, September 1997

77 See for example, C Barnes, *Disabled People in Britain and Discrimination: a case for anti-discrimination legislation*, Hurst, 1991

78 E Grundy et al, *Disability in Great Britain*, DSS Research Report 94, 1999

79 Devised by the then Office of Population, Censuses and Surveys for an

earlier disability survey in 1985.

80 Further discussed in R Berthoud et al, *The Economic Problems of Disabled People*, Policy Studies Institute, 1993

81 D Acheson, *Independent Inquiry into Inequalities in Health Report*, The Stationery Office, 1998

82 M Bartley and C Owen, 'Relation Between Socio-economic Status, Employment and Health During Economic Change, 1973-1993', *British Medical Journal*, vol 313, 24 August 1996

83 L Finlayson et al, *The British Lone Parent Cohort 1991-1998*, DSS Research Report 128, Corporate Document Services, 2000

84 R Berthoud, *Disability Benefits: a review of the issues and options for reform*, Joseph Rowntree Foundation, 1998

85 See note 78

86 See note 84

87 A Kestenbaum, *Disability-Related Costs and Charges for Community Care*, The Disablement Income Group, 1997

88 H Barnes, *Working for a Living? Employment, benefits and the living standards of disabled people*, The Policy Press, 2000

89 Audit Commission, *Charging with Care: how councils charge for home care*, 2000

90 See note 78

91 Disability Rights Commission, *Disability Briefing*, August 2000

92 See note 6

93 Department of Social Security, *Households Below Average Income 1999/2000*, Corporate Document Services, 2001

94 T Burchardt, *Enduring Economic Exclusion*, Joseph Rowntree Foundation, 2000

95 See note 94

96 See note 94

97 R Dorsett et al, *Leaving Incapacity Benefit*, DSS Research Report 86, Corporate Document Services, 1998

98 See note 10

99 See note 84

100 P Craig and M Greenslade, *First Findings from the Disability Follow-up to the Family Resources Survey*, DSS, 1998

101 See note 26

102 HM Government, *Caring about Carers: a national strategy for carers*, 1999

103 Social Policy Research Unit, 'Informal carers: a moving target', *Cash and Care*, Winter 1999

104 House of Lords, *Hansard*, 28 October 1999, WA 46

105 E Holzhausen and V Pearlman, *Caring on the Breadline: the financial implications of caring*, Carers National Association, 2000

106 See note 8

107 K Rake (ed), *Women's Incomes over the Lifetime: a report to the Women's Unit*, Cabinet Office, 2000

108 See note 105

109 See note 105

110 Carers National Association, *The True Cost of Caring: a survey of carers' lost income,* 1996

111 D Madden and I Walker, *Labour Supply, Health and Caring: evidence from the UK,* University College, Dublin

112 See note 105

113 E McLaughlin, *Social Security and Community Care,* DSS Research Report 4, 1991

114 See note 10

115 National Statistics, *Health Statistics Quarterly,* II, Autumn 2001, population tables

116 The Pension Provision Group, *We All Need Pensions: the prospects for pension provision,* The Stationery Office, 1998

117 Department of Social Security, *The Changing Welfare State: pensioner incomes,* DSS Paper 2, 2000

118 See note 117

119 See note 117

120 Department of Social Security, *The Pensioners' Incomes Series 1999/00,* National Statistics, 2000

121 Department of Social Security, *A New Contract for Welfare: partnerships in pensions,* Cm 4179, 1998

122 See note 6

123 See note 117

124 See note 116

125 R Berthoud, *The Incomes of Ethnic Minorities,* Joseph Rowntree Foundation, 1998

126 See note 84

127 R Disney et al, *The Dynamics of Retirement,* DSS Research Report 72, Corporate Document Services, 1997

128 E Bardasi, S Jenkins and J Rigg, *Retirement and the Economic Well-being of the Elderly: a British perspective,* ISER working paper, 2000–33

129 See note 117

130 See note 26

131 See note 26

4 Effects of poverty and deprivation

'You're more tired. I mean just the thing that being poor is so much work your whole life. You see people going into a shop they buy what they want and they leave. But you're there, you're having to calculate how much money you've got as you go round, you're having to look at one brand then another, and meanwhile the store detective is looking over your shoulder which is also work having to cope with that kind of scrutiny, because you're poor they expect you to take something...There's that pressure there all the time.'

(Group of women involved in campaigns:
P Beresford et al, *Poverty First Hand*)[1]

The last chapter looked at some of the circumstances which can lead to poverty. This chapter highlights some of the effects of poverty and deprivation, which can be practical, psychological, physical and relational.[2] The specific impact on children is considered in Chapter 5.

Notwithstanding the confusion alluded to in Chapter 1, new research into the dynamics of poverty, notably studies analysing data from the British Household Panel Survey, can highlight the potential impact of living on a low income over time.

This chapter includes evidence from those analyses as well as smaller scale qualitative studies. It also includes results from a large-scale survey which reveals the extent to which people lacked items that the majority of the population perceive as essential, and whether their incomes were too low to afford them; this Poverty and Social Exclusion (PSE) Survey, discussed in detail in Chapter 2, also investigated exclusion (from services, social activities and social relationships).[3]

LIVING ON A LOW INCOME

Life on a low income means going without, which in turn can lead to longer-term problems such as poor health, debt, poor housing and homelessness.[4] These effects will be considered later in the chapter; here we examine the extent to which people go without basic essentials.

THE BARE NECESSITIES

As noted in Chapter 1, one approach to poverty is to adopt the 'consensual' approach, along the lines of the *Breadline Britain* surveys.[5] This entailed asking a representative sample of the population, with those items attracting 50 per cent or more support being considered 'essential'. Using this approach, the PSE Survey found that 35 out of 54 items were 'essential'.[6] As noted in Chapter 2, people were then classified as 'poor' if lacking two or more essentials *because they could not afford them*. Some people might lack items but have a relatively high income (eg, having obtained a job), so were classified as having 'risen out of poverty'; conversely those who did not lack items but had a low income (eg, having recently lost a job) were 'vulnerable to poverty'. Using this definition:

- 25.6 per cent were poor;
- 10.3 per cent were vulnerable to poverty;
- 1.8 per cent had risen out of poverty;
- 62.2 per cent were not poor.

GOING WITHOUT HOUSEHOLD ITEMS

According to the PSE Survey, 14 per cent of adults could not afford to keep their home decorated, 12 per cent could not afford to replace electrical goods and 12 per cent could not afford to replace worn out furniture.[7] Table 4.1 below shows the proportion of households that could not afford items in the 1999 survey, compared with the comparable *Breadline Britain* surveys in 1990 and 1983.

TABLE 4.1: **Percentage of households lacking items because they cannot afford them 1999, 1990 and 1983**

	1999	1990	1983
Beds and bedding	1	1	1
Damp-free home	6	2	7
Fridge	*	1	2
Home decorations	15	15	–
Contents insurance	10	10	–
Washing machine	2	4	6
Telephone	2	7	11
Carpets	2	2	2
TV	*	1	*

Note: * less than 0.5%
Source: D Gordon et al *Poverty and Social Exclusion in Britain*, Joseph Rowntree Foundation, 2000, p51

CUTTING BACK ON FOOD

Money for food can be used as a reserve to iron out fluctuations in income and to meet emergencies; hence people on low incomes often go without food, or eat less well than people who are better off. A poor diet can cause cognitive defects, and even short-term nutritional deficiencies can influence children's behaviour, ability to concentrate and perform complex tasks:[8]

- The PSE Survey showed that 4 per cent of adults could not afford fresh fruit and vegetables daily.[9]
- Another survey published in 1997 found that one in 20 mothers sometimes went without food to meet the needs of their children, with lone mothers on income support 14 times more likely to go without than mothers in two-parent families not on benefit.[10]
- A survey of carers carried out by Carers UK during 2000 showed more than one in five (22 per cent) cutting back on food.[11]
- Many young people living in poverty in 1998 went without food.[12]

As well as cutting back, people on low incomes may not be getting a nutritious diet:

- According to the 1998 National Food Survey, households with less than £160 per week spent 22 per cent less on food than the average.[13]

- Working households ate 85 per cent more vegetables than workless households; only a third of unemployed men ate fruit on five or six days a week, compared with half of employed men.[14]
- A study of lone parents found that those on income support had worse nutrient and iron intakes than those with earned income, and the further from benefit collection day, the worse their diets were.[15]
- People living in deprived areas in England were likely to have a less healthy diet than those in better-off areas.[16]

Poor people also pay proportionately more for their food; low-income families tended to shop 'little and often' at local discount supermarkets as they could not commit themselves to buying in bulk or in advance from large supermarkets.[17]

'Worst thing about being poor, you can't go to the supermarkets and buy top quality food like they advertise on telly and things like that.' (Women's group)[18]

CUTTING BACK ON FUEL

Research also shows the caution of many low-income families in the use of heating, particularly if at home all day, or for those who need to stay warm for health reasons or because of young children.

Individual rooms were heated as needed – normally during the coldest part of the late evening. Central heating, even where it was available, was not used.[19]

The poorest spend only half as much as the better off on fuel, but what they do spend represents a higher proportion of their income. The Family Expenditure Survey for 1999/2000 showed that households in the lowest 10 per cent of income distribution spent £7.80 a week on fuel and power, compared with £15.90 in the top tenth and an average of £11.30.[20]

When households *need* to spend more than 10 per cent of their income to provide adequate heat and energy, they are commonly considered by the Government to be in 'fuel poverty'.[21] On this basis, one household in five – or almost five million – is fuel poor according to the latest English House Condition Survey (1996), with those aged over 60 most at risk. One in 20 households could also be described as in severe fuel poverty because they need to spend 20 per cent or more of their income for warmth.

CUTTING YOUR CLOTH – GOING WITHOUT CLOTHING

The PSE Survey showed that, in 1999, 4 per cent of adults could not afford a warm, waterproof coat, and 5 per cent could not afford two pairs of all-weather shoes; 11 per cent of children lacking two items or more did not have a warm coat, and 11 per cent lacked properly fitted shoes, because their parents could not afford it.[22]

Most low-income families bought second-hand clothes for themselves, and sometimes for their children, although parents would often try to ensure that children had new clothes as far as possible:

> 'Most of his and my clothes we get in Erdington second-hand shops... you know, the Spastics Society (now Scope) – they do have some nice stuff...The children get new quite often...they're never handed dow2the kids have something every five or six weeks – you know, if it's only a pair of shorts.'[23]

BUDGETING AND BUDGETING STRATEGIES

While many people on low incomes manage their finances well, living on a limited income can lead to difficulties with money management. This can result partly from having to set up home, a problem faced by many young single mothers.[24]

People may experience acute worry about finances when initially falling into a low income, through a period of coping, and finally chronic despair. In the early stages there may be a high risk of arrears as existing commitments become unmanageable or savings are eroded. Many people who have been poor for a long time feel depressed, and diets become worse the longer they spend on benefit.[25] Although people live on low incomes for long periods, in some cases the more practice they have at money management, the better they become.

> '...you make mistakes and you learn by them.'[26]

People develop strategies to deal with a low income. A study of 74 low-income families with children found that:

- 36 were balancing the books – 'keeping their heads above water';
- 6 had been making ends meet but were falling into arrears – 'sinking';
- 16 were in multiple arrears but reducing the amounts owed to creditors – 'struggling to the surface';
- 20 were struggling to make ends meet, had multiple arrears and saw no prospect of things getting better – 'drowning'.[27]

So, for some people, one effect of poverty is falling into debt.

DEBT

One in seven referrals to the National Association of Citizens Advice Bureaux (NACAB) during 1998/99 concerned debt, a 12 per cent increase on the previous year.[28] A survey of long-term unemployment in Germany, Sweden and Britain found that debt was more common among British than other respondents, where three-quarters incurred debts during unemployment; many were excluded from other forms of credit available to working people, such as interest-free loans, credit and overdrafts.[29]

INDICATORS OF DEBT

- A survey of clients from 29 Citizens Advice Bureaux in the north of England showed that about half were in debt to fuel companies.[30]
- In 1996/97, one in five households in England with an unemployed head were in arrears with their mortgage, compared with only one in 50 of employed households.[31]

Some claimants can be living below the basic income support level because their benefit is reduced at source. Benefit deductions can be made for social fund loans, overpayment of benefit, debt or fines. Where there is more than one debt or charge, deductions are made in the following priority order:

1. Housing costs.
2. Rent arrears.
3. Fuel charges.
4. Water charges.
5. Council tax and community charge (poll tax) arrears.
6. Unpaid fines, costs and compensation orders.
7. Child maintenance.[32]

The maximum amount that can be deducted from benefit each week for arrears and child maintenance is £8.10 (April 2001 figures); for housing and utility costs, the combined cost of consumption and arrears has to be no more than 25 per cent of the total eligible benefit.

In May 2001, 1.22 million income support claimants had one or more deductions from benefit, the largest groups being lone parents (755,000) and disabled people (582,000);[33] 204,000 unemployed claimants of income-based jobseeker's allowance had one or more deductions.[34]

While deductions can help with budgeting, they can be problematic because benefit levels are low.[35] Research for the DSS revealed that deductions increased with length of time on benefit: a third of the sample had more than one deduction, and only 40 per cent reported that they still had sufficient to live on.[36] One claimant described the impact of obtaining a social fund loan, which resulted in £3.25 a week being deducted from her benefit as repayment:

'It's so difficult – even though it's just like £3 odd – but I'm finding that at the end of the week I'm stuck. You know what I mean? I've been borrowing off my mother and everything…Definitely more, I don't know why, I'm just spending more. I think it's also because the kids are getting bigger as well. They need more food, they're eating more…'[37]

WHO FALLS INTO DEBT?

Debt results from either a sudden disruption to income (for example, as a result of unemployment or relationship breakdown or illness), where previous commitments are difficult to sustain, or from a slower, cumulative effect of a persistently low and inadequate income (for example, as a result of living on benefit for a sustained period)…

(J Ford, *Consuming Credit: debt and poverty in the UK*)[38]

A combination of low incomes and high costs can also cause debt; disabled people can incur expenses, such as special diets, extra heating and hot water, higher transport costs, and so are often at risk of falling into debt.[39]

One and a half million households in Britain (7 per cent) are without bank or building society accounts, savings, or insurance; they tend to be on income support or other low incomes, living in social housing or in areas with a high level of deprivation.[40] Lacking access to short-term credit makes it more difficult to budget, leading to arrears and/or recourse to high-cost moneylenders.

IMPACT OF DEBT

The *Hard Times*[41] survey revealed the impact of debt:

• Going without essential items, or reducing family contact and staying in so as to avoid additional cost and embarrassment, or 'robbing Peter to pay Paul'.

- Feelings of shame and having done something wrong.
- Ill-health, such as severe anxiety attacks resulting from court proceedings, or respiratory problems from living in a damp home, including where rent arrears could prevent re-housing to a better property.
- Further debt: the pressure of having to meet urgent demands often drives people into seeking secured loans on their property or borrowing from moneylenders. The first brings the danger of losing the home, the second, exorbitant rates of interest.
- Deploying bailiffs to obtain payment: using 'distress' (removal of domestic goods to settle a debt) can result in further hardship. Over 1.3 million warrants to authorise bailiff action were issued during 1997/98.[42]
- Fear of further family disruption: people with mortgage arrears feared that their home could be repossessed and their children taken into care.[43]

Those who juggled bills and got into debt often did so by adopting social conventions about what to buy in an attempt not to appear different from others. This motivation was most keenly felt in relation to their children. The second group, whose approach was to cut back, tried to conceal their poverty by cutting themselves off from social interaction and avoiding, at all costs, stigmatising debt. In their own way, both groups were adopting social conventions; either they kept up appearances or they avoided debt. Living on a low income meant they could not do both. (*Hard Times* p286)

As we have seen, debt can create further problems, such as more debts and homelessness. Hence another effect of poverty can be living in poor housing, perhaps with high costs or arrears, in some cases being vulnerable to homelessness. This is considered in the next section.

HOUSING AND HOMELESSNESS

POOR HOUSING

Despite improvements to housing conditions, nearly three million English households live in poor housing (ie, which is unfit, in need of repair or essential modernisation). In England, lone parents and people from minority ethnic communities were more likely to experience poor housing in 1996 than in 1991.[44] The PSE Survey of Britain also revealed that 6 per cent of adults could not afford to live in a damp-free home, and 14 per cent could not afford to keep the home in a decent state of decoration.[45]

Poor housing can lead to poor health, such as asthma resulting from damp homes.[46] A report by the Scottish Executive highlighted that:

- cold, damp and mouldy conditions pose the greatest risk to health, and the prevalence of illness appears to increase with the level of dampness;
- overcrowding and living in high-rise flats are associated with psychological symptoms, such as depression;
- anxiety and depression increase with the number of housing problems.[47]

HIGH HOUSING COSTS AND ARREARS

Changes in the housing market over the past 20 years have tended to make it more difficult for people on low incomes to find and keep affordable accommodation.[48] Rents have risen ahead of inflation as a result of subsidy reduction in the social housing sector and the effects of decontrol in the private sector. In the 15 years to 1997, housing costs rose across the board with a shift away from local authority tenancies, which tended to cost less.[49] Private sector rents increased six-fold between 1980 and 1994.[50] The structure and administration of housing benefit has been a key factor in rent arrears and homelessness;[51] a third of all unemployed heads of households in rent arrears attributed this to problems with their housing benefit.[52]

HOMELESSNESS

Official statistics can underestimate the extent of homelessness. The *Households Below Average Income* statistics cover only private households, excluding people sleeping rough or in bed and breakfast (B&B) accommodation. Homelessness statistics also exclude those who have not been accepted by local authorities as homeless according to the criteria, such as priority need (eg, families with children or a pregnant woman, households that are considered vulnerable, perhaps because of illness, or those homeless in an emergency). Fewer than half of housing applications are accepted as homeless. In 2000, 110,790 households in England were accepted as homeless.[53] This is below the 1994 figure of 122,660, but twice that of the 55,530 acceptances in 1979.[54] Just under 14 per cent of those accepted as homeless were housed in B&B in 2000, compared with 10 per cent in 1997.

- Over one million households in England were homeless at some time during the ten years ending 1998/99. Most at risk were those from minority ethnic communities, lone-parent families and under 45-year-olds.[55]
- 137,000 court warrants were issued to repossess homes in 1999, above the previous peak of 134,000 in 1991.[56]
- An estimated 2,000 people in England may be sleeping rough, with as many as 10,000 drifting in and out of rough sleeping over a year.[57] Most rough sleepers are male, and about a quarter are aged between 18 and 25. Up to a half also have mental health problems, the majority of whom became ill before they became homeless.

CAUSES OF HOMELESSNESS

A principal cause of homelessness is a shortage of affordable housing, primarily affecting people on low incomes.[58] However, the immediate triggers for becoming homeless include the following:

- In 2000, 30 per cent of homeless people in England lost their last home because friends or relatives could no longer accommodate them; 23 per cent because of relationship breakdown; and 3 per cent because of mortgage arrears.[59]
- Domestic violence can also cause homelessness, mainly among women.[60]

In 1998/99, lone parents in England were more than twice as likely as couples with children to have problems with mortgage payments, including arrears, and unemployed people more likely than full-time workers (43 per cent compared with 14 per cent).[61]

IMPACT OF HOMELESSNESS

Homelessness can have a negative impact on health and on a child's education. According to the Acheson report:[63]

- homeless people, especially rough sleepers and hostel dwellers, have very high mortality rates;
- twice as many people in B&B experience psychological distress than in the general population, and are more likely to have infections and skin conditions, and children have more accidents;
- a higher proportion of homeless people experience major mental health problems, notably schizophrenia and very high levels of suicide;
- single homeless people have higher rates of respiratory conditions, including tuberculosis, as well as arthritis, skin diseases and problems related to alcohol and substance misuse;
- child development is impaired through lack of space for safe play and exploration.

Over half of homeless young people have been excluded from school.[62]

The association between housing situation and illness highlights another effect of poverty – poor health, which is considered next.

POOR HEALTH

There are many factors that appear to contribute to the differences in health that people experience. However, the link between poverty and ill-health is clear. In nearly every case the highest incidence of illness is experienced by the worst off social classes. (Department of Health, *Our Healthier Nation*, 1998, p24)

The widening income inequalities of the 1980s and early-1990s have been accompanied by a parallel trend in health inequalities, although the precise causal relationship is still debated.[64] These inequalities are also reflected in death rates.

DEATH RATES

During the twentieth century there has been a sizeable decline in death rates.[65] However, inequalities remain:

- Life expectancy differences between social class I and V is 5.2 years in men and 3.4 years in women.[66]
- Children in the bottom social class are five times more likely to die from an accident than those at the top.[67]

DEATHS IN CHILDHOOD

Although overall death rates for babies and young children have declined over time, disparities remain. In 1999, infant mortality (ie, death within the first year) inside marriage was almost twice as high in unskilled manual classes (6.5 per thousand) than in professional classes (3.8 per thousand) and ninety-seven times higher for very low birthweight babies (less than 1,500 grammes) than for usual birthweight (2,500 grammes or more).[68] Differences are even greater between deprived and better-off areas; for example, male infants were three times as likely to die in Stoke on Trent as in the Isle of Ely towns.[69] The poorest areas have failed to match the overall improvement; in London's Bethnal Green, child mortality rates for males were higher in 1992 than in 1950.

ADULT DEATH RATES

As noted above for child deaths, there is a geographical pattern in premature adult death. In areas like Glasgow, Manchester and London, death rates have risen rapidly, much of which could be accounted for by inequality, unemployment and poverty in the 1970s and 1980s.[70]

TABLE 4.2: **Perinatal and infant mortality rates per 1,000 births (within marriage only) by social class 1978/79 and 1999**

Social class	Perinatal		Infant	
	1978/79	1999	1978/79	1999
I	11.9	5.8	9.8	3.8
II	12.3	6.2	10.1	3.8
III (non-manual)	13.9	8.2	11.1	5.0
III (manual)	15.1	7.7	12.4	5.1
IV	16.7	9.9	13.6	6.5
V	20.3	11.0	17.2	8.4
Other	20.4	9.7	23.3	7.3
Ratio Class V:I	1.71	1.89	1.8	2.21

Source: *Mortality Statistics, Perinatal and Infant: social and biological factors 1978-79 and 1992*, HMSO, 1995; *Mortality Statistics: childhood, infant and perinatal, 1999*, DH3 series, 2001 (Table 20 – all ages, within marriage)

- Unemployed men in England and Wales have a 20 per cent higher risk of death than average.[71]
- Among unemployed men aged between 16 and 44, mortality from injuries and poisonings, including suicide, is 90 per cent higher than for employed men of the same age.[72]

> 'I used to belong to the Job Club and this chap was really looking for work hard, really really looking for work. And he thought he had a job and he came in to celebrate then they told him the job wasn't his and he tried to kill himself because he'd looked so long.' (Group of unemployed people, London) [73]

- Death rates increase during the winter months by around 30 per cent, three times that of colder Scandinavian countries, with older people more at risk. During 1999/2000, provisional figures show that there were over 54,000 'excess winter deaths'[74] in Great Britain.[75]

POVERTY AND POOR HEALTH

Poverty and social exclusion is associated with poor health. About two-thirds of the families interviewed in *Hardship Britain* reported sickness or disability, most commonly asthma, bronchitis and eczema. Ill-health was associated with the stress of poverty, inability to meet extra expenses caused by illness, and not being able to heat homes sufficiently.

> 'I have asthma and when I get worried or I'm not warm, I get worse...we put on the heaters for the children because you have to, but for ourselves we say no.'[76]

A survey of English adults in 1998 asked people whether their health was good or 'less than good'. Those most likely to report 'less than good health' were from manual social classes; on incomes below £10,000; economically inactive; with no qualifications; in local authority housing; and single unemployed people.[77] The General Household Survey has also revealed that people from manual groups have been more likely to report longstanding illness and suffer from conditions like musculo-skeletal problems and heart complaints (see Figure 4.1).

Poverty also seems to be associated with poor mental health:

- One in four unemployed people have a neurotic disorder compared

TABLE 4.3: **Percentage with limiting longstanding illness by socio-economic group, total of all ages, 1998**

Socio-economic group	Men	Women
Professional	12	13
Employers/managers	15	17
Intermediate non-manual	17	20
Junior non-manual	15	23
Skilled manual	22	22
Semi-skilled manual	23	27
Unskilled manual	27	29
All	19	21

Source: 1998 General Household Survey, p94

with only one in eight of those working full time, and for workless women the rate is twice as high as for workless men.[78]

● Higher reported stress also seems to be connected with isolation, economic inactivity in men and lone motherhood.[79]

As well as health, poverty can also affect relationships and participation in society.

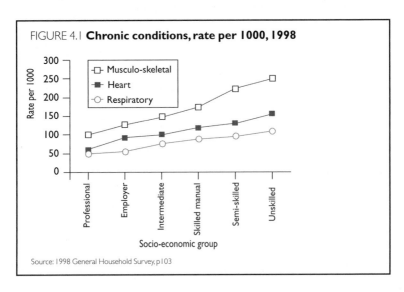

FIGURE 4.1 **Chronic conditions, rate per 1000, 1998**

Source: 1998 General Household Survey, p103

EXCLUSION

The PSE Survey also examined the links between poverty and other experiences, including being unable to afford to use services and exclusion from social relationships.

EXCLUSION FROM SERVICES

Lack of access to basic services can occur outside of the home (like transport) or inside (like power supplies). Outside the home, the PSE Survey found that:

- 24 per cent of respondents were excluded from two or more services because they were unaffordable or unavailable;
- one in ten respondents found services unaffordable, mainly affecting evening classes and visits to the pub or cinema/theatre. Eleven per cent found train services unavailable or unaffordable.[80]

Within the home, 6 per cent of PSE Survey respondents had experienced disconnection from a power supply, and 11 per cent had restricted their consumption.[81] Gas disconnections rose from 18,600 in 1991 to 29,500 in 1998.[82] Around 30 per cent of those in the lowest tenth of incomes use pre-payment meters for gas and 10 per cent for electricity, despite this being one of the most expensive forms of payment.[83] About a third of people with such meters 'self-disconnected' during 1999; some people preferring this to being in debt.

> 'I try to cut down on me electric. Many a Sunday afternoon our electric has gone. We've just waited 'til Monday.' (Trudy in *Hard Times*)[84]

Though since 1 July 1999 water companies no longer have the power to disconnect, in the past disconnections peaked at 18,636 in 1992/93, and were concentrated among low-income households.[85]

EXCLUSION FROM SOCIAL ACTIVITIES

Basic necessities included in the PSE Survey were *social customs, obligations and activities. Customs* include celebrations on special occasions, such as Christmas, weddings and funerals, and presents for family and friends once a year. *Obligations and activities* include a hobby or leisure activity, as well as those involving reciprocation and care of others, such as visits to family or friends, having family/friends round for a meal.

The PSE Survey found that:

- a fifth of the population were excluded from three or more social activities because they could not afford to participate;
- poor people were less likely to be active in their local community;
- 18 per cent of adults could not afford a holiday away from home;
- 7 per cent could not afford a hobby or leisure activity.[86]

Other studies show the isolation and exclusion experienced by people on low incomes. Some lose contact with friends as their financial problems increase and they can not afford to go out:

> 'Just to be able to go out and mix with people. It's not just having a social life in the first place, you don't meet people, you don't make contacts, you don't develop in any way...It just restricts your opportunities.' (Group of homeless people)[87]

The Family Expenditure Survey for 1999/2000 also showed that the poorest tenth of the income distribution spent £11.50 a week on leisure services – over £32 a week less than the average (£43.90). [88]

Another effect of poverty is in the self-perceptions of poor people, the impact on dealings with authorities and the effect on family life.

PERCEPTIONS ABOUT BEING POOR

The PSE Survey asked people whether they felt poor (leaving open how 'poor' was defined). Of those who said they felt poor all the time, 86 per cent were actually poor, though 11 per cent of those who were poor said they never felt poor.[89] The more often they believed they were poor in the past, the more likely they were to be poor at the time of the survey:

- Nearly three-quarters of people who felt isolated or depressed as a result of lack of money during the previous year were currently poor (at the time of the survey).
- Those who were dissatisfied with their area, or felt unsafe walking in the neighbourhood or being alone at home, were more likely to be poor.[90]

STIGMA AND MARGINALISATION

Many people on low incomes express feelings of marginalisation and exclusion. Although researchers organising group discussions did not use the term 'stigma', it dominated the understanding of poor people about their poverty:

> 'Poor is stigma.' (Group for low-income families)[91]

Some people found that once others knew they were on benefit, their attitudes would change:

> 'Even in the church which I belong to, when they were collecting, somebody said, "We're collecting for 'you people'". I thought all of a sudden I have become 'you people', you know...' (Group of unemployed people, London)[92]

Many people also felt that where they lived could affect their chances of moving out of poverty, perhaps by getting a job; living in an area with a 'notorious' reputation could also limit social life or ability to gain credit.[93] In a study of two poor estates in Sheffield and York, where only a third of residents were employed at the time of the survey, one resident said:

> 'As soon as you say you live on Bell Farm, you're some sort of deranged monster...a criminal, can't look after your children, you're in the pub all day'.[94]

Perceptions about the effects of the process of obtaining free school meals on families with children are discussed in Chapter 5.

PSYCHOLOGICAL EFFECTS OF POVERTY

Discussion groups of people living in poverty revealed some of the psychological effects, such as powerlessness, loss of self-esteem, stress, depression and anger.

> 'Constant worrying, 24 hours a day about money and having to manage for the rest of the week, month, year whatever.' (Lone parents' group, Bristol)[95]

Men and women can experience the effects of poverty differently: men may struggle to come to terms with failing to succeed as breadwinners, while women bear the brunt of having to manage inadequate resources.[96]

TREATED AS POOR: DEALING WITH OFFICIALS

Asking for help can also lead to feelings of stigma, possibly also leading to being further investigated. One mother with a new baby, whose father had just died, had her electricity cut off and was in debt. Asking social services for help, she found herself called to a case conference to assess her ability as a mother.[97] Young people can also feel they are not treated as adults:

> 'Careers and social services and dole – fill this form in, bring it back next week. And social services do treat you like kids 'cos they don't let you make your own decisions.' (Emily, Hull)[98]

Claimants describe their lives as being 'governed by the DSS' and being treated like 'dirt'.[99] Research with unemployed people in 1997 and 1998 uncovered frustration at dealing with officials:

> 'It's a joke, a waste of paper. You sit there with a person who knows nothing about you and they're obviously in a rush so you get about ten minutes of their time and then you sign it and then go.'[100]

Life on a low income has entailed form-filling, numerous contacts with different offices, and queuing. *Hardship Britain* documented some of the difficulties faced by claimants in the early 1990s, when the emphasis on postal and computerised claiming had reduced most direct contact with officials to changing circumstances, emergencies, errors or delays.[101]

The introduction of more personalised services and new agencies, such as the proposed 'working-age agency', combining different offices into one, may change this experience. However, poor people feel that officials have great power over their lives, and often believe they are not treated with respect.[102] Simply changing names, such as from 'claimants' to 'customers', may result in little difference if the balance of power remains the same.

IMPACT ON FAMILY LIFE

While some relationships are strong and people help each other out financially, poverty can also place strains on family life. Lack of money can drive a wedge between family members if someone cannot repay a debt or afford to meet family obligations, as encountered by one woman who could not afford to buy a wreath for her father's funeral.[103]

Relationship breakdown can be another effect of poverty. Evidence from six years of the British Household Panel Survey revealed that people receiving income support were three times more likely to have a relationship breakdown than those not on income support. Also at risk were people whose financial situation was worsening, and social tenants.[104] Another analysis focussing more specifically on divorce found that important precursors were unemployment, reliance on benefits, disability and financial difficulties.[105]

A notable effect of separation is that the mothers tend to become poor lone parents. Among couples separating between 1991 and 1994, the median net income of mothers dropped by 17 per cent the following year, 30 per cent of mothers were new income support claimants and 28 per cent were on income support both before and after separation.[106]

THE IMPACT ON CHILDREN

Many poor parents feel that financial constraints have a negative impact on their children, excluding them from the lifestyle of their peers because of the poverty of their parents. For instance, a child might have to make sacrifices or go without a desired item, simply because the parents cannot afford to buy it. Compared with workless people in Germany and Sweden, British families are concerned that their unemployment might have a psychological and social impact on their children.[107]

> 'When you're not working and you're having to claim, you can't take your kids out to the shop and say can I buy you this? Can I buy you that? You can't. You've got to say 'Oh I'll try and buy it for you next time.'' (Group of unemployed people, Yorkshire)[108]

Poverty can also affect children by diminishing their parents' capacity and resources to bring them up.

> Good parenting requires certain permitting circumstances. There must be the necessary life opportunities and facilities. Where these are lacking even the best parents may find it difficult to exercise their skills. (Rutter, quoted in Utting, *Family and Parenthood: supporting families, preventing breakdown*)[109]

Chapter 5 considers the impact on children in more detail, including parental sacrifice to protect children from poverty and the longer-term impact of growing up in a low-income household.

CRIME AND FEAR OF CRIME

People on low incomes may be disproportionately affected by crime. Firstly, while unemployed people have the same chance of experiencing crime as those in work, the former are more likely to be victims of different offences, such as car crime, burglary, household theft.[110] Secondly, being a victim of crime can have a more devastating effect on people on low incomes; for instance, living in high-risk areas and being less likely to have home contents insurance.[111] Thirdly, poor people are also more likely to feel unsafe or that their quality of life is significantly affected by fear of crime.[112]

Some poor people believed that the restricted choices faced by people on low incomes could push them into crime, though it was also recognised that this could simply result in a vicious circle of further financial limitations:

> 'You just can't get a car unless you just went illegal, then you get arrested and get into trouble, get fined and then it's taken out of your benefit so your benefit goes down.' (Group of young people)[113]

CONCLUSION

Poverty casts a long shadow, and can affect many aspects of life from being unable to afford the basics to being excluded from social activities and services. Poverty can have many effects, and we have focussed on just some of them, such as debt, a higher risk of ill-health and premature death, living in poor housing and sometimes homelessness. While not all people who are poor experience these problems, and people who are not poor may also encounter them, people who live on low incomes, especially for a prolonged period, are more likely to be vulnerable to multiple deprivation.

NOTES

1 P Beresford et al, *Poverty First Hand: poor people speak for themselves*, CPAG, 1999
2 See note 1
3 D Gordon et al, *Poverty and Social Exclusion in Britain*, Joseph Rowntree Foundation, 2000
4 E Kempson, *Life on a Low Income*, Joseph Rowntree Foundation, 1996

5   For example, J Mack and S Lansley, *Poor Britain*, Allen and Unwin, 1985
6   See note 3
7   See note 3
8   Quoted in S Leather, *The Making of Modern Malnutrition: an overview of food poverty in the UK*, The Caroline Walker Trust, 1996
9   See note 1
10 S Middleton, K Ashworth and I Braithwaite, *Small Fortunes: spending on children, childhood poverty and parental sacrifice*, Joseph Rowntree Foundation, 1997
11 E Holzhausen and V Pearlman, *Caring on the Breadline: the financial implications of caring*, Carers National Association, 2000
12 D Roker, *Worth More Than This: young people growing up in family poverty*, The Children's Society and Trust for the Study of Adolescence, 1998
13 Ministry of Agriculture, Fisheries and Food, *National Food Survey 1998*, The Stationery Office, 1999
14 J Pullinger and C Summerfield, *Social Focus on the Unemployed*, Office for National Statistics, 1999
15 E Dowler and C Calvert, *Nutrition and Diet in Lone-Parent Families in London*, Family Policy Studies Centre, 1995
16 L Rainford et al, *Health in England 1998: investigating the links between social inequalities and health*, Office for National Statistics, 2000
17 B Dobson et al, *Diet, Choice and Poverty: social, cultural and nutritional aspects of food consumption among low-income families*, Family Policy Studies Centre, 1994
18 See note 1
19 See note 4
20 D Down (ed), *Family Spending: a report on the 1999-2000 Family Expenditure Survey*, National Statistics, 2000
21 See for example, section on fuel poverty in Department of Trade and Industry, *Energy Report*, 1999
22 See note 3
23 E Kempson, A Bryson and K Rowlingson, *Hard Times? How poor families make ends meet*, Policy Studies Institute, 1994
24 See note 4
25 See note 4
26 See note 4
27 See note 23
28 National Association of Citizens Advice Bureaux, *Undue Distress: CAB clients' experience of bailiffs*, 2000
29 J Clasen, A Gould and J Vincent, *Long-Term Unemployment and the Threat of Social Exclusion*, Joseph Rowntree Foundation, 1997
30 Social Welfare Research Unit, *Multiple Debt and Fuel Costs: a review of the literature and a survey of CAB clients: a report to NACAB (North Region)*, University of Northumbria, 1999
31 See note 14

32 C George et al, *Welfare Benefits Handbook 2000-2001*, CPAG, 2000

33 Department of Social Security, *Income Support Quarterly Statistical Enquiry*, May 2001

34 Department of Social Security, *Jobseeker's Allowance Quarterly Statistical Enquiry*, May 2001

35 National Association of Citizens Advice Bureaux, *Make or Break? CAB evidence on deductions from benefit*, 1993

36 R Mannion, S Hutton and R Sainsbury, *Direct Payments from Income Support*, DSS Research Report 33, 1994

37 R Cohen et al, *Hardship Britain: being poor in the 1990s*, CPAG, 1992

38 J Ford, *Consuming Credit: debt and poverty in the UK*, CPAG, 1991

39 L Grant, *Disability and Debt: the experience of disabled people in debt*, Sheffield Citizens Advice Bureaux Debt Support Unit, 1995

40 E Kempson and C Whyley, *Kept Out or Opted Out? Understanding and combating financial exclusion*, Joseph Rowntree Foundation/The Policy Press, 1999

41 See note 23

42 See note 28

43 See note 23

44 Department of the Environment, Transport and the Regions, *The English House Condition Survey, 1996*

45 See note 3

46 See note 4

47 Scottish Office, 'Poor Housing and Ill Health: a summary of the evidence 1999', *NCH Factfile 2000*, p321

48 See note 4

49 E Kempson and F Bennett, *Local Living Costs: variations in the costs borne by low-income households*, Policy Studies Institute, 1997

50 That is, by comparing private sector rents in 1980 with those of de-regulated tenancies in 1994; E Kempson, M White, and J Forth, *Rents and Work Incentives*, Policy Studies Institute, 1997

51 See for example, L Phelps, *Falling Short: the CAB case for housing benefit reform*, NACAB, 1999

52 See note 14

53 Department for Transport, Local Government and the Regions, *Housing: Key figures*, July 2001

54 J Newton, *All in One Place*, CHAS, 1994

55 Department of the Environment, Transport and the Regions, *Housing in England: 1998/99 Housing Survey*, 2000

56 J Matheson and C Summerfield (eds), *Social Trends 31*, National Statistics, 2001

57 Social Exclusion Unit, *Rough Sleeping*, Cm 4008, July 1998

58 See note 4

59 See note 53

60 See note 47

61 See note 55

62 See note 60

63 D Acheson, *Independent Inquiry into Inequalities in Health Report*, The Stationery Office, 1998

64 See note 63

65 See for example, G Davey Smith and D Gordon, 'Poverty Across the Life-Course and Health', in C Pantazis and D Gordon (eds), *Tackling Inequalities: where are we now and what can be done?*, The Policy Press, 2000

66 See note 65

67 Department of Health, *Our Healthier Nation*, Cm 3852, February 1998

68 National Statistics, *Mortality Statistics: Childhood, infant and perinatal, 1999*, DH3 series, 2001 and *Health Statistics Quarterly*, No. 8, Winter 2000

69 D Dorling, *Death in Britain: how local mortality rates have changed: 1950s-1990s*, Joseph Rowntree Foundation, 1997

70 R Mitchell, D Dorling and M Shaw, *Inequalities in Life and Death: what if Britain were more equal?*, The Policy Press, 2000

71 See note 63

72 See note 14

73 See note 1

74 Excess winter deaths are defined as the number of deaths in the four months from December to March, minus the average of the numbers in the preceding autumn (August-November) and the following summer (April-July).

75 House of Commons, *Hansard*, 8 November 2000, col 271w

76 See note 37

77 See note 16

78 See note 14

79 See note 16

80 See note 3

81 See note 3

82 Department of Trade and Industry, *UK Energy Report*, 1999

83 See note 82

84 See note 23

85 See note 4

86 See note 3

87 See note 1

88 See note 20

89 See note 3

90 See note 3

91 See note 1

92 See note 1

93 See note 1

94 P Lawless and Y Smith, 'Poverty, Inequality and Exclusion in the Contemporary City', in P Lawless, R Martin, and S Hardy, *Unemployment*

and Social Exclusion: landscapes of labour inequality, Regional Studies Association, 1998
95 See note 1
96 See note 4
97 ATD Fourth World, *Participation Works: involving people in poverty in policy-making*, 2000
98 T Bentley et al, *The Real Deal: what young people really think about government, politics and social exclusion*, Demos, 1999
99 See note 1
100 D Finn, M Blackmore and M Nimmo, *Welfare to Work and the Long-Term Unemployed*, Unemployment Unit and Youthaid, 1998
101 See note 37
102 UK Coalition Against Poverty, *Listen Hear: the right to be heard*, Report of the Commission on Poverty, Participation and Power, The Policy Press, 2000
103 See note 4
104 R Boheim and J Ermisch, *Breaking Up: financial surprises and partnership dissolution*, Institute for Social and Economic Research, University of Essex, 1999
105 K Kiernan, 'Divorce/Family Breakdown', in *Persistent Poverty and Lifetime Inequality: the evidence*, proceedings from a workshop held at HM Treasury, 17 and 18 November, CASE report 5, March 1999
106 S Jarvis and S Jenkins, *Marital Dissolution and Income Change: evidence for Britain*, University of Essex Working Paper, 1997
107 See note 29
108 See note 1
109 D Utting, *Family and Parenthood: supporting families, preventing breakdown*, Joseph Rowntree Foundation, 1995
110 See note 14
111 C Whyley, J McCormick and E Kempson, *Paying for Peace of Mind: access to home contents insurance for low-income households*, Policy Studies Institute, 1998
112 C Howarth et al, *Monitoring Poverty and Social Exclusion 1999*, New Policy Institute and Joseph Rowntree Foundation, 1999
113 See note 1

5 Children

Children from poor homes have lower life expectancy and are more likely to die in infancy or childhood; they have a greater likelihood of poor health, a lower chance of high educational attainment, a greater risk of unemployment, a higher probability of involvement in crime and of enduring homelessness. Girls from poor homes are at greater risk of teenage pregnancy.

(Sally Holtermann, *All our Futures: the impact of public expenditure and fiscal policies on Britain's children and young people*, Barnardo's 1995)

The costs of a child can fall disproportionately on low-income households and the combination of higher costs and lower incomes can push some families into poverty. In Chapter 2 we discussed child poverty as revealed by the *Households Below Average Income* statistics and the Povety and Social Exclusion Survey, and in Chapter 3 the circumstances leading to poverty were examined; here we consider the costs of children, and the different measures which can be applied to child poverty, and the longer-term impact of a childhood of poverty (such as low educational achievement).

THE COSTS OF A CHILD

A child reaching her/his 17th birthday may have cost an estimated £50,000 (at 1997 prices).[1] These costs include one-off items like baby equipment and ongoing spending on essentials. The mother may also have given up work, losing earnings.[2] Costs can be both direct (like food, clothing and toys) and indirect (such as earnings foregone).

DIRECT COSTS

The direct costs of a child have been estimated through pricing a specific 'basket of goods and services' (the budget standards approach).[3] The *Small Fortunes* survey[4] used expenditure information from children and parents, finding that costs varied by age and income. More was spent on older children, but income constrained spending.

Using a similar approach, bringing up a severely disabled child has been costed as three times higher than the average for children.[5]

Receipt of income support was more significant than family type in explaining differences in spending on children, suggesting that it is being in a lone-parent family on income support which makes the difference rather than being in a lone-parent family *per se*. However,

TABLE 5.1: **Parents' spending by age of child, 1997**

	Babies (under 2)		Pre-school (2-5)		Primary (full-time school, under 11)		Secondary (11-16)	
	Mean £	%	Mean £	%	Mean £	%	Mean £	%
Food	13.95	32	16.08	39	17.78	38	21.70	41
Clothes	7.45	17	5.26	13	4.12	9	3.51	7
Nappies	6.63	15	1.81	4	–	–	–	–
School	–	–	–	–	3.85	8	5.82	11
Babysitting	0.42	1	1.01	2	0.58	1	0.37	1
Phone	–	–	–	–	0.15	0	0.72	1
Other regular	5.91	13	5.97	14	3.32	7	3.72	7
Other	0.36	1	0.24	1	0.42	1	1.41	3
Christmas	2.38	5	2.59	6	3.06	7	4.03	8
Birthdays	1.30	3	1.62	4	1.49	3	1.85	4
Trips/holidays	3.77	9	4.30	10	5.78	12	4.28	8
Weekly average	**44.21**		**41.28**		**46.30**		**52.38**	
Childcare	7.64	+17	10.52	+25	3.16	+7	0.86	+2
Average including childcare	**51.85**		**51.80**		**49.46**		**53.24**	

Source: S Middleton, K Ashworth and I Braithwaite, *Small Fortunes: spending on children, childhood poverty and parental sacrifice*, Joseph Rowntree Foundation, 1997

childcare was 12 per cent more expensive for working lone parents than for two-parent working families, perhaps due to the number of hours and type of care used. Most of the higher income from work in a lone-parent family was swallowed up in the increased use of childcare rather than spending on the child directly.

For all parents, the cost of childcare can be high. The Day Care Trust has estimated that the cost of childcare for a family with two children, one pre-school and one at school needing after-school and holiday care would typically amount to almost £6,000 a year.[6]

INDIRECT OR OPPORTUNITY COSTS

The indirect cost of having a child (in giving up work) tends to be born mainly by women. A report to the Cabinet Office Women's Unit showed that the gap in lifetime earnings between women with children and those without could be as great as half a million pounds, with those least skilled losing most:[7]

- Earnings foregone by a low-skilled woman with two children were £269,000 and for four children £426,000.
- Earnings foregone by a high-skilled woman with two children were £19,000 and £90,000 for four children.

CHILD POVERTY

Chapter 1 discussed some of the different discourses and definitions of poverty. Two approaches are considered in this chapter: the first uses the 'statistical percentage' as adopted by the Government. The second is the consensual approach to establish what are essential items and families with children who lack these items because they cannot afford them.

In contrast to previous official denials of poverty, the Labour Government has set ambitious targets to end child poverty within 20 years (2020), halving it within ten and reducing it by a quarter by 2004. The DSS uses a range of income thresholds (50, 60 and 70 per cent below median and 40, 50 and 60 per cent below mean) as a poverty baseline.[8] As discussed in Chapter 2, we use '50 per cent of mean income after housing costs' (AHC), as a proxy for the poverty line, so this measure is used in this chapter except where only other measures are available.

TRENDS IN CHILD POVERTY

As we saw in Chapter 2, child poverty rates have risen fast over the past 30 years, despite a fall in both family size and numbers of families with children, and remains high relative to other countries (discussed in Chapter 9).

Looking at *incomes*, the number of children in households on below half average incomes grew from one in ten to just under one in three between 1968 and 1995/96:[9]

- In 1968, 9 per cent of children living in two-parent households and 31 per cent of children in lone-parent households were poor (below half mean income AHC).
- By 1995/96, 24 per cent of children living in two-parent households and 65 per cent of children in lone-parent households were poor.
- Poverty rose twice as fast for families with children (21 per cent) as for those without (10 per cent).[10]

Comparing income distribution with *spending* shows a similar pattern. Dividing households into high and low 'expenditure quintiles' for 1968 and 1995/96:

- families with children in the lower fifth of expenditure spent substantially less than other families in both 1968 and 1995/96;
- the higher spending groups spent considerably more on children's clothes in 1995/96 than in 1968, but those in the bottom fifth saw no increase;
- spending on fresh fruit and vegetables actually fell in the lowest expenditure groups.[11]

CHILDREN AT RISK OF POVERTY

Some children, such as those in lone-parent households, from workless families and many from minority ethnic families, are more at risk of poverty than others.[12] The 1999/2000 *Households Below Average Income* revealed:

- half of couples with children and lone parents lived below 50 per cent of mean incomes (AHC);
- three-quarters of children in lone-parent families and two-thirds in two-parent families where no one was in full-time work were living in the bottom fifth of incomes (AHC);

• children from minority ethnic households were more at risk of falling into a low-income group; while 26 per cent of children in White households were on incomes below 50 per cent of the mean (AHC), 44 per cent of Indian, 47 per cent of Black, and 66 per cent of Pakistani and Bangladeshi children, were below this level.

Overall, a third of children lived in households with below half average incomes (50 per cent mean AHC) in 1999/2000.[13] Figure 5.1 below shows the proportion of children living below half average income by family type.

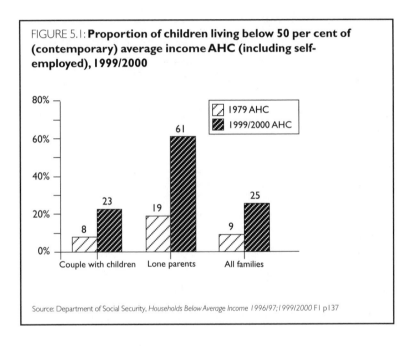

FIGURE 5.1: **Proportion of children living below 50 per cent of (contemporary) average income AHC (including self-employed), 1999/2000**

Legend: 1979 AHC / 1999/2000 AHC

	Couple with children	Lone parents	All families
1979 AHC	8	19	9
1999/2000 AHC	23	61	25

Source: Department of Social Security, *Households Below Average Income 1996/97; 1999/2000* F1 p137

Children are more likely to live on means-tested benefits, such as income support; 17 per cent of households with children receive half or more of their income from means-tested benefits, compared with only 7 per cent of households without children.[14] In 1998, over 800,000 children had spent at least five years on means-tested benefits.[15]

CHILDREN PERSISTENTLY POOR

Thus children, particularly those under five, have a greater risk of staying in poverty for long periods than adults.[16] One analysis of the British Household Panel Survey, over a six-year period (1991–96), found that 14 per cent of children, but only 9.7 per cent of adults, were poor[17] at least three times.[18] According to *Households Below Average Income*,[19] almost one in five children were in the bottom three deciles for four consecutive years in the 1990s, with lone parents more likely to remain poor relative to couples with children and childless working-age adults.[20]

TABLE 5.2: **Proportions in persistent poverty by family type, 1991–99**

	% in bottom 30 % in all four years		
	1991–94	1995–98	1996–99
Couples with children	12	13	13
Lone parents	42	32	31
Couple no children	(3)	(4)	(4)
Single no children	(6)	7	(6)

Note: estimates in brackets are based on less than 100 sample cases
Source: Department of Social Security, *Households Below Average Income* 1994/95 to 1999/2000, July 2001, p96

DEPRIVATION

Another approach to child poverty has been to examine the extent to which children go without essentials because their parents cannot afford them. The 1997 *Small Fortunes* survey constructed a 'childhood deprivation index' based on parents' views about which items were essentials (21 out of 32):[21]

- One in ten children lacked three or more items because their parents could not afford them.
- Three per cent lacked five or more items.
- Children in lone-parent families were more likely to lack five or more items than in two-parent families, irrespective of work status.[22]

The Poverty and Social Exclusion (PSE) Survey in 1999 refined the *Small Fortunes* list of essentials into 27. A threshold was then established through statistical analysis of the likelihood of lacking an item because the parents could not afford to buy it from their income.[23] A child was 'deprived' if lacking one or more necessities because her/his parents could not afford them.

TABLE 5.3: **Percentage of children lacking certain basic necessities, 1999**

	% lacking one	% lacking two
Food		
Fresh fruit and vegetables daily	5	9
Three meals a day	(3)	(5)
Meat/fish/vegetarian twice daily	11	21
Clothing		
New fitted shoes	7	12
Warm waterproof coat	6	11
School uniform	6	12
New, not second-hand, clothes	9	18
Participation/activities		
Celebrations	10	20
Hobby/leisure	9	18
School trip once a term	5	(10)
Swimming once a month	21	34
Holiday away from home	64	68
Leisure equipment	9	17
Friends round for tea/snack	11	21
Developmental		
Books of own	0	(1)
Play group	(4)	(7)
Educational games	12	21
Toys	(1)	(3)
Construction toys	10	19
Bike: new/second-hand	10	18
Environmental		
Bed and bedding for self	(2)	(3)
Bedrooms each child of different sex over age 10	10	10
Bedroom carpet	(4)	(9)
Garden for play	10	8

Note: figures in brackets indicate less than 20 weighted cases
Source: D Gordon et al, *Poverty and Social Exclusion in Britain*, Joseph Rowntree Foundation, 2000

Thirty-four per cent of children lacked one or more items; 18 per cent lacked two or more (see also Table 2.8).

Children who were deprived of essentials did not necessarily equate to those who were poor by income measures; 45 per cent of children who lived in 'income-poor' households (defined as below 60 per cent of median household income) were not 'necessity deprived' (according to the 'one item' threshold). For those deprived of two or more essentials, 65 per cent were income poor but not necessities-deprived.[24]

THE IMPACT OF GROWING UP IN POVERTY

As we noted in Chapter 4, many families on low incomes cannot afford to spend enough on food – one quarter of children in lone-parent families where the parent is not working is deprived of at least one essential food item.[25]

PARENTAL SACRIFICE

However, the *Small Fortunes* survey showed that parents were often more likely to go without basic items than their children; half of the parents defined as 'poor' (ie, lacking three or more essentials) themselves had children who were not similarly 'poor', suggesting a significant degree of parental sacrifice.[26] Two-parent families seemed more able to protect their children from poverty than lone-parent families, which may have been due to the longer periods which lone parents spent out of work and on income support.

STIGMA AND SCHOOL MEALS

Parents may also be wary of poverty 'stigmatising' their children. One example is free school meals entitlement (now only for families receiving income support or means-tested jobseeker's allowance). Sometimes children can be identified (such as by separate queues) which, in some cases, can result in bullying from other pupils and deter take-up – with one in five children failing to take up their entitlement.[27]

'I am on income support and my two children rely on free school meals. However, West Sussex has recently decided to scrap our hot school meals. It is now even more obvious who the free school meal children are, as better-off parents are resorting to a packed lunch. I have, therefore, forfeited my entitlement to school meals and provide my own packed lunch for my children. This is very hard financially and makes a very significant difference to our budget, but I do not feel that it is fair to put my children through this stigmatisation.'[28]

POOR CHILD HEALTH

Inability to afford essentials like food means a poor diet; for instance, young people from lower socio-economic groups, particularly boys, have lower intakes of energy, fat, and most vitamins and minerals.[29] This can lead to poor health.

- A study of lone-parent families during 1991-95 found a quarter had at least one child with a long-standing illness, with child ill-health more likely in workless families or those which had experienced material hardship.[30]
- Children under age 15 from families in manual classes are more likely to report long-standing illness than those from professional classes.[31]

A survey of British 5–15-year-olds revealed that 10 per cent had mental health problems, and half were from families where the parents had separated.[32] High risk factors included living in households with weekly incomes under £200 a week, being in social class V, families with five or more children, living in social rented housing, in a lone-parent family, and where neither parent was working.

Furthermore, *some* poor children may be at risk of abuse or neglect; several studies associated unemployment, lone parenthood and receipt of means-tested benefits with child protection registrations.[33] It may, though, simply be that poor families are more easily detected; in some poor neighbourhoods, numbers on the 'at risk' register are five times higher than in other parts of the same city.[34]

CHILD DEVELOPMENT

Poverty can also affect child development; low birthweight and shorter height are both more pronounced in deprived and urban areas:[35]

- Low birthweight is 25 per cent higher in children from social classes

IV/V than I/II, and 45 per cent greater for lone parents registering the baby without the father.[36]

- Five-year-olds from a deprived area are on average 2.25 cm shorter than children from a better-off area.[37]

Poverty can also have an effect on a child's intellectual development:

- An analysis of children aged 6 to 17 in the National Child Development Study found those in the top fifth of incomes scored on average 3.7 per cent higher on a test of cognitive functioning, the Peabody Picture Vocabulary Test, than children on the lowest incomes.[38]
- From as early as 22 months, children of parents in social classes I/II with higher educational levels are already 14 percentage points higher up the scale of educational development than children of class IV/V parents with low educational attainment.[39]

EDUCATIONAL DISADVANTAGE

Poverty also affects the likelihood of progressing through school to attain formal educational qualifications.[40] In 1998:

- truants were more likely to have parents from poorer backgrounds, in low-skilled rather than managerial jobs, living in local authority housing;[41]
- children excluded from school were more likely to be from poorer families, have disrupted family circumstances or be from schools with a high level of disadvantage.[42]

Roughly one in twelve school leavers have no GCSE passes, and the gap between the highest and lowest attaining pupils has grown.[43] Up to 75 per cent of the difference can be explained by factors affecting the pupil intake, including low income:[44]

- Low income, as indicated by eligibility for free school meals, could account for 66 per cent of the difference in GCSE attainment at local authority level.[45]
- In nine schools, GCSE success was associated with higher levels of home ownership and lower levels of unemployment.[46]

In 2000, 9 per cent (170,000) of English 16–18-year-olds were neither in education, training nor work, a rise of 10,000 over the previous year.[47] These young people were more likely to have disadvantages associated with poverty, such as having neither parent in work, or with parents in manual occupations.[48] The Government's third annual poverty report shows progress on some educational indicators, such as increasing attainment and reducing school exclusions.[49]

CHILDREN LEARNING TO BE POOR

Interviews with children aged between five and sixteen revealed that poor children had learned to moderate their demands on parents:[50]

- Children of lone parents were more likely than those in two-parent families to restrict their requests for items believing their parent could not afford them (57 per cent and 47 per cent respectively), as were children in income support families (54 per cent) compared with those not on income support (48 per cent).
- Children from families receiving income support were over five times as likely, and from lone-parent families four times more likely, to believe that their family did not have enough money to live on.

LONGER-TERM OUTCOMES OF CHILDHOOD POVERTY

Poorer children's lower educational attainment explains much of the disadvantage they take with them into adulthood. However, statistical research shows that financial disadvantage has a further, distinct effect, over and above its impact on education.[51]

Children who grow up in poor families are more likely as adults to have a low income and other disadvantages.[52] An analysis of the National Child Development Study found that:

- children who grew up in families with financial difficulties faced joblessness rates at age 23 which were between 5 per cent (men) and 9 per cent (women) higher than those without these difficulties;
- having been brought up in poverty was likely to lead to lower wages and more unemployment in men at age 33.[53]

The rate of teenage pregnancies is higher in some of the poorest areas,[54] with risks ten times higher for girls from social class V than I, and for girls who have suffered financial hardship.[55] A teenage mother with a childhood spent in poverty stands six times the risk of remaining unqualified at age 33 as older mothers.[56]

CONCLUSIONS

Children bring costs as well as joy, and families with children tend to spend more on the basics than households without children. Whether measured by incomes, spending, or deprivation of basic necessities, families with children tend to be 'poor', with lone-parent families the poorest of all.

Although parents may sacrifice their own needs to protect their children from having to go without or face the stigma of being poor, for many this is a losing battle, with poor children facing greater risks of ill-health, poor development and low educational attainment. Poverty can follow a child into adulthood, leading to educational and employment disadvantage. As a result, plans to reduce child poverty need to tackle both the immediate and longer-term effects of childhood deprivation.

NOTES

1 S Middleton, K Ashworth and I Braithwaite, *Small Fortunes: spending on children, childhood poverty and parental sacrifice*, Joseph Rowntree Foundation, 1997

2 See for example, E Kempson, *Living on a Low Income*, Joseph Rowntree Foundation

3 N Oldfield and A C S Yu, *The Cost of a Child*, CPAG, 1993

4 See note 1

5 B Dobson and S Middleton, *Paying to Care: the cost of childhood disability*, Joseph Rowntree Foundation, 1998

6 Day Care Trust, *The Childcare Gap*, Briefing Paper 1, 1997

7 K Rake (ed), *Women's Incomes over the Lifetime: a report to the Women's Unit*, The Stationery Office, 2000

8 Department of Social Security, *Opportunity for All: tackling poverty and social exclusion*, First Annual Report 1999, Cm 4445

9 P Gregg, S Harkness and S Machin, *Child Development and Family Income*, Joseph Rowntree Foundation, 1999

10 P Gregg, S Harkness and S Machin, 'Poor Kids: trends in child poverty in Britain, 1968–96', *Fiscal Studies*, Vol 20 No 2, June 1999

11 See note 9

12 HM Treasury, *Supporting Children Through the Tax and Benefit System: the modernisation of Britain's tax and benefits system*, Number Five, November 1999

13 Department of Social Security, *Households Below Average Incomes, 1994/95 to 1999/2000,* Corporate Document Services, 2001

14 Department of Social Security, *Family Resources Survey 1999/2000*, DSS, 2001, p46

15 See note 12

16 HM Treasury, *Tackling Poverty and Extending Opportunity: the modernisation of Britain's tax and benefits system*, Number Four, March 1999

17 Defined as incomes below half of the 1991 mean (ie, a fixed threshold).

18 M Hill and S Jenkins, *Poverty Among British Children: chronic or transitory?*, Institute for Social and Economic Research, Essex University working paper, 1999

19 See note 13

20 This could be due to small sample size and methodological changes.

21 See note 1

22 See note 1

23 D Gordon et al, *Poverty and Social Exclusion in Britain*, Joseph Rowntree Foundation, 2000

24 See note 23

25 See note 1

26 See note 1

27 T Smith and M Noble, *Education Divides: poverty and schooling in the 1990s*, CPAG, 1995 and P Storey and R Chamberlin, *Improving the Take-up of Free School Meals,* DfEE Research Report 270, 2001

28 T Marsh and W McMahon, *Filling the Gap: free school meals, nutrition and poverty*, CPAG 1999

29 Department of Health and Food Standards Agency, *National Diet and Nutrition Survey: young people aged 4–18 years, volume 1: report of the diet and nutrition survey,* The Stationery Office, 2000

30 R Ford, A Marsh and L Finlayson, *What Happens to Lone Parents*, DSS Research Report 77, The Stationery Office, 1998

31 A Bridgwood et al, *Living in Britain: results from the 1998 General Household Survey*, Office for National Statistics, 2000

32 National Statistics, *Mental Health of Children and Adolescents in Great Britain,* 2000

33 D Acheson, *Independent Inquiry into Inequalities in Health*, The Stationery Office, 1998

34 Joseph Rowntree Foundation, *Inquiry into Income and Wealth, Volume 1,* February 1995

35 S Holtermann, *All our Futures: the impact of public expenditure and fiscal policies on Britain's children and young people,* Barnardo's, 1995

36 C Howarth et al, *Monitoring Poverty and Social Exclusion: Labour's inheritance,* New Policy Institute and Joseph Rowntree Foundation, 1998

37 C Wright et al, 'A Comparison of Height, Weight and Head Circumference of Primary School Children Living in Deprived and Non-deprived Circumstances', *Early Human Development*, 1992, 31:157-62, cited in British Medical Association, *Growing up in Britain: ensuring a healthy future for our children; a study of 0–5-year-olds*, BMJ Books, 1999

38 A McCulloch and H Joshi, *Child Development and Family Resources: an exploration of evidence from the second generation of the 1958 British birth cohort*, Institute for Social and Economic Research Paper 99-15, 1999

39 See note 16

40 For example, see note 16

41 Social Exclusion Unit, *Truancy and School Exclusion*, Cm 3957, May 1998

42 N Pearce and J Hillman, *Wasted Youth: raising achievement and tacking social exclusion*, IPPR, 1998.

43 J Sparkes, *Schools, Education and Social Exclusion*, CASE paper 29, November 1999

44 S Thomas and P Mortimore, 'Comparison of Value Added Models for Secondary School Effectiveness', Research Papers in Education, 1996, 11 (1) p279-95, in J Sparkes, *Schools, Education and Social Exclusion*, CASE paper 29, November 1999

45 A West et al, 'The Financing of School-Based Education: end of award report to ESRC', Centre for Educational Research, 1999, in J Sparkes, *Schools, Education and Social Exclusion*, CASE paper 29, November 1999

46 I McCallum and G Redhead, 'Poverty and Educational Performance', *Poverty*, Summer 2000, CPAG

47 Department for Education and Skills, *Participation in Education, Training and Employment by 16–18-Year-Olds in England*, Statistical First Release, June 2001

48 Department for Education and Employment, *Youth Cohort Study: education, training and employment of 16–18-year-olds in England and the factors associated with non-participation*, Statistical Bulletin 02/2000, May 2000

49 Department of Social Security, *Opportunity for All: making progress*, Third Annual Report, Cm 5260, 2001

50 J Shropshire and S Middleton, *Small Expectations: learning to be poor?*, Joseph Rowntree Foundation, 1999

51 See note 16

52 See note 16

53 See note 9

54 Social Exclusion Unit, *Teenage Pregnancy*, Cm 4342, June 1999

55 K Kiernan, 'Family Forms and Intergenerational Links' in A Lee and J Hills, *New Cycles of Disadvantage? Report of a conference organised by CASE on behalf of the ESRC for HM Treasury*, July 1998

56 J Hobcraft and K Kiernan, *Childhood Poverty, Early Motherhood and Adult Social Exclusion*, Centre for Analysis of Social Exclusion, CASE paper 28, July 1999

6 Ethnicity and poverty

*In comparison to their representation in the population, people from
minority ethnic communities are more likely than others to live in
deprived areas; be poor; be unemployed, compared with white people with
similar qualifications; suffer ill-health and live in overcrowded and
unpopular housing. They also experience widespread racial harassment
and racial crime and are over-represented in the criminal justice system,
from stop and search to prison. But there is much variation within and
between ethnic groups in all of these areas.*

(Social Exclusion Unit, *Minority Ethnic Issues in Social Exclusion
and Neighbourhood Renewal*, Cabinet Office, 2000)

Until relatively recently, few studies explored the nature and extent of
poverty faced by people from minority ethnic communities in Great
Britain.[1] Information has not always been available by ethnic group, or
the numbers involved have been too small to use results confidently.[2]
However, more research is revealing varying experiences *between*
different ethnic groups, such as the fourth national survey of ethnic
minorities published by the Policy Studies Institute (PSI) in 1997.[3]

Households Below Average Income (HBAI)[4] now contains information
about ethnicity, and race is increasingly recognised as a policy concern,
following the inquiry into the death of Stephen Lawrence.[5] Subsequently the Social Exclusion Unit has published a summary of initiatives on minority ethnic issues,[6] and the Runnymede Trust Commission
has reported on the future of multi-ethnic Britain.[7]

This chapter considers some of the indicators of poverty, notably
low incomes and unemployment, followed by other associated aspects
of poverty, such as educational disadvantage, poor housing and poor
health. Finally, we consider ethnicity and the benefits system.

Throughout this chapter we use the terms 'minority ethnic', though in tables and figures the terminology follows the classification used in the original source.

INDICATORS OF POVERTY

INCOMES

Poverty does not automatically flow from minority ethnic status, but it can be a common experience, such as for Pakistani and Bangladeshi people.[8] In 1999/2000, more minority ethnic individuals were in the bottom fifth of the income distribution; 61 per cent of Pakistani and Bangladeshi individuals were in the lowest fifth – three times more than White, and almost twice as many as Black Caribbean, individuals.[9]

The composition of working-age families varied by ethnic group. Compared with Whites:

- Caribbeans and Africans had more lone-parent families, Asians had fewer;
- Indians had more disabled people;
- Pakistanis and Bangladeshis had more unemployed people.[10]

Minority ethnic households overall were more likely to be receiving means-tested benefits than White households, Pakistani/Bangladeshi households in particular because they were unemployed, Caribbean households because more were lone-parent families.

Table 6.3 shows the proportions of jobless working-age families with unearned income, insurance benefits, means-tested benefits and 'other' (mainly disability benefits and child benefit).[11]

Older people from minority ethnic groups also tend to be over-represented in the bottom of the income distribution. Many arrived in the UK in the middle of their working lives, leaving less time to build up pension entitlements, and spend longer unemployed or low paid, so have limited national insurance or occupational provision.[12]

UNEMPLOYMENT

The unemployment rate of people from minority ethnic groups relative to White groups was higher in the late 1990s than in the mid–late 1980s, unemployment being twice as high for minority

TABLE 6.1: **Percentage of individuals in income fifths, after housing costs, by ethnic group, excluding self-employed, 1999/2000**

(bottom)	5	4	3	2	1 (top)	millions
White	18	20	20	20	21	47.3
Black Caribbean	26	20	21	20	14	0.6
Black Non-Caribbean	49	16	10	14	11	0.4
Indian	32	22	20	19	7	0.7
Pakistani/Bangladeshi	61	28	4	3	4	0.7
Other	37	13	17	17	16	0.7
Total	20	20	20	20	20	50.6

Source: Department of Social Security, *Households Below Average Income 1999/2000*, 2001

TABLE 6.2: **Proportions receiving benefit by ethnic origin, 1999/2000**
(per cent of benefit units)

	White	Black	Indian	Pakistani/ Bangladeshi	Other	Total
Means-tested benefits						
Family credit/Working families' tax credit	2	4	4	8	3	2
Income support	10	19	14	22	16	11
Housing benefit	14	28	9	19	19	14
Council tax benefit	18	29	15	29	20	18
Contributory benefits						
Retirement pension	25	13	8	6	6	24
Widows' benefits	1	–	1	2	1	1
Incapacity benefit	5	2	4	3	2	5
Non-contributory, non-means-tested						
Invalid care allowance	1	1	1	4	1	1
Disability living allowance (care)	4	3	3	6	2	4
Disability living allowance (mobility)	5	4	3	5	3	5
Attendance allowance	3	1	1	1	1	3
Child benefit	22	30	34	42	27	23
Jobseeker's allowance	3	8	4	9	4	3

Notes: Jobseeker' allowance is not separated into contributory or means-tested elements in *Family Resources Survey*
Source: Department of Social Security, *Family Resources Survey 1999/2000*, 2001

TABLE 6.3: **Sources of income of non-working families**
Per cent

	White	Caribbean	African	Indian	Pakistani/ Bangladeshi	Others
Unearned income	58	54	59	56	62	62
Insurance benefits	26	13	6	34	18	12
Any means-test	78	88	83	76	89	78
Income support	68	81	77	71	84	67
Other benefits	70	73	66	70	77	66

Source: Department of Social Security, *Family Resources Survey* 1994/95 amd 1995/96

ethnic groups than for White groups with the same broad level of qualifications.[13]

Among minority ethnic men, unemployment is three times higher, and for minority ethnic women, four times higher, than for White men and women, even allowing for age and qualifications.[14]

Minority ethnic jobseekers complete more job applications than White jobseekers, but this does not achieve any more interviews. Over two years, fewer minority ethnic (66 per cent) than other claimants (76 per cent) leave benefit for paid jobs, and even when finding work, spells of employment are shorter.[15]

Unemployment of minority ethnic groups, relative to White, was higher in the mid-1990s than during the mid-1980s.[16] Black unemployment appears to rise faster and higher when the economy is contracting, but when it is expanding, unemployment falls more quickly than for White people.[17] For people of Pakistani and Bangladeshi origin, unemployment is consistently high:

- 79 per cent of Pakistani/Bangladeshi men were out of work for over a year, as were men of Caribbean (75 per cent), Indian/African Asian (62 per cent), and White (45 per cent) origin.[18]
- 96 per cent of unemployed Pakistani/Bangladeshi people had no partner in work, compared with 65 per cent of Indian/African Asian, 61 per cent of Caribbean, and 56 per cent of White couples.[19]
- 12 per cent of young people aged 16–24 with higher qualifications

TABLE 6.4: **Indicators of economic resources among people aged over 60, by ethnic origin, 1991-96**

Per cent

	White (exc. Irish)	Irish	Indian/ Bangladeshi	Pakistani	Black Caribbean
Bottom income 1/5th	21	27	50	56	34
Top income 1/5th	9	7	10	3	3
National insurance pension	91	88	62	68	84
Income support	33	39	45	76	58
Occupational pension	45	39	22	13	32

Source: M Evandrou, 'Social Inequalities in Later Life: the socio-economic position of older people from ethnic minority groups in Britain', *Population Trends*, Autumn 2000, National Statistics

from minority ethnic groups were unemployed compared with 7 per cent of similarly qualified Whites; of those with no qualifications, 45 per cent of young people were unemployed compared with 29 per cent of Whites.[20]

Employment rates after completing Work-Based Training for Young People are lower for Bangladeshi (37 per cent), Black African (37 per cent) and Pakistani (39 per cent) than White trainees (63 per cent); fewer entrants to the New Deal for young people from minority ethnic groups move into employment than White (25 per cent compared with 33 per cent), more going into education and training (59 per cent compared with 44 per cent), despite being better qualified.[21]

EMPLOYMENT RATES

In 2000, Pakistani and Bangladeshi men had the lowest employment rate, and Pakistani and Bangladeshi women were less than half as likely to work as all other minority women – perhaps due to religious or cultural factors and the structure of the labour market.[22]

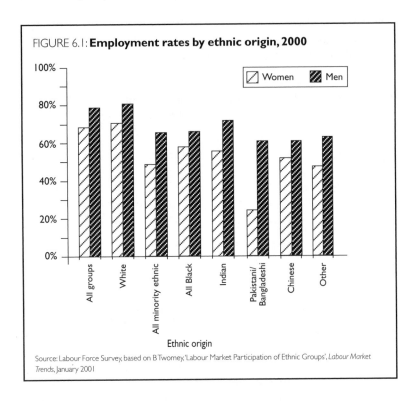

FIGURE 6.1: **Employment rates by ethnic origin, 2000**

Legend: Women, Men

Ethnic origin

Source: Labour Force Survey, based on B Twomey, 'Labour Market Participation of Ethnic Groups', *Labour Market Trends*, January 2001

LABOUR MARKET SEGREGATION

Segregation into particular industries, manual work, and being concentrated in deprived areas, made many workers from minority ethnic groups especially vulnerable to the decline in manufacturing and the rise in unemployment. However, during the 1980s and 1990s, the position became more differentiated both *between* and *within* minority groups.

While women from minority ethnic groups had similar occupational patterns as White women, men from minority ethnic groups were more likely than White men to work in textiles, distribution, transport, communications and public health, and less likely to be in construction.[23] About a third of Caribbean and White men worked in manufacturing, whereas more than half of Bangladeshi men worked as waiters or kitchen staff in restaurants:[24]

• Caribbean men were more likely to undertake shift work (30 per cent) than White men (20 per cent).[25]

- Minority ethnic workers were less likely to be in the top occupational category or work in large establishments, and fewer were in supervisory or managerial positions compared with White employees.[26]

While labour market changes have had an impact on these patterns, racial discrimination also appears to have been a factor:

- In 1997, one in five minority ethnic, but one in 20 White, respondents believed employers discriminated – a significant increase over earlier surveys.[27]
- White job applicants were three times more likely to obtain interviews than those with equivalent qualifications from Asian backgrounds, and five times more likely than Black people.[28]

LOW PAY

Workers from minority ethnic groups are also more likely to be low paid; the TUC has found twice as many Black and Asian workers in the notoriously low-paid sector of hotels and restaurants.[29] In 1998/99, Pakistani/Bangladeshi full-time workers had the lowest average gross hourly rates of pay in Great Britain (£6.87 for men and £6.33 for women). However, Chinese men and women, White men, and Indian men were paid at over £9.00 per hour.[30] Bangladeshis and Pakistanis were almost three times as likely as Whites to be earning less than half male median hourly pay (£3.85 in 1999 when the prevailing minimum wage was £3.60).[31]

The relative position of different minority ethnic groups has changed; in 1982 average earnings for Asian men were nearly 15 per cent below White men, but by 1997 there was little difference between African Asian[32] and White men.[33]

OTHER ASPECTS OF POVERTY

EDUCATIONAL DISADVANTAGE

Educational progress varies by ethnic origin; the gap between children from minority ethnic groups and White children widens during primary school, but at secondary school the trend reverses for Indian

TABLE 6.5: **Mean weekly earnings of full-time employees by ethnic origin, 1997**

	Men	Women
White	£336	£244
Caribbean	£306	£267
Indian	£287	£252
African Asian	£335	£254
Pakistani	£227 ⎱	£181
Bangladeshi	£191 ⎰	
Chinese	(£336)	£287
All ethnic minority	£296	£259

Note: figures in brackets denote small sample size
Source: T Modood and R Berthoud, *Ethnic Minorities in Britain: diversity and disadvantage*, Policy Studies Institute, 1997

and Chinese pupils, who tend to do better than their White counterparts.[34]

OFSTED research has found that Black pupils' position relative to their White peers worsened between the start and end of compulsory schooling; in one large urban authority, African-Caribbean children entered school as the highest achieving group but left as the group least likely to attain five high-grade GCSEs.[35]

African-Caribbean children have been six times more likely to be excluded from school than other pupils,[36] but no more likely to be persistent truants.[37] The exclusion rate for other minority groups (Chinese, Indian, Bangladeshi, Pakistani) is below average.[38]

While more pupils from minority ethnic groups have gained five or more GCSEs at grades A-C, by 1998 only 29 per cent of Pakistani and Black pupils, and 33 per cent of Bangladeshi pupils, had reached that level compared with 47 per cent of White and 54 per cent of Indian pupils.[39] There were differences by social class and gender:

- One study showed that, within each gender and ethnic group, those entitled to free school meals were least likely to obtain five or more GCSE grades; boys tended to do less well than girls.[40]
- Comparing GCSE attainment between 1988 and 1995, the OFSTED report indicated that, while all groups had improved, within each ethnic group, girls had higher attainments; ethnic inequalities remained even when controlling for gender and class.[41]

LIVING IN DEPRIVED AREAS

Minority ethnic households are not evenly spread across Great Britain; the highest concentration being in London (25 per cent) and the West Midlands (10 per cent).[42]

In 1998, more than half of people from minority ethnic groups lived in the 44 most deprived local authorities in England, as a result of historical, social, economic and geographical considerations.[43] Those 44 areas contained four times as many people of ethnic minority origin as other areas.[44] Only one in 20 Black and Asian people lived in an area of low unemployment, compared with one in five Whites.[45] In 1999 within some London boroughs, around half of the population was from an ethnic minority group.[46]

POOR HOUSING

In the 1990s, many minority ethnic groups in England lived in poor housing; 15 per cent of minority ethnic households (24 per cent of Pakistani/Bangladeshi households) lived in overcrowded conditions compared with 2 per cent of White households.[47] The English House Condition Survey 1996 showed that minority ethnic households were more likely to live in poor housing – that is, homes needing repair or modernisation or which were unfit:

- 34.8 per cent of Pakistani/Bangladeshi households and 22.9 per cent of Black households lived in poor housing compared with Whites (13.7 per cent).
- 28 per cent of Pakistani and Bangladeshi older people, and 24 per cent of Black Caribbean older people, had no central heating.[48]

Minority ethnic households are also more likely to experience homelessness; the 1998/99 survey, *Housing in England*, found 15 per cent of minority ethnic households had been homeless at some time during the past ten years, compared with only 5 per cent of households overall.[49]

POOR HEALTH AND PREMATURE DEATH

Minority ethnic groups can be more at risk of poor health. Indian, Chinese and African Asian people have similar levels of self-reported health as White people, but Pakistani/Bangladeshi people were one and a half times more likely to report poor health, and African-Caribbean people a third more likely.[50]

Some conditions, such as diabetes, are more common in certain minority ethnic groups; compared with Whites, Pakistani/Bangladeshi people are over five times, and Indian/South Asian people three times, more likely to have diabetes.[51]

Health variations may be explained in part by the socio-economic status of minority ethnic groups, associated with the process and consequences of migration and the process of discrimination.[52] Evidence about minority ethnic health in London showed that:

- Pakistani elderly people aged 60 and over had the highest rates of long-term limiting illness of any group;
- conditions such as TB affected disproportionate numbers of asylum seekers and refugees.[53]

The prevalence of mental ill-health also varies across ethnic groups; for example, depression appears more common in African-Caribbeans than Whites.[54] A follow-up of the fourth PSI survey found that:

- African-Caribbean women had higher rates of diagnosis of psychotic conditions relative to the White population;[55]
- South Asian groups appeared to have low rates of mental ill health, though one unexplained finding was that those who were born in Britain or who had migrated to Britain at an early age, were more likely to have a mental illness, as were South Asian women relative to men.[56]

Infant mortality was 100 per cent higher for children of African-Caribbean and Pakistani mothers than White; suicide rates were high among young South Asian women born in India, and death rates in people aged under 15 and over 65 were higher in migrants from Ireland and the Indian sub-continent than those born in England and Wales.[57]

ETHNICITY AND THE BENEFITS SYSTEM

People from minority ethnic communities can face particular problems within the benefits system:

- The emphasis on non–interruption of contributions for some benefits militates against those who have irregular earnings, absences abroad or short working lives in the UK.
- The consequent over-reliance on means-tested benefits means that minority ethnic families are more likely to suffer from the associated problems, such as low take-up, administrative complexity and the poverty trap.
- Direct and indirect discrimination through conditions placed on 'people from abroad' such as sponsorship, and tests of residence.
- Direct and indirect discrimination in the administration of social security, including the failure to provide interpretation and trans-lation facilities.[58]

IMMIGRATION STATUS AND SOCIAL SECURITY

Most social security benefits now have immigration conditions attached to them; immigration status[59] can affect benefit entitlement, and vice versa. Although immigration status is not the same as 'race' these issues may have a greater impact on claimants from minority ethnic groups.[60] Some people may also be deterred from claiming benefits, fearing that their immigration status would be questioned.[61]

'Residence' conditions are attached to most benefits and tax credits. For example, in 1994 a 'habitual residence test' was introduced to determine entitlement to the main means-tested benefits to deter social security abuse by European nationals. However, in its first year most of the 25,000 people who failed the test were either British nationals (21 per cent) or from outside Europe (42 per cent), and there was some evidence that Black and Asian people were being dis-proportionately affected.[62]

Many asylum seekers no longer have rights to benefit, though they may receive a support package worth 70 per cent of income support rates, paid largely in vouchers with a small amount of cash. This has been described by the Runnymede Trust as a system which 'under-mines economic and social self-sufficiency' and by organisations like Oxfam as leaving many asylum seekers hungry.[63]

Contributory benefits are usually payable on the basis of national insurance contributions having been paid over a set period of time, such as a 'working life' for retirement pension. In practice, contributory benefits disadvantage people with shorter working lives, an interrupted work pattern or low pay, and so lead to greater reliance on means-tested benefits.

A major problem with means-tested benefits is low take-up. Although official estimates do not include ethnic origin, there is other evidence that people from minority ethnic groups communities are less likely to take up their entitlement. One study suggested that perceptions of benefits were strongly influenced by culture and religion, with negative perceptions leading to underclaiming and delayed claims, particularly among Chinese and Bangladeshi households.[64] Shame and stigma were most strongly felt among Bangladeshi, Pakistani and Chinese households and least strongly by African-Caribbeans.

Older people may feel there is shame and stigma attached to claiming,[65] and take-up of the minimum income guarantee by pensioners from minority ethnic groups has received relatively little attention, perhaps requiring a more personalised approach to overcome such barriers as language.[66]

BENEFITS ADMINISTRATION

Hardship Britain described how some Asian claimants encountered difficulties with the Benefits Agency. Language was sometimes a problem where a claimant did not speak or understand English, and at the time of the study there was a lack of interpreting facilities in the relevant Benefits Agency offices. Some claimants also believed they were treated differently by officials because they were Asian:

> 'There is no doubt that they don't look too well on us people that is why it takes so long to get an answer from them, or when it's late they take even longer. It's more difficult if you don't know the language or can't read or write English.'[67]

Lone Asian women, particularly orthodox Muslim women who had a dependent economic role prior to the death of, or separation from, a spouse, also encountered difficulties as a result of their social role not normally involving them in dealing with outside authorities.

Several reports have documented excessive delays in processing claims, with some files lost due to incorrect use of some Black claim-ants' names.[68] Some evidence may not be easy to produce, such as a marriage licence; the increasing emphasis on national insurance num-bers for benefit claims may also have led to delays.[69] A Commission for Racial Equality report on claims by Asian people in Manchester showed that supporting evidence was more often required, and fraud officers drawn in more frequently, for Asian than for other claims.[70]

CONCLUSION

The minority ethnic population has been at greater risk of being excluded from many aspects of society as a result of discrimination in employment and in the wider society. People from minority ethnic groups are more at risk of unemployment and worklessness, low pay and poor working conditions, poor health, housing and low incomes. However, the experiences of each ethnic group differs, and has changed over time.

NOTES

1 The most recent information on different ethnic groups is from the Labour Force Survey (LFS), which covers Great Britain not the UK. In Northern Ireland LFS respondents are not asked their ethnic origin.
2 See for example, Social Exclusion Unit, *Minority Ethnic Issues in Social Exclusion and Neighbourhood Renewal*, Cabinet Office, June 2000
3 T Modood and R Berthoud, *Ethnic Minorities in Britain: diversity and dis-advantage*, Policy Studies Institute, 1997
4 Department of Social Security, *Households Below Average Income 1994/95-1999/2000*, Corporate Document Services 2001
5 *The Stephen Lawrence Inquiry: report of an inquiry by Sir William MacPherson of Cluny*, The Stationery Office, Cm 4262-I, 1999
6 See note 2
7 B Parekh, *The Future of Multi-Ethnic Britain*, The Runnymede Trust, 2000
8 R Berthoud, *The Incomes of Ethnic Minorities*, Essex University, 1998
9 See note 4
10 See note 8
11 Department of Social Security, *Family Resources Survey 1999/2000*, DSS, 2001
12 Department of Social Security, *The Changing Welfare State: pensioner incomes*, DSS Paper No. 2, March 2000
13 B Twomey, 'Labour Market Participation of Ethnic Groups', *Labour Market*

Trends, January 2001

14 Department for Education and Employment, *Race Research for the Future*, Research Topic Paper RTP01, March 2000

15 J Shropshire, R Warton and R Walker, *Unemployment and Jobseeking: the experience of ethnic minorities*, DfEE Research Report RR106, 1999

16 F Sly, T Thair and A Risdon, 'Trends in the Labour Market Participation of Ethnic Groups', *Labour Market Trends*, December 1999

17 See note 2

18 See note 3

19 See note 3

20 LFS data in Department for Education and Employment, *Report of Policy Action Team 1: Jobs for All*, 1999

21 See note 14

22 See note 8 and note 13

23 See note 7

24 See note 3

25 See note 3

26 See note 3

27 See note 3

28 Commission for Racial Equality, *We Regret to Inform You: testing for racial discrimination in youth employment in the north of England and Scotland*, 1996

29 Trades Union Congress, *Black and Excluded: Black and Asian workers in the 1990s*, 1999

30 See note 13

31 C Howarth et al, *Monitoring Poverty and Social Exclusion 1999*, New Policy Institute and Joseph Rowntree Foundation, 1999

32 Defined in the PSI survey as people of Asian origin, mainly but not exclusively Indian, who had spent some time in Africa, or whose parents/ grandparents had done so.

33 See note 3

34 J Sparkes, *Schools, Education and Social Exclusion*, CASE paper 29, November 1999

35 D Gillborn and H Mirza, *Educational Inequality: mapping race, class and gender: a synthesis of research evidence*, OFSTED, 2000

36 Department for Education and Employment, *Statistics of Education: schools in England*, 1999

37 Social Exclusion Unit, *Truancy and School Exclusion*, Cm 3957, May 1998

38 Home Office, *Race Equality in Public Services: driving up standards and accounting for progress*, 2000

39 See note 2

40 See note 2

41 See note 34

42 National Statistics, *Regional Trends* 35, 2000

43 See note 8

44 Social Exclusion Unit, *Bringing Britain Together: a national strategy for*

neighbourhood renewal, Cm 4045, September 1998

45 See note 7

46 Association of London Government, *Sick of Being Excluded: improving the health and care of London's black and minority ethnic communities*, 2000

47 See notes 7 and 2

48 M Evandrou, 'Social Inequalities in Later Life: the socio-economic position of older people from ethnic minority groups in Britain', *Population Trends*, No. 101, Autumn 2000

49 M McConahy et al, *Housing in England 1998/99*, National Statistics, 2000

50 See note 2

51 J Nazroo, *The Health of Britain's Ethnic Minorities*, Policy Studies Institute, 1997

52 See note 50

53 See note 45

54 D Acheson, *Independent Inquiry into Inequalities in Health*, The Stationery Office, 1998

55 J Nazroo, *Ethnicity and Mental Health*, Policy Studies Institute, 1997

56 See note 54

57 See note 53

58 G Craig, 'Race, Social Security and Poverty' in J Ditch (ed), *Introduction to Social Security*, Routledge, 1999

59 For a more detailed discussion of immigration policy, see the Parekh report for the Runnymede Trust, note 7; for its interaction with benefit rules, see CPAG's *Migration and Social Security Handbook*.

60 S McKay and K Rowlingson, *Social Security in Britain*, Macmillan, 1999

61 A Bloch, 'Ethnic Inequality and Social Security Policy', in A Walker and C Walker (eds), *Britain Divided: the growth of social exclusion in the 1980s and 1990s*, CPAG, 1997

62 National Association of Citizens Advice Bureaux, *Failing the Test: CAB clients' experience of the habitual residence test in social security*, February 1996

63 See note 7 and Oxfam et al, *Token Gestures: the effects of the voucher scheme on asylum seekers and organisations in the UK*, Oxfam, 2000

64 I Law et al, *Racial Equality and Social Security Service Delivery: a study of perceptions and experience of black minority ethnic people eligible for benefit in Leeds*, Leeds University, 1994

65 See note 45

66 House of Commons Social Security Select Committee, *Pensioner Poverty*, HC 606, July 2000

67 R Cohen et al, *Hardship Britain: being poor in the 1990s*, CPAG, 1992

68 National Association of Citizens Advice Bureaux, *Barriers to Benefit: black claimants and social security*, CAB evidence E/1/91, 1991

69 National Association of Citizens Advice Bureaux, *A Person before the Law: the case for a statement of rights for people with limited leave to remain in the UK*, February 2000

70 Commission for Racial Equality, *The Provision of Income Support to Asian and Non-Asian Claimants*, Manchester CRE, 1995

7 Unequal shares

It might be possible to justify a growth in inequality – a widening gap between incomes of rich and poor – on the grounds that the beneficial effects on growth would raise the living standards of the poorest, but there is no evidence that this has occurred in the UK: there is no sign of 'trickle-down.'

(*Joseph Rowntree Foundation Inquiry into Income and Wealth,*
Volume 1, 1995)

The UK has one of the most unequal distribution of incomes in the industrialised countries of the world (international comparisons are further discussed in Chapter 9). While income inequality declined during the 1960s, it rose in the late 1970s to peak in the 1980s,[1] and by the mid-1990s was still greater than at any time since the Second World War.[2] Between 1979 and 1998/99, average incomes grew by 52 per cent, driven by relatively large increases in numbers of people with high incomes, while those at the bottom experienced below average increases.[3] More data is becoming available about disparities in incomes and wealth, including a new statistical series, *Social Inequalities,* produced by National Statistics.[4]

This chapter examines the unequal shares in income, expenditure, earnings and wealth, and the impact of government policy (tax and social security) on these trends.

UNEQUAL INCOMES

As noted in Chapter 2, over the past 20 years the incomes of the poorest have fallen in real terms (ie, allowing for inflation) as the richest have grown. Between 1979 and 1999/2000, the poorest tenth in the income distribution saw a real rise of only 6 per cent in their 'after housing costs' (AHC) incomes, compared with an average rise of 80 per cent, while the top tenth gained 86 per cent.[5]

TABLE: 7.1 **Percentage changes in real incomes**

Between 1979 and 1996/97, including self-employed

Decile group	Income BHC*	Income AHC
1 (bottom 10%)	12	-9
2 (10-20%)	18	5
3 (20-30%)	21	2
4 (30-40%)	24	23
5 (40-50%)	30	31
6 (50-60%)	34	36
7 (60-70%)	38	41
8 (70-80%)	41	46
9 (80-90%)	49	54
10 (top 10%)	62	70
Total population (mean)	**42**	**44**

Between 1994/95 and 1999/2000, including self-employed

Decile group	Income BHC	Income AHC
1 (bottom 10%)	(0 to +12)	(+6 to +3)
2 (10-20%)	(10)	(11)
3 (20-30%)	10	13
4 (30-40%)	10	13
5 (40-50%)	(11)	13
6 (50-60%)	(10)	12
7 (60-70%)	10	12
8 (70-80%)	11	13
9 (80-90%)	(10)	(13)
10 (top 10%)	(+6 to +18)	(+8 to +22)
Total population (mean)	**12**	**15**

*BHC = before housing costs
( ) denotes uncertain
Source: Department of Social Security, *Households Below Average Incomes 1979-1996/97; 1994/95-1999/2000*, Table A1

Different income measures include 'original income' (ie, income from sources such as earnings, occupational pensions and investments before taxes or benefits) and 'post-tax income' (ie, after direct and indirect taxes and benefits have been paid). According to each of the income measures, the top fifth have gained in the share of income. Between 1978 and 1999/2000:

- the richest fifth's share of original income grew from 43 per cent to 52 per cent;
- the richest fifth's share of post-tax income rose from 37 per cent to 45 per cent;
- the poorest fifth's share of original income increased slightly from 2.4 per cent to 3 per cent in 1998/99, and dropped back again in 1999/2000 to 2 per cent;
- the poorest fifth's share of post-tax income dropped from 9.5 per cent to 6 per cent.[6]

TABLE 7.2: **Original and post-tax income distribution by quintile group (fifths): percentage shares of equivalised income, per cent**

	1979	1999/2000
	Original income	
Quintile group		
Bottom	2.4	2
Second	10	7
Third	18	15
Fourth	26	25
Top	43	52
	Post-tax income	
Quintile group		
Bottom	9.5	6
Second	13	11
Third	18	16
Fourth	23	22
Top	37	45

Source: *Economic Trends*: December 1994 and April 2001, ONS

As well as original and post-tax income, other measures include 'gross income' (original income plus cash benefits, such as state pensions, etc) and 'disposable income' (gross income minus direct taxes, employee national insurance contributions, etc).

Figure 7.1 below shows the trends for each of these stages of distribution, namely original income, gross income, disposable income and post-tax income. Each of these four income measures is expressed as the 'Gini co-efficient' (a measure of inequality, where the higher the figure, the greater the inequality).

Another approach is to consider the income of the richest relative to the poorest; this includes taking the ratio of the top tenth in the income distribution to the bottom tenth (called the 90th percentile and the 10th percentile respectively), or the ratio of incomes in the top fifth to the bottom fifth (the 75th percentile to the 25th) as shown in Table 7.3.

All of these income measures show greater income inequality in the 1980s, with a steadier distribution in the 1990s. During 1999/2000, however, the figures show a worrying drop in the share of the poorest fifth of original incomes as well as an increase in inequality as measured by disposable income.

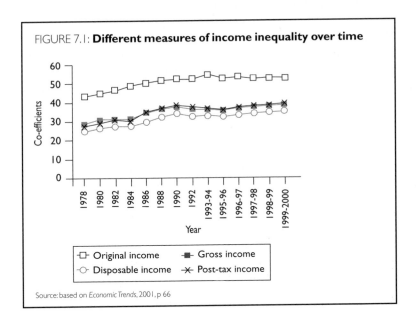

FIGURE 7.1: **Different measures of income inequality over time**

Source: based on *Economic Trends*, 2001, p 66

TABLE 7.3: **Ratios for disposable income, 1978-1999/2000**

	P90/P10	P75/P25
1978	3.2	1.9
1980	3.5	2.0
1982	3.3	2.0
1984	3.3	2.0
1986	3.7	2.1
1988	4.4	2.4
1990	4.9	2.5
1992	4.6	2.4
1993/94	4.5	2.3
1995/96	4.2	2.2
1996/97	4.4	2.3
1997/98	4.5	2.3
1998/99	4.5	2.3
1999/2000	4.6	2.4

Source: *Economic Trends*, 2001
Note: The higher the ratio, the bigger the gap between rich and poor

UNEQUAL EXPENDITURE

Household spending can be another indicator of inequality, though may not reflect income trends (for example, people may choose to spend beyond their means by using savings or borrowing or falling into debt; alternatively some income may be diverted into savings). In reflecting expectations of future income, *expenditure* may be more stable than measures of current income. A poverty line defined by *income* concerns the right to a minimum level of resources, while one defined by *expenditure* is about a standard of living.[7]

Hence, spending and income trends may be different. For example, the Institute for Fiscal Studies (IFS) analysed changes in expenditure and income between 1979 and 1992, showing that there was a rise in spending inequality but this was not as large as the growth in income inequality. The authors suggest that this could have been influenced by increasing numbers of unemployed people, who may have high spending patterns, especially if expecting their spell of unemployment to be short, as well as the growth in self-employment:[8]

• Spending by the bottom tenth of spenders (excluding housing costs) rose by 14 per cent whereas the AHC income of the bottom tenth of income distribution fell by 18 per cent.

- Comparing the lower spending groups with the lower income groups, pensioners were more likely to be low spenders but were less likely to be found in low-income groups; only 8 per cent of the lowest tenth of income distribution in 1992 were pensioners, but they comprised 40 per cent of the lowest tenth in spending.

Other studies of income and spending have shown the following:

- Between 1981-83 and 1991-93, spending of the lowest income group was 20 per cent higher than at the start of the ten-year period. At the same time, at the top, incomes grew by 52 per cent – more than spending (42 per cent).[9]
- Comparing 'cohorts' of people born in each of four ten-year periods from 1920–29 to 1950–59, all of those below retirement age faced considerably greater income and expenditure inequality by the end of the period between 1970–1992, suggesting that later cohorts faced greater inequality of both income and spending than preceding cohorts at a similar age.[10]

A study of child poverty between 1968 and 1995/96 also found a large increase in expenditure inequality since 1968, the fastest rise in

TABLE 7.4: **Households with children: income and expenditure ratios, 1968–1995/96**

	1968	1979	1990	1995/96
Income ratio poor/not poor	0.432	0.413	0.326	0.321
Spending ratio poor/not poor	0.625	0.599	0.557	0.529
Couples spending ratio non-working/working	0.644	0.822	0.571	0.546
Singles spending ratio non-working/working	0.631	0.585	0.618	0.591

Source: P Gregg, S Harkness and S Machin, *Poor Kids: trends in child poverty in Britain, 1968-96*, Fiscal Studies Vol 20 No 2, June 1999

spending being by working couples, the lowest being for workless couples and lone parents.[11]

UNEQUAL EARNINGS

Earnings can generate inequality as those without work lag further behind earnings growth, and those in work who are low paid may find it hard to increase their earnings. There has been a growing gap between the highest and lowest paid since the 1980s:

- Earnings for men in the top tenth rose at double the rate of the bottom tenth over 20 years; for women, earnings at the top grew by five times as much as the bottom.[12]
- Wage dispersion seems to follow the overall trends in income inequality;[13] rapid wage growth between 1984 and 1988 contrasted with the 1990s, when wage growth slowed and lagged behind Gross Domestic Product (GDP) growth; these trends may provide an explanation for the relative slow-down in income inequality in the 1990s.[14]
- In 1978, the poorest tenth of men in full-time manual work earned 69 per cent of the average and the richest tenth, 146 per cent; by 2000, the poorest tenth earned 62.4 per cent and the richest 160 per cent (see Figure 7.2 below).[15]

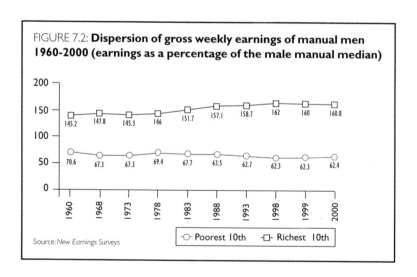

FIGURE 7.2: **Dispersion of gross weekly earnings of manual men 1960-2000 (earnings as a percentage of the male manual median)**

Source: *New Earnings Surveys*

-O- Poorest 10th   -□- Richest 10th

Some of the earnings dispersion in the 1980s could be explained by:

- higher wages for more experience or qualifications, especially for young people;
- the declining importance of trade unions and wages councils;
- a growing polarisation between 'work-rich' and 'work-poor' households;
- a rise in self-employment.[16]

Research covering the early 1990s shows that wage mobility is limited and the individuals who do increase their earnings tend not to move very far.

- Only 30 per cent of employed men in the bottom decile in 1989 had moved up the wage distribution by 1994 (mainly to the next two deciles), whereas almost half (48 per cent) in the top decile were still there five years later.[17]
- During a three-year period to 1994, 28 per cent of men saw their wages rise by a fifth; but 12 per cent experienced a fall of a fifth or more.[18]
- Ninety per cent of men in the top quarter of earnings remained in work over three years, but only 70 per cent of those who started in the bottom quarter of earnings distribution did so.[19]

CONTEMPORARY LOW PAY

The Labour Government introduced a national minimum wage in April 1999, initially set at an hourly rate of £3.60 for workers over age 22, and £3.00 for workers aged 18-21. The higher rate increased to £4.10 in October 2001.

- In 1999, one in ten employees earned less than £4 an hour, and more than one in five earned £12 an hour or more.[20]
- Over two million people were paid below half male median earnings (£3.85 an hour) in 1999.[21]

Between 1.7 and 2.1 million employees (9 per cent of all workers) were expected to gain from the minimum wage, particularly part-time workers, women and those working in the hotel/restaurant, wholesale and retail industries.[22] Between April 1999 and April 2000 weekly earnings of the bottom 10 per cent increased faster than the top (by 4.2 per cent and 2.2 per cent respectively).[23] By Spring 2000 an estimated

300,000 jobs held by people over age 18 were still paid below the minimum wage.[24]

UNEQUAL WEALTH

In the late 1990s a number of studies examined the distribution of wealth as well as, or instead of, income.[25] Wealth is even more unequally distributed than incomes, changing little over 20 years. By the late 1990s, the top 1 per cent of the UK population owned almost a quarter of marketable wealth, and the wealthiest half owned almost all wealth – 94 per cent (see Table 7.5 below).[26]

Comparing the identifiable wealth of the richest thousand people and families in the UK and the least wealthy half of the population (some 28 million people) the former had, on average, *15,000 times more wealth* than the least wealthy.[27]

The IFS has analysed trends in assets and wealth:

- During the 1980s, ownership of assets, like housing and pensions, grew when income inequality was rising.
- Most individuals did not have large amounts of wealth – the median figure in 1996 was £750.
- One tenth of the population (10.2 per cent) did not have any assets at all in 1996, twice as many as in 1978, when 5.9 per cent had none.
- Households in the top quarter of income distribution were more likely to own stocks and shares (37.9 per cent) than households in the bottom quarter (13.4 per cent), and the difference has widened over time.[28]

More households have no assets and so face 'financial exclusion'.[29] This can be a dynamic process, some people currently without assets having

TABLE 7.5: **Distribution of marketable wealth, 1976-1998**

	1976	1979	1983	1987	1992	1996	1997	1998
Most wealthy 1%	21	20	20	18	18	20	22	23
Most wealthy 10%	50	50	50	51	50	52	55	56
Least wealthy 50%	8	8	9	9	7	7	7	6

Source: Inland Revenue statistics, 1994 and 2000, Table 13.5

TABLE 7.6: **Ownership of assets by income: percentage of households, 1979-1996**

Income:	Poorest 25th	Richest 25th
		Interest-bearing accounts
1979	47.4	77.4
1996	44.0	76.1
		Stocks and shares
1979	4.1	16.6
1996	13.4	37.9
		Home ownership
1979	38.3	71.4
1996	47.5	86.1
		Life assurance
1979	66.3	82.6
1996	53.0	73.1

Source: J Banks and S Tanner, *Household Saving in the UK*, Institute for Fiscal Studies, 1999

had them in the past, and perhaps likely to have them in the future.[30] Some disparity in the ownership of wealth partly concerns age and stage of the lifecycle – for instance new households having less time to accumulate wealth than older ones.

According to the 1999/2000 *Family Resources Survey*, the following had no savings account:

- 29 per cent of lone-parent households.
- 15 per cent of households with one or more sick or disabled people under pension age.
- 20 per cent of working-age households with one or more unemployed.
- 9 per cent of pensioners.[31]

HOUSING AS A SOURCE OF WEALTH

In Chapter 4 some of the effects of poverty on housing, including homelessness, were documented. Here, housing is examined as an increasingly important source of *wealth*. In 1997, about a third of all

TABLE 7.7: **Median housing wealth by lifecycle groups**

Young singles	£0
Older singles	£0
Young childless couples	£8,900
Lone parents	£0
Young couples, young children	£14,000
Older couples, young children	£37,000
Couples, school-age children	£43,800
Older childless couples	£48,500
Pensioner couples	£59,400
Single pensioners	£0

Source: K Rowlingson, C Whyley and T Warren, *Wealth in Britain: a lifecycle perspective*, Policy Studies Institute, 1999
Note: £0 = zero median housing wealth – ie, at least half of the people in these groups have no housing wealth

wealth was from house ownership.[32] The Policy Studies Institute examined housing wealth across 'lifecycle' groups, finding that lone parents and single people were least likely to have housing wealth, as Table 7.7 shows.

Changes in tenure reflect the more affluent people moving into home ownership, and the least affluent moving into council housing (the largest groups moving from the private rented sector or newly-formed households[33]). This process has been affected by changes in the economy, demographic trends (such as more older people and lone parents), and policies like the 'Right to Buy' and changes in benefits, especially housing benefit.[34] Table 7.8 shows the continuing polarisation of tenure by work status.

THE IMPACT OF SOCIAL SECURITY AND TAX POLICY

It has been argued that ill-health and premature death, some of the effects of poverty examined in Chapter 4, could be reduced through greater equality of incomes and wealth.[35] Social security and taxation systems can be tools to either reduce or increase inequality. Before government intervention (taxes and benefits), in 1998/99 the top fifth had incomes 17 times as great as the bottom fifth; after taxes and benefits the ratio was reduced to 4:1.[36]

TABLE 7.8: **Analysis of tenure by economic status, 1979 to 1999/2000**

	Self-employed %	In work %	Head 60+ %	Unemployed %	Other %
Owned outright					
1979	8	50	35	2	5
1999/2000	9	38	46	2	6
Mortgage					
1979	9	86	2	1	2
1999/2000	13	79	3	1	4
Private rented					
1979	5	67	18	3	6
1999/2000	6	55	8	8	23
Local authority/ housing association					
1979	3	67	17	5	8
1999/2000	3	38	22	9	28

Source: Department of Social Security, *Households Below Average Income 1979-1992/93* (1995) and DSS analysis of HBAI 1999/2000, 2001

Cash benefits are higher for households lower down the income distribution than at the top, so have a more equalising effect.[37]

Direct taxes[38] tend to be progressive, taking a larger proportion of income from the richest (24 per cent of gross income of the top fifth of households, compared with 12 per cent from the poorest fifth), contributing towards reducing inequality, though not by as much as cash benefits.

Indirect taxes take relatively more from people on low incomes, partly due to the proportionately higher spending of some low-income households on items which attract indirect tax. In addition, some higher income households channel their income into savings and mortgages, which do not attract indirect taxation.[39]

Services in kind, like health and education, are not included in *Housing Below Average Income* (HBAI) figures, but lower incomes groups tend to benefit more from them.[40] Adding in an element for this 'social wage' was found to have reduced the growth in income inequality, but only by about a fifth, and hardly at all after adjusting for the particular rate of inflation for each of these items.[41]

It is clear that tax and benefit policies are important drivers for changing the distribution of income and wealth; during the 1980s when income inequality grew, the top rate of income tax dropped from 83 per cent to 40 per cent. Changes to the tax system between 1985 and 1995 entailed:

- reduction in the tax rates (income tax and national insurance), particularly for the better off;
- a shift towards indirect taxation;
- a widening of the tax base with the restriction of tax reliefs such as mortgage interest and the married couple's allowance.[42]

As a result, the poorest tenth lost on average £3 a week (2.9 per cent of their net income), while the top tenth gained £31 (5.8 per cent of their net income); unemployed couples with children and lone parents lost out by £4.47 a week and £1.69 a week respectively.[43]

The Joseph Rowntree Foundation's inquiry into income and wealth also concluded that the tax system had little impact, as the shift in the tax burden from higher to lower and middle income groups cancelled out the progressivity of income tax.[44] They also found that social security policy slowed the growth of inequality in the early 1980s but not in the 1990s (eg, the impact of uprating future pension levels with prices and not earnings).[45]

Between 1996/97 and 1998/99, income inequality rose by one percentage point.[46] The effects of policy changes to taxes and benefits announced between 1997 and the March 2000 Budget have been estimated to change the distribution of incomes of households with children, potentially reducing the proportion of children below half average incomes from 26 per cent to 17 per cent.[47] This represents a start but, as the official statistics suggest, there are signs that inequality of incomes could be rising again. Much more is needed to reduce the scale of inequalities in Britain.

CONCLUSION

There is no doubt that the gap between rich and poor, however measured, increased during the 1980s and 1990s. In the mid-1990s the trend appears to have stabilised. Nonetheless, changes in taxation and social security policies have played a part in maintaining these divisions over the past 20 years. Many of the more progressive changes since 1997 have yet to take effect.

NOTES

1 A Goodman, P Johnson and S Webb, *Inequality in the UK*, Oxford University Press, 1997

2 J Hills, *Income and Wealth: the latest evidence*, Joseph Rowntree Foundation, 1998

3 Figures from Department of Social Security, *Households Below Average Income*, on the after housing costs measure

4 F Drever et al, *Social Inequalities: 2000 edition*, National Statistics, 2000

5 Comparisons for the period to 1998/99 can only be made from 1994/95 when the larger Family Resources Survey was used in the HBAI series, replacing the earlier Family Expenditure Survey; the two series are not directly comparable.

6 T Harris, 'The Effects of Taxes and Benefits on Household Income, 1998-99', *Economic Trends* No 557, April 2000; C Lakin, 'The Effects of Taxes and Benefits on Household Income, 1999-2000', *Economic Trends* No 569, April 2001, Table 1, Appendix 2

7 A Atkinson, *Poverty and Social Security*, Harvester Wheatsheaf, 1989

8 A Goodman and S Webb, 'The Distribution of UK Household Expenditure, 1979-1992', *Fiscal Studies*, Vol 16 No 3, pp55-60, 1996

9 See note 1

10 R Blundell and I Preston, 'Income, Expenditure and the Living Standards of UK Households', *Fiscal Studies*, Vol 16 No 3, pp40-54

11 P Gregg, S Harkness and S Machin, 'Poor Kids: trends in child poverty in Britain, 1968-96', *Fiscal Studies*, Vol 20 No 2, June 1999

12 HM Treasury, *Tackling Poverty and Extending Opportunity: the modernisation of Britain's tax and benefit system*, Number 4, March 1999

13 The IFS here uses the BHC measure.

14 T Clark and J Taylor, 'Income Inequality: a tale of two cycles?' *Fiscal Studies*, Vol 20 No 4, December 1999

15 National Statistics, *New Earnings Survey 2000, Part A: streamlined analyses*, National Statistics, 2000

16 J Hills, *Inquiry into Income and Wealth*, Vol 2, Joseph Rowntree Foundation, 1995

17 Though the period of this data includes the recession of the early 1990s; R Dickens, 'Wage Mobility in Great Britain', in CASE, *Persistent Poverty and Lifetime Inequality: the evidence*, proceedings from a workshop held at HM Treasury 17 and 18 November 1998, CASE report 5, March 1999

18 A Gosling et al, *The Dynamics of Low Pay and Unemployment in Early 1990s Britain*, Joseph Rowntree Foundation, 1997

19 See note 18

20 J Matheson and C Summerfield, *Social Trends 30*, 2000 edition, National Statistics, 2000

21 C Howarth et al, *Monitoring Poverty and Social Exclusion 1999*, New Policy

Institute and Joseph Rowntree Foundation, December 1999

22 D Wilkinson, 'Who are the Low Paid?' *Labour Market Trends*, December 1998

23 House of Commons Library, *Economic Indicators*, Research Paper 00/85, 31 October 2000

24 See note 23

25 J Banks and S Tanner, *Household Saving in the UK*, Institute for Fiscal Studies, 1999

26 Inland Revenue Statistics, 2001

27 D Gordon, 'Inequalities in Income, Wealth and Standard of Living in Britain', in C Pantazis and D Gordon (eds), *Tackling Inequalities: where are we now and what can be done?*, The Policy Press, 2000

28 See note 25

29 E Kempson and C Whyley, *Kept Out or Opted Out? Understanding and combating financial exclusion*, Joseph Rowntree Foundation and The Policy Press, 1999

30 K Rowlingson, C, Whyley and T Warren, *Wealth in Britain: a lifecycle perspective*, Policy Studies Institute, 1999

31 Department of Social Security, *Family Resources Survey 1999-2000*, DSS, July 2001, p88

32 See note 30

33 M McConaghy et al, *Housing in England 1998/99*, ONS/DETR

34 P Lee and A Murie, *Poverty, Housing Tenure and Social Exclusion*, The Policy Press, 1997

35 R Mitchell, D Dorling and M Shaw, *Inequalities in Life and Death: what if Britain were more equal?*, The Policy Press, 2000; A Glyn and D Miliband (eds), *Paying for Inequality: the economic costs of social injustice*, IPPR, 1994

36 See note 6

37 See note 6

38 Except for local taxes

39 See note 6

40 See note 2

41 T Sefton, *The Changing Distribution of the Social Wage*, STICERD Occasional Paper 21, LSE, 1997

42 C Giles and P Johnson, 'Tax Reform in the UK and Changes to the Progressivity of the Tax System, 1985-1995', *Fiscal Studies*, Vol 15 No 3, 1995

43 See note 42

44 See note 2

45 See note 2

46 J Hills, *Taxation for the Enabling State*, CASE paper 41, LSE, August 2000

47 H Sutherland, *The British Government's Attempt to Reduce Child Poverty: a Budget 2000 postscript*, Microsimulation Unit Research Note No 36, June 2000

8 Geographical divisions

...a key theme to emerge from the analysis in this report is that the disparity within regions is at least as great as that between them.
(Cabinet Office, *Sharing the Nation's Prosperity: variation in economic and social conditions across the UK,* report to the Prime Minister, December 1999)

Poverty is not evenly spread across the United Kingdom (UK). Although some regions and countries are poorer than others, each contain diverse areas and cities with different poverty levels.

Since 1997, the UK's countries and regions have become increasingly important as powers have been devolved. At the same time, smaller territories have become the focus for area-based policies such as health action zones. More data is available down to ward level, and income statistics now contain a breakdown by region/country.[1]

This chapter is an overview of data on poverty at different geographical levels, starting with the UK, then, following the lines of devolved powers, the small nations within the UK and London as the capital city are examined. This is followed by consideration of poverty by constituencies, districts and wards, and finally rural poverty.

Both Great Britain (excluding Northern Ireland) and the UK are referred to, depending on the source; 'regions' are the government office regions of England, following the convention in *Regional Trends*.

GEOGRAPHICAL DIVISIONS ACROSS THE UK

THE UK ECONOMY

The UK economy can be measured by Gross Domestic Product (GDP), the total annual value of all goods and services produced within a country. In 1998, London and the South East had the highest levels of per-capita GDP in the UK and the highest levels of disposable household income.[2]

INCOMES

The Department of Social Security's *Households Below Average Income* (HBAI) statistics now include countries and regions within Great Britain (GB). During 1999/2000, almost one and a half times as many people were in the bottom fifth of incomes after housing costs (AHC) in the North East than in the South East (see Table 8.2).

Some of the poorer areas of the UK also had a higher proportion of their income from benefits, especially Wales and Northern Ireland.

TABLE 8.1: **GDP per head across the UK, 1999**

	£ per head p.a.	As a % of UK
North East	10,000	77.3
North West	11,300	86.9
Yorkshire and Humberside	11,400	87.9
East Midlands	12,100	93.6
West Midlands	11,900	91.7
East	15,100	116.4
London	16,900	130.0
South East	15,100	116.4
South West	11,800	90.8
England	13,300	102.4
Wales	10,400	80.5
Scotland	12,500	96.5
Northern Ireland	10,100	77.5
UK total	**13,000**	**100.0**

Source: National Statistics, Regional GDP, News Release 27 February 2001

TABLE 8.2: **Percentages of quintile groups of individuals, after housing costs, excluding self-employed, Great Britain 1999/2000**

Quintile	1 (lowest)	2	3	4	5 (highest)
North East	24	23	23	16	14
North West	21	23	20	20	17
Yorkshire and Humberside	22	22	23	18	16
East Midlands	17	20	23	21	19
West Midlands	18	23	21	21	16
East	16	18	21	21	24
London	27	16	15	17	26
South East	16	15	18	21	29
South West	19	22	20	22	17
England	20	20	20	20	21
Wales	21	22	22	20	14
Scotland	19	21	20	22	18
GB total	**20**	**20**	**20**	**20**	**20**

Source: Department of Social Security, *Households Below Average Income 1999/2000*

As described in other chapters, the Poverty and Social Exclusion (PSE) Survey defined poverty as being unable to afford two or more basic necessities.[3] On this definition, the pattern is different from income data – see Figure 8.1.

EMPLOYMENT AND WORKLESSNESS

As with poverty, employment is not evenly spread; a Trades Union Congress (TUC) report concluded that there was a clear 'jobs divide' between the level of worklessness in the south of England (excluding London) and the rest of the UK.[4] Between 1997 and 1999 worklessness rates rose in the North East, whereas they fell in areas with already lower worklessness rates, like the South East.

The employment rate also varies, with Northern Ireland, Wales and the North East having the lowest proportion of adults in employment.

TABLE 8.3: **Average gross weekly household income and proportion of income from social security benefits across the UK, 1997/98–1999/2000**

	£ per week	% of income from benefits
North East	363	19
North West	421	15
Yorkshire and Humberside	401	15
East Midlands	439	12
West Midlands	445	13
East	484	10
London	571	9
South East	538	9
South West	427	13
England	469	12
Wales	364	19
Scotland	403	15
Northern Ireland	362	21
UK total	455	12

Source: *Family Spending: a report on the 1999/2000 Family Expenditure Survey*, 2000 edition, ONS, p143

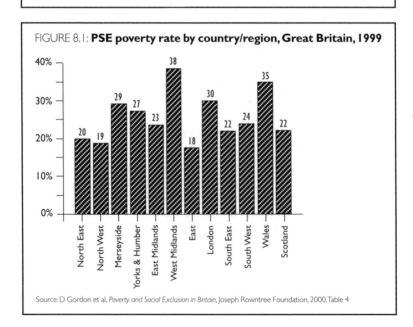

FIGURE 8.1: **PSE poverty rate by country/region, Great Britain, 1999**

Source: D Gordon et al, *Poverty and Social Exclusion in Britain*, Joseph Rowntree Foundation, 2000, Table 4

TABLE 8.4: **Working-age people in workless households, UK, 1997 and 1999 (per cent)**

	1997	1999
North East	17%	20%
North West	15%	15%
Yorkshire and Humberside	15%	13%
East Midlands	12%	10%
West Midlands	13%	13%
East	11%	9%
London	15%	15%
South East	9%	7%
South West	10%	10%
England	13%	12%
Wales	16%	16%
Scotland	15%	15%
Northern Ireland	15%	15%
UK	**13%**	**13%**

Source: House of Commons Library, *Regional Social Exclusion Indicators*, Research Paper 00/71, 3 August 2000, revised

FIGURE 8.2: **Working-age people in employment, UK, 1997 and 1999**

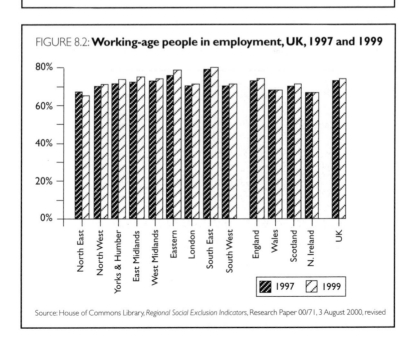

Source: House of Commons Library, *Regional Social Exclusion Indicators*, Research Paper 00/71, 3 August 2000, revised

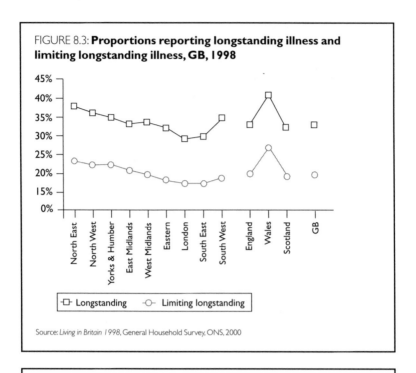

FIGURE 8.3: **Proportions reporting longstanding illness and limiting longstanding illness, GB, 1998**

Legend: -☐- Longstanding -○- Limiting longstanding

Source: *Living in Britain 1998*, General Household Survey, ONS, 2000

TABLE 8.5: **UK death rates, by NHS regional office area, 1999**

Rate per 1,000

	All deaths	Infant mortality
UK total	10.6	5.8
Northern and Yorkshire	10.9	6.0
North West	11.3	6.6
Trent	10.8	6.1
West Midlands	10.6	6.9
Eastern	10.1	4.6
London	8.5	6.0
South East	10.2	4.9
South and West	11.4	4.6
England	10.4	5.7
Wales	11.9	6.4
Scotland	11.8	5.0
Northern Ireland	9.3	6.4

Source: *Regional Trends* 36, The Stationery Office, 2001, Table 7.1

POOR HEALTH AND DEATH RATES

The poorest GB countries/regions have poorer health and higher death rates, as shown by Figure 8.3 and Table 8.5.

Table 8.5 shows death rates, including infant mortality (deaths under the age of one), by NHS regions (not the Government Office regions).[5]

POVERTY IN THE SMALL NATIONS

In this section child poverty in the small nations is considered (as indicated by numbers below half average incomes; in workless households; free school meals entitlement), followed by poverty in each nation in turn.

Of the countries, Wales and Northern Ireland had the greatest child poverty; Wales had the highest proportion of children living in households below half average income and the highest proportion of children living in households without work.

However, Northern Ireland had the highest proportion of children eligible for free school meals (one in four). In all countries, data for primary schools reveals that more pupils were eligible for a meal than took it up.

SCOTLAND

About a quarter of poor Scots live in rural areas, but there are also notable concentrations in Glasgow.[6] A major cause of poverty has been unemployment and economic inactivity, particularly due to the erosion of manufacturing industries from the early 1980s.[7]

Scots have a higher risk of premature death, especially in the Glasgow area.[8] Scotland also has a higher proportion of hypothermia cases per head of population than England and Wales, and more excess winter deaths in the coldest part of the year.[9] An estimated 750,000 households are unable to afford adequate warmth in the home.[10]

There has also been an increase in the number of people in Scotland on very low incomes – below 40 per cent of the average (after housing costs) – the highest risk being for lone parents and pensioners, the lowest being for couples without children.[11]

In 1999/2000, 29 per cent of children in Scotland lived in households with below half mean incomes AHC (excluding self-employed), lower than the GB average (32 per cent), though on the before housing costs (BHC) measure Scotland had a higher proportion of children in poverty than GB as a whole.[12]

WALES

Two-thirds of the Welsh population lives in South Wales, where levels of deprivation are high. Wales has higher inactivity rates and sickness levels than England.

- In 1997–98, one in five Welshmen (21 per cent) was economically inactive, compared with 15 per cent in England.
- Illness rates were a fifth higher in 1998 than in 1991, with over 34 per cent reporting a limiting long-term illness – higher in some areas (43 per cent in Merthyr Tydfil and 41 per cent in Blaenau Gwent).[13]

Fewer people are employed in Wales (68 per cent) compared with GB as a whole (73 per cent), and employment rates are even lower in some areas (60 per cent in Merthyr Tydfil and 58 per cent in Blaenau Gwent).[14]

In 1999/2000, Wales had a higher proportion of individuals with incomes below 50 per cent of the mean; income distribution in Wales is skewed towards the bottom, with only 14 per cent of individuals in the top fifth (AHC). Benefits make up a larger proportion of total gross income in Wales than in England or Scotland.

- Children in Wales are more at risk of living on a low income than the rest of GB: 36 per cent of children in Wales lived in households below 50 per cent of the mean (AHC) (excluding self-employed).
- Wales had the highest proportion of working-age people below all income thresholds.[15]

NORTHERN IRELAND

As many statistics are GB-based, Northern Ireland is often excluded from a wider analysis. It is the smallest UK territory, with a younger population containing a higher proportion of children and lone parents. There are long-standing demographic differences between the two communities, the Catholic community being younger with larger

TABLE 8.6: **Percentage of children below 50% mean income after housing costs in GB countries, excluding self-employed, 1999/2000**

	Below 50% mean %	Total children millions
England	32	9.8
Scotland	29	0.9
Wales	36	0.6
GB	32	11.3

Source: Department of Social Security, *Households Below Average Income 1999/2000*, 2001

TABLE 8.7: **Proportion of children living in workless households by UK country, 1999**

England	18%
Scotland	17%
Wales	21%
Northern Ireland	19%
UK	18%

Source: House of Commons Library, *Regional Social Exclusion Indicators*, Research Paper 00/71, 3 August 2000, revised

TABLE 8.8: **Eligibility and take-up of free school meals in primary schools, 1999/2000**

	% eligible	% receiving meals
England	18.3	15.0
Scotland	21.7	17.9
Wales	21.8	20.5
Northern Ireland	24.0	15.0

Sources: Scottish Executive, *School Annual Survey of School Meals 1999-00*;
National Assembly for Wales, *Schools in Wales: general statistics, 1999*;
Department for Education and Employment, *Education Statistics: schools in England 2000*; Northern Ireland Department of Education communication, 2000

average household size. The Catholic community has incomes 15 per cent lower than Protestant households, largely as a result of the greater dependency on social security benefits (30 per cent compared with 18 per cent).

Northern Ireland is the poorest country; even at the top tenth of incomes, households in Northern Ireland received only 81 per cent of the UK equivalent in 1998,[16] when earnings for both men and women in manual occupations were lower than in other parts of the UK.[17] There are also fewer high earners:

- The proportion earning more than £20,000 a year was four percentage points lower than in the UK, while the proportion earning below £7,5000 was 2 per cent higher than in the UK.
- The average annual net income in Northern Ireland (£10,700) was lower than the UK average (£11,800).[18]

POVERTY IN THE CAPITAL CITY

As the capital, London attracts much wealth, but also has many of the features of inner city poverty, such as high death rates. Between 1981 and 1991, death rates in the most deprived wards had risen by a quarter, whereas those in affluent areas fell by 20 per cent.[19]

On a measure after housing costs, in 1999/2000, 27 per cent of individuals in London were in the bottom fifth of incomes, but there were more in the top fifth (26 per cent) than the England average (21 per cent).[20] Before housing costs the proportions were 20 per cent in the bottom fifth and 28 per cent in the top. London also had a bigger earnings gap; in 1997 the highest paid tenth of employees earned 4.5 times more than the poorest tenth.[21]

Inner London had over twice the proportion of primary school pupils taking free school meals as the England average; in 2000, 32.9 per cent of children in Inner London received free school meals, although 39.5 per cent were eligible, compared with Outer London where 15.6 per cent received meals and 19.3 per cent were eligible.[22]

In 1999, 27 per cent of children lived in workless households – the highest proportion within UK countries/regions.[23] In 2000, unemployment in some London boroughs was more than three times higher than for Greater London overall; 14.6 per cent in Haringey compared with the London average of 4.5 per cent.[24]

POVERTY AT LOCAL LEVEL

Many districts contain 'pockets' of deprivation in inner city areas and social housing estates, although in other areas it can be spread more thinly.[25] As poverty and inequality grew during the 1980s and 1990s, people on low incomes became more concentrated in poor areas, with the gap between richer and poorer wards widening.[26]

BRITISH PARLIAMENTARY CONSTITUENCIES

More statistics are being produced at constituency level. One example is the *Human Development Report* on the UK, using the United Nation's (UN) Human Poverty Index.[27]

The UN Human Poverty Index for industrialised countries (HPI-2) consists of the following indicators:

1. The percentage of people not expected to survive to age 60.
2. The long-term unemployment rate (12 months or more).
3. The percentage of people living below the income poverty line (50 per cent of median disposable income).
4. The functional illiteracy rate.

DISTRICTS AND WARDS

The former Department of the Environment, Transport and the Regions (DETR) developed deprivation indicators for English districts and wards, most recently in 2000. While the earlier 1998 Index consisted of 12 equally weighted indicators covering crime, housing, health and incomes, the revised 2000 Index comprised 33 indicators, with different weightings across six different 'domains'.[28] These domains and weightings are:

Income	25%
Employment	25%
Health deprivation and disability	15%
Education, skills and training	15%
Geographical access to services	10%
Housing	10%

Districts and wards can be ranked according to the extent and concentration of indicators in these domains. The top ten districts (ie, the most

TABLE 8.9: **Poorest and least poor British parliamentary constituencies according to HPI-2 indicators**

	HPI-2 indicator				
	1	2	3	4	HPI-2
10 poorest					
Glasgow Shettleston	27.2	2.3	35	26	27.1
Glasgow Springburn	25.3	2.6	34	25	26.0
Glasgow Maryhill	23.4	2.5	34	25	25.8
Birmingham Ladywood	18.6	2.9	35	27	25.7
Manchester Central	21.4	2.5	34	23	24.7
Camberwell and Peckham	17.1	2.6	34	25	24.6
Glasgow Bailleston	21.6	2.1	33	24	24.5
Liverpool Riverside	21.4	3.3	35	20	24.5
Hackney South/Shoreditch	17.0	2.3	34	23	24.0
Bethnal Green and Bow	17.8	1.6	32	24	23.6
10 least poor					
Beaconsfield	9.4	2.0	9	10	8.6
Rayleigh	9.7	1.9	8	10	8.5
North East Hampshire	9.2	1.2	9	10	8.4
Romsey	8.5	1.9	9	10	8.3
Chesham and Amersham	8.8	1.6	8	10	8.3
Buckingham	9.2	1.8	9	9	8.2
Woodspring	8.4	1.1	8	10	8.1
Cheadle	9.2	1.3	8	9	7.9
Northavon	9.1	0.9	8	9	7.9
Wokingham	8.4	1.0	7	9	7.5

Note: 1-4 refer to the numbered indicators on page 183

Source: J Seymour, *Poverty in Plenty: a human development report for the UK*, UNED-UK, 2000

deprived) on the income scale tend to be mainly in the North and Midlands, whereas London appears more prominent on combined deprivation indicators. The *extent* order shows the most deprived districts according to the percentage of the population in wards that rank within the most deprived 10 per cent of wards in England.

In 1998, the Social Exclusion Unit (SEU) found that 44 English local authority districts had the highest concentrations of deprivation according to the DETR's 1998 Index, which, compared to the rest of England, included:

TABLE 8.10: **Top ten English districts ranked by income, combined deprivation and extent of deprivation, DETR Index 2000**

Income ranking	Combined ranking	Extent ranking
1. Birmingham	1. Tower Hamlets	1. Hackney
2. Liverpool	2. Hackney	2. Tower Hamlets
3. Manchester	3. Newham	3. Newham
4. Leeds	4. Easington	4. Manchester
5. Bradford	5. Liverpool	5. Knowsley
6. Sheffield	6. Knowsley	6. Easington
7. Newham	7. Manchester	7. Liverpool
8. Kirklees	8. Islington	8. Middlesborough
9. Sandwell	9. Southwark	9. Islington
10. Nottingham	10. Hartlepool	10. South Tyneside

Source: derived from the 2000 *Index of Deprivation* at district level

- nearly two-thirds more unemployment;
- almost one and a half times more lone-parent households;
- a quarter more children without a single GCSE;
- 30 per cent higher death rates;
- two to three times the levels of poor housing, vandalism and dereliction.[29]

The SEU has subsequently suggested that between 20 and 30 per cent of all wards in England could have rates of worklessness and child poverty of *double* the national average.[30]

POVERTY IN RURAL AREAS

Rural poverty is more dispersed and therefore more hidden, reinforced by a mistaken belief that poverty is an urban problem. An analysis of the British Household Panel Survey (BHPS) between 1991 and 1996 indicated that 30 per cent of rural households had experienced poverty, compared with 40 per cent in urban areas; periods on a low income were shorter, and fewer were 'persistently poor'.[31]

However, the gap between rich and poor may be wider in rural areas; in one Wiltshire village, 40 per cent of households had annual incomes of over £40,000 while a further 40 per cent had incomes below £8,000.[32]

Rural unemployment tends to be lower (4.2 per cent compared with 6.1 per cent in England in 1998). However, one study found a mismatch between people's skills and the jobs available, together with difficulties getting to work and the costs of working, including transport and childcare.

> 'So I was in a bit of a catch-22 situation, I couldn't get a job, I couldn't get a car until I got a job and I couldn't get a job until I got a car.' (Andrew, Lincs).[33]

Young people were also affected by poor transport and lack of affordable housing; living in the parental home tended to disguise personal poverty, and parents only nominally received 'digs money'.[34]

Low-income children in rural areas have expressed feelings of isolation, boredom and a growing conflict with adults, perhaps as a result of the more restricted opportunities locally; nearly half of children on low incomes had no family car.[35]

Factors influencing rural poverty include more older people retiring to these areas, and the prevalence of low pay.[36] The latter is more common in rural areas, fewer people escaping from low pay if employed in smaller rural workplaces.[37] The *New Earnings Survey* showed that, in 2000, average gross weekly pay in agriculture was £286.30, over 30 per cent lower than the national average for all industries (£410.60).[38]

CONCLUSION

A precise 'geography of poverty' is hard to define, as regions, countries and large cities contain wide variations in poverty and wealth, and even idyllic rural areas contain poverty, although often less visible.

With devolution to countries within the UK, and more powers to bodies at regional level, better information may emerge about poverty within these areas and aid the process of policy development.

NOTES

1 Department of Social Security, *Households Below Average Income 1999/2000*, Corporate Document Services, 2001

2 Cabinet Office, *Sharing the Nation's Prosperity: variation in economic and social conditions across the UK*, report to the Prime Minister, December 1999

3 D Gordon et al, *Poverty and Social Exclusion in Britain*, Joseph Rowntree Foundation, 2000

4 Trades Union Congress, *The Regional Jobs Divide*, March 2000

5 Before their reorganisation in 1999 – see *Regional Trends* 35, p239

6 House of Commons, Scottish Affairs Select Committee, *Poverty in Scotland*, HC 59-I, July 2000

7 See note 6

8 M Shaw et al, *The Widening Gap: health inequalities and policy in Britain*, The Policy Press, 1999

9 Scottish Poverty Information Unit, *Poverty in Scotland 1999*, Glasgow Caledonian University, 1999

10 See note 6

11 P Kenway, and M Rahman, *Indicators of Poverty in Scotland: a report for the Joseph Rowntree Foundation*, New Policy Institute, 2000

12 See note 1

13 The National Assembly for Wales, *Welsh Health Survey 1998*, 1999

14 Department of Social Security evidence to the House of Commons Select Committee on Welsh Affairs Inquiry into Social Exclusion in Wales, 1999/00

15 See note 1

16 T Wong and M Morrissey, *Just How Poor is Northern Ireland? A review of the data*, Northern Ireland Anti-Poverty Network, 1999

17 E Bradley (ed), *Northern Ireland Annual Abstract of Statistics 1999*, Northern Ireland Statistics and Research Agency, 1999

18 P Geddis (ed), *Focus on Northern Ireland: a statistical profile*, Northern Ireland Statistics and Research Agency, 1997

19 P Edwards and J Flatley, *The Capital Divided: mapping poverty and social exclusion in London*, London Research Centre, 1996

20 See note 1

21 London Research Centre, *Monitoring Poverty and Social Exclusion in London*, July 1998

22 Department for Education and Employment, *Statistics of Education: schools in England*, 2000

23 House of Commons Library, *Regional Social Exclusion Indicators*, Research Paper 00/71, 3 August 2000, revised

24 National Statistics, *Labour Market Trends*, August 2000, Table C.22

25 G Smith, *Area-Based Initiatives: the rationale and options for area targeting*, CASE paper 25 May 1999

26 Described in J Hills, *Inquiry into Income and Wealth*, Vol 2, Joseph Rowntree Foundation, 1995

27 J Seymour, *Poverty in Plenty: a human development report for the UK*, UNED-UK, 2000

28 Department of the Environment, Transport and the Regions, *Indices of Deprivation 2000*, Regeneration Research Summary No 21, 2000

29 Social Exclusion Unit, *Bringing Britain Together: a national strategy for neighbourhood renewal*, Cm 4045, September 1998

30 Social Exclusion Unit, *National Strategy for Neighbourhood Renewal: a framework for consultation*, Cabinet Office, April 2000

31 P Chapman et al, *Poverty and Exclusion in Rural Areas: the dynamics of low income and employment*, Joseph Rowntree Foundation, 1998

32 P Milbourne et al, *Poverty and Social Exclusion in Wiltshire*, Cheltenham and Gloucester College of Higher Education, quoted in Performance and Innovation Unit, *Rural Economies Report*, Cabinet Office, December 1999

33 S Monk et al, *Finding Work in Rural Areas: bridges and barriers*, Joseph Rowntree Foundation, 1999

34 S Pavis, S Platt and G Hubbard, *Young People in Rural Scotland: pathways to social inclusion and exclusion*, Joseph Rowntree Foundation, 2000

35 J Davis and T Ridge, *Same Scenery, Different Lifestyle: rural children on a low income*, The Children's Society, 1997

36 Performance and Innovation Unit, *Rural Economies Report*, Cabinet Office, December 1999

37 See note 31

38 National Statistics, *New Earnings Survey 2000: Part A: Streamlined analyses*, 2000

9 International comparisons

The persistence of child poverty in rich countries undermines both equality of opportunity and commonality of values. It therefore confronts the industrialised world with a test of both its ideals and of its capacity to resolve many of its intractable social problems.
(*A League Table of Child Poverty in Rich Nations*, UNICEF, 2000)

Many countries experienced rising inequality during the 1980s and early 1990s. The Joseph Rowntree Foundation's *Inquiry into Income and Wealth* found that, during the 1980s and early 1990s:

- not all countries experienced greater inequality, but it increased in most;
- the rise in inequality in the UK was faster than in any other country except New Zealand;
- the UK's level of income inequality was in the middle of the range of 11 countries;
- increasingly wide earnings dispersion was a major cause of rising inequality in the USA, Canada and the UK;
- the tax and benefit systems in Australia, Canada, France and Germany acted as a brake on growing inequalities, contrasting with other countries like the UK, Sweden and the USA.[1]

Since then, more data has emerged (such as from the European Household Panel and the Luxembourg Income Study of industrialised countries), highlighting the persistence of inequality in some nations, and the differences between them.

In this chapter trends across the European Union are examined. Poverty in other industrialised countries and across the world is also considered.

THE EUROPEAN UNION

Looking at trends in Gross Domestic Product (GDP) per head, the European Union (EU) countries differ, ranging from the highly industrialised, like Germany, to those, such as Greece, Portugal and Spain, with large agricultural sectors. There are also large in-country differences. In 1999, 12 per cent of the workforce in Southern Italy worked in agriculture compared with 5.4 per cent in Italy as a whole.[2] GDP per head in this region was 64 per cent of the EU average, in Italy as a whole 101 per cent of the EU average.

TABLE 9.1: **European Union GDP per head, 1998**

EU	100
Austria	112
Belgium	111
Denmark	119
Finland	102
France	99
Germany	108
Greece	66
Ireland	108
Italy	101
Luxembourg	176
Netherlands	113
Portugal	75
Spain	81
Sweden	102
UK	102

Source: National Statistics, *Regional Trends* 36, 2001, Table 2.3

PATTERNS OF POVERTY IN THE EUROPEAN UNION

The data available for poverty in Europe comes from the European Commission (Eurostat). The definition of 'poverty' is based on a 'statistical percentage' approach, as described in Chapter 1. Thresholds differ, but most commonly 50 per cent or 60 per cent of the median or

TABLE 9. 2: **Percentage in poverty in the European Union, 1988 and 1995**

	1988	1995
EU-14	n/a	17
EUR-12	15	n/a
Belgium	9	17
Denmark	4	11
Finland	n/a	12
France	17	16
Germany	12	16
Greece	21	21
Ireland	19	18
Italy	22	19
Luxembourg	12	12
Netherlands	5	12
Portugal	25	22
Spain	18	21
UK	15	19

Source: European Anti-Poverty Network, *Poverty in Europe*, 2000

mean equivalised net income is used for European comparisons.[3] The definition of 'poverty' used in Table 9.2 is *household incomes below 50 per cent of the average* within a country, though figures for the late 1980s are based on expenditure rather than income levels.

During the 1980s, poverty increased in all of the then 12 member states of the European Community, with Italy, Germany and the UK experiencing the sharpest rises.[4] Eurostat figures released in 2000 for 1995 showed that 62 million individuals were poor.[5]

Whatever the threshold, countries like Denmark, the Netherlands and Germany have the lowest proportion of their population in poverty – Greece, Spain and Portugal the highest.

In 1995, there were three times more lone parents among the low-income population than in the European population as a whole (six times more than in the general population in the UK).[6] Similarly, EU unemployed people were three times more likely to be living on a low income (four times in the UK). The smallest difference between

TABLE 9.3: **Poverty rates in the European Union, 1994**
(percentage of the population)

	60% of median	50% of median	50% of mean
EU	20.5	13.6	18.5
Austria	17.7	12.1	15.0
Belgium	18.4	11.4	15.7
Denmark	9.7	4.4	6.3
France	16.6	9.9	14.0
Germany	17.9	10.9	14.7
Greece	21.1	14.9	21.1
Ireland	22.2	9.4	24.8
Italy	19.4	12.5	17.2
Luxembourg	15.0	9.5	14.7
Netherlands	10.1	5.2	7.6
Portugal	22.5	15.9	24.0
Spain	21.2	14.7	20.7
UK	20.9	11.6	22.6

Source: C Blum, 'Income: disparities and poverty', Social Portrait of Europe, Eurostat, 1998

unemployed people in the low-income population compared with the population overall was in Denmark.

The EU poor in 1993 consisted of:

- 35 per cent of working people;
- 33 per cent of pensioners;
- 36 per cent of lone parents with children under age 16;
- 20 per cent of children (highest in the UK – 32 per cent – and lowest in Denmark – 5 per cent).

The largest groups living in poverty were people over age 65 living alone (19 per cent of the poor) followed by childless couples (18 per cent).[7]

The European Household Panel also contains information about households lacking basic essentials. In 1995, 59 per cent of households in Portugal could not afford a holiday, compared with 11 per cent in Germany.[8]

TABLE 9.4: **Households in the European Union lacking items and unable to make ends meet, 1995**
(per cent)

	Cannot afford a week's holiday	Cannot afford new clothes	Difficulty making ends meet
Austria	24	10	54
Belgium	28	12	42
Denmark	15	5	31
France	32	9	51
Germany	11	14	30
Greece	50	32	78
Ireland	38	8	60
Italy	38	15	68
Luxembourg	13	5	17
Netherlands	14	13	31
Portugal	59	47	78
Spain	46	8	63
UK	42	16	62

Source: C Blum, 'Income: disparities and poverty', *Social Portrait of Europe*, Eurostat, 1998

INCOME AND INCOME INEQUALITY IN THE EUROPEAN UNION

Income inequality rose in most EU countries between 1980 and 1995. In 1994, the top tenth of the income distribution received ten times more of the total income than the bottom fifth.[9] The inequality gap was widest in Greece, Spain and Portugal, with Ireland and the UK around the EU average.

Table 9.5 shows two measures of inequality across EU countries, also used in Chapter 7:

- **P90/P10**: the ratio of the top tenth in the income distribution to the bottom tenth (90th percentile to the 10th percentile).
- **The Gini co-efficient**: a more general measure of inequality, where the higher the figure, the greater the inequality.

These measures place the UK at a little above average, only behind Greece, Spain, Portugal and Ireland.

TABLE 9.5: **Inequality measures in the European Union**

	P90/P10	Gini co-efficient
EU	4.5	0.322
Austria	4.1	0.297
Belgium	3.9	0.296
Denmark	2.6	0.227
France	3.7	0.290
Germany	3.9	0.296
Greece	5.3	0.351
Ireland	4.6	0.357
Italy	4.4	0.314
Luxembourg	4.0	0.304
Netherlands	3.0	0.247
Portugal	5.6	0.368
Spain	4.9	0.340
UK	4.5	0.345

Source: C Blum, 'Income: disparities and poverty', *Social Portrait of Europe*, Eurostat, 1998

EMPLOYMENT AND UNEMPLOYMENT IN THE EUROPEAN UNION

Although the number of people employed has been climbing since 1995, more than three million jobs were lost in the EU between 1991 and 1996, and unemployment grew from 13.6 million to 18.2 million.[10] In 1999 the UK had the highest proportion of children in workless households in the EU.[11]

Employment rates in Europe also varied between member states. In 1999/2000, the UK was above average in the employment rate and below average for unemployment (as measured by the International Labour Organisation (ILO) definition).[12]

TABLE 9.6: **European employment and ILO unemployment rates 2000**

(per cent)

	Employment rate	ILO unemployment rate
EU-15	65.3	7.6
EUR-11 (in euro)	63.5	8.3
Austria	70.3	3.9
Belgium	63.2	6.8
Denmark	78.3	4.3
Finland	70.2	9.0
France	63.7	8.5
Germany	68.4	7.9
Greece	57.8	11.1
Ireland	65.7	3.8
Italy	55.5	9.4
Luxembourg	64.9	2.5
Netherlands	75.1	2.2
Portugal	69.5	4.4
Spain	56.4	13.0
Sweden	72.3	4.7
UK	74.6	5.1

Source: National Statistics, *Labour Market Statistics*, October 2001

POVERTY IN INDUSTRIALISED NATIONS

Children are kept in poverty not by a padlock to which there is a single key but by a combination lock that requires an alignment of factors if it is to be released.

(*A League Table of Child Poverty in Rich Nations*, UNICEF, 2000)

Some of the worst levels of child poverty exist in the richest countries of the world. A UNICEF study of 23 countries in the Organisation for Economic Co-operation and Development (OECD) showed that, in the 1990s:

- one in six children – 47 million – were living in poverty (defined as below 50 per cent of the national median);
- child poverty rates in the richest nations varied from 3 per cent to over 25 per cent;

- a child was four times more likely to be poor if living in a lone-parent family;
- poverty rates were not related to the proportion of lone-parent families in the countries;
- poverty was higher where there were more workless and low-paid households (where full-time workers earned less than two-thirds of the national median wage.[13]

In the league table for child poverty (defined as income below 50 per cent of the national median), the bottom four places were occupied by:

- the UK;
- Italy;
- the USA;
- Mexico.

The UNICEF report also analysed the duration of child poverty in six OECD countries, tracking the poorest fifth of families over a period of years.

- In all countries, around six or seven out of ten children in the poorest fifth remained there the next year, and between 6 and 9 per cent were poor for five consecutive years.
- US children were least likely to move out of poverty.

Another analysis of child poverty in 25 nations in 1999 showed a similarly wide variation.[14] The poverty measures were: half of the median income for all persons within a country; half of the median for children only (ie, a child is poor if her/his disposable income is below

TABLE 9.7: **The persistence of child poverty in six OECD countries**
% of children in the poorest fifth

	in 1 year	in 2 consecutive years	in all 5	in all 10
Ireland	20	13	–	–
Spain	20	13	–	–
Hungary	20	13	7	–
UK	20	14	6	–
Germany	20	14	6	5
USA	20	14	9	6

Source: UNICEF, *A League Table of Child Poverty in Rich Nations*, June 2000

half of that of the average child); and the US official poverty line. Here we concentrate on the measures of adult and child median (see Chapter 1 for a critique of different approaches).

- On 50 per cent of the *overall* median, the UK was ranked as third worst, after Russia and the USA, with over a fifth of children in poverty, and greater child poverty than countries like Taiwan.
- For most countries child poverty was about a third lower when measured against the *child* rather than the adult median, as children's

TABLE 9.8: **Child poverty rates in 25 countries by adult and child median**

Country	Year	50% overall median	50% child median
Russia	1995	26.6	25.4
USA	1994	26.3	18.6
UK	1995	21.3	11.0
Italy	1995	21.2	15.7
Australia	1994	17.1	11.0
Canada	1994	16.0	11.2
Ireland	1987	14.8	6.5
Israel	1992	14.7	10.3
Poland	1992	14.2	10.9
Spain	1990	13.1	9.7
Germany	1994	11.6	7.1
Hungary	1994	11.5	10.1
France	1989	9.8	6.8
Netherlands	1991	8.4	5.8
Switzerland	1982	6.3	3.9
Taiwan	1995	6.3	4.1
Luxembourg	1994	6.3	1.9
Belgium	1992	6.1	4.2
Denmark	1992	5.9	5.1
Austria	1987	5.6	3.3
Norway	1995	4.5	3.5
Sweden	1992	3.7	3.2
Finland	1991	3.4	2.5
Slovakia	1992	2.2	1.5
Czech Republic	1992	1.8	1.6

Source: B Bradbury and M Jantti, *Child Poverty Across Industrialised Nations*, Innocenti Occasional papers No 71, September 1999

incomes are lower; there were however differences, for instance between Russia (where child median was high) and the UK and Ireland (where child averages were relatively low).

Although children were generally more likely to be poor if living with a lone mother, variations in rates of lone motherhood could not explain the differences. The authors concluded that higher market incomes (through access to paid work) marked out countries with the lowest levels of child poverty, so low pay and worklessness may be significant factors in the UK.

The association between employment rates and poverty was also explored in another study of OECD countries.[15] Working-age poverty was concentrated in workless households, the greatest risk being in the UK, USA and Canada.

Countries with fewest low-paid workers also had low poverty rates overall. Using the OECD definition of low pay (66 per cent of the median gross wage), countries like Belgium, Finland and Sweden had fewer than 10 per cent of full-year, full-time workers who were low

TABLE 9.9: **Poverty rates in workless households in OECD countries**

% in poverty

	Single workless adult	Workless couples
Australia	65.6	47.5
Belgium	16.1	18.0
Canada	63.7	46.5
Denmark	20.1	7.9
Finland	30.3	8.9
France	32.5	25.6
Germany	44.2	32.4
Italy	27.1	23.5
Netherlands	27.8	17.1
Norway	28.3	11.2
Spain	28.7	27.3
Sweden	32.4	13.6
UK	57.7	52.3
USA	72.8	48.9

Source: I Marx, 'Low Pay and Poverty in OECD Countries', Employment Audit, Issue 10, Winter 1999

paid, and in France, Germany and the Netherlands, 15 per cent were low paid. In contrast, in the UK, about one in five full-time workers was low paid.

The UK has also been ranked 16th out of 18 OECD countries for which the Human Poverty Index was estimated (see below), putting the UK third from bottom.[16] An important factor in this poor ranking seemed to be the high rates of illiteracy, with more than a fifth of the population unable to read instructions on a medicine bottle, fill out a form or read a bedtime story to a child.

In comparison to countries with similar levels of income and average human development, the UK has more serious problems of gender disparities in empowerment, human poverty, income poverty and income inequalities.[17]

POVERTY ACROSS THE WORLD

Chapter 1 highlighted the need for better tools to identify who is poor and what needs to be done. Poverty in developing countries can be seen as different from the industrialised world, but increasingly there are parallels between 'North and South'[18] within research and policy debates, where causes and consequences can be similar.

To date, the UN has devised a 'Human Development Index' (HDI) to rank countries, and from 1997 included a 'Human Poverty Index' (HPI).

> *Human development* focuses on expanding capabilities important for all people, capabilities so basic that that their lack forecloses other choices. *Human poverty* focuses on the lack of these same capabilities – to live a long, healthy and creative life, to be knowledgeable, to enjoy a decent standard of living, dignity, self-respect and the respect of others.[19]

While the HDI measures overall progress towards development within a country, the HPI reflects the distribution of progress and the 'backlog of deprivation' that still exists.[20] The HPI has been constructed separately for developing countries (HPI-1) and for industrialised countries (HPI-2), as human deprivation varies with the social and economic conditions of a community, and to reflect the additional data available in the latter countries.

The HPI-1 for developing countries includes indicators such as adult illiteracy rates and the percentage of underweight under-fives. The HPI-2 for industrialised countries includes the percentage of people:

TABLE 9.10: **Number of children in poor and non-poor households in 22 developing countries**
(numbers)

Country	Family characteristics	Poor	Non-poor	All
Argentina	No. of children under 15	3.0	0.4	1.3
Bolivia	''	3.4	1.3	2.3
Brazil	''	3.6	0.8	1.8
Cameroon	% households 6+	59.0	30.0	45.0
Chile	No. of children under 15	2.5	0.9	1.5
Costa Rica	''	3.3	1.0	2.0
Ecuador	''	3.4	1.4	2.9
El Salvador	''	3.7	1.1	2.4
Guyana	No. of children under 17	2.6	1.4	1.8
Honduras	No. of children under 15	4.2	1.7	3.1
Indonesia	No. of children under 9	1.7	n/a	1.2
Malawi	Household size	5.4	4.2	5.0
Mali	''	11.5	9.2	10.4
Mexico	No. of children under 15	4.0	1.1	2.3
Nepal	No. of children under 14	3.5	2.5	n/a
Nicaragua	No. of children under 15	4.9	1.8	3.3
Panama	''	3.2	0.8	1.9
Paraguay	''	4.3	1.3	2.8
Peru	''	3.7	1.1	2.4
Philippines	Household size	6.0	5.0	n/a
Tanzania	''	7.2	5.0	6.0
Uruguay	No. of children under 15	2.8	0.5	1.2

Source: UNICEF, *Poverty Reduction Begins with Children*, March 2000

- born today who are expected to die before age 60;
- whose ability to read and write is not adequate to be functional;
- living below an income poverty line (50 per cent of median personal disposable income);
- who are long-term unemployed (12 months or more).

The international community commonly measures income poverty according to the US $1 a day yardstick (adjusted to local currency using purchasing power parities), though as Chapter 1 points out, there are limitations to this approach.[21] During the 1990s, there was some progress in reducing the proportion of the world's population living in poverty. Between 1990 and 1998 the proportion living in income poverty according to this measure decreased from 29 per cent to 24 per cent. However:

- there are 1.2 billion people living on less than $1 a day in developing countries and 130 million people in OECD countries living below half average income;[22]
- the richest 1 per cent of the world's people received as much income as the poorest 57 per cent;[23]
- a study of 77 countries showed that 45 had experienced widening inequality since the 1950s; only 16 had improved;[24]
- combining the results of household budget surveys across 91 countries, growth in the income share of the top tenth had increased at the expense of the poorest; between 1988 and 1993 the Gini co-efficient increased from 62.5 to 66.0.[25]

Households with more children have a higher risk of being poor. UNICEF has estimated that about half of the 1.2 billion income-poor in developing countries are children, suggesting that 600 million children under 18 live on less than $1 a day, representing 40 per cent of all children in developing countries.[26]

A new generation of anti-poverty plans is needed to focus on 'making growth more pro-poor, target inequality and emphasise empowering the poor.'[27]

CONCLUSION

Poverty and inequality have tended to increase across the EU and industrialised countries, with disparities between and within countries. However, the UK has a record of child poverty which remains among the worst in the EU and other industrialised countries, due partly to high levels of worklessness and low pay. Its ranking according to UN indicators suggests that more progress is needed.

NOTES

1   J Hills, *Inquiry into Income and Wealth*, Vol 2, Joseph Rowntree Foundation, 1995
2   National Statistics, *Regional Trends* 36, 2001
3   C Blum, 'Income: disparities and poverty', in *Social Portrait of Europe*,

Eurostat, 1998

4 For a further discussion of trends during this time, see the 1996 edition of *Poverty: the facts.*

5 European Anti-Poverty Network, *Poverty in Europe*, EAPN, 2000

6 Eurostat, *Social Exclusion in EU Member States: single-parent households and unemployed people particularly exposed*, News Release, 31 January 2000

7 See note 4

8 See note 5

9 See note 5

10 J Recktenwald, 'Labour Market – Creating Jobs and Combating Unemployment: the challenge ahead', in *Social Portrait of Europe*, Eurostat, 1998

11 HM Treasury, *Supporting Children Through the Tax and Benefit System: the modernisation of Britain's tax and benefit system*, Number Five, November 1999

12 Defined as people who are out of work, want a job, have sought work in the past four weeks and are available to start within a fortnight, or are out of work and accepted a job they are waiting to start within a fortnight.

13 UNICEF, *A League Table of Child Poverty in Rich Nations*, Innocenti Report Card Issue No 1, June 2000

14 B Bradbury and M Jantti, *Child Poverty Across Industrialised Nations*, Innocenti Occasional papers No 71, September 1999

15 I Marx, 'Low Pay and Poverty in OECD Countries', *Employment Audit*, Issue 10, Winter 1999

16 J Seymour, *Poverty in Plenty: a human development report for the UK*, UNED-UK, 2000

17 See note 16

18 Terminology in this debate is developing, but the term 'developing countries' is used here, meaning those to which the UN Human Poverty Index -1 applies.

19 United Nations Development Programme, *Human Development Report 2000*, Oxford University Press, 2000

20 See note 19

21 United Nations Development Programme, *Human Development Report 2001*, Oxford University Press, 2001

22 See note 21

23 See note 21

24 UNICEF, *Poverty Reduction Begins with Children*, March 2000

25 Quoted in UNICEF, *Poverty Reduction Begins with Children*, March 2000, p44

26 See note 24

27 United Nations Development Programme, *Overcoming Human Poverty*, Poverty Report 2000, 2000

Conclusion

In setting out the facts about poverty at the beginning of the new century, we have ranged over a considerable amount of data relating to various dimensions of economic and social disadvantage and deprivation. As we said at the beginning of this book, such information has a number of uses, one of which is to feed into and inform the efforts of CPAG and others to influence government policy. In these concluding pages, we shall seek to draw out some of the main lessons and issues which will feature in CPAG's lobbying and campaigning efforts between now and the next edition of this book – and doubtless for some time afterwards. Naturally, there is a close relationship here with the agenda which we sought to promote earlier this year in the run-up to the general election.[1]

MINIMUM INCOME STANDARDS

Lord Morris, speaking in a debate on the Welfare Reform and Pensions Bill in October 2000, made the following point:

> When people apply for income support the Benefits Agency undertakes a means inquiry and then notifies applicants whether or not they are entitled to it. If they are entitled the Agency's letter tells them: '...how much money the law says you need to live on each week'. If they are not entitled the letter says: 'You have more money coming in than the law says you need to live on'. Yet there is no list, quantification or costing by Government of need. The law 'says' but the law does not 'know' because need is not defined. It is a remarkably misleading letter in the absence of any official and empirical research into essential needs to enable the setting of minimum income standards.[2]

This is very well put. If governments are to be serious about eradicating poverty, then they will need targets at which to aim, notably in planning levels of benefits, tax credits, tax thresholds and minimum wages. If financial poverty is to be conceived of in terms of incomes below which ability to participate in the mainstream of society is impaired, then we need to know what these incomes are. Whatever else their uses, the *Households Below Average Income* statistics cannot tell us this. Nor can the current benefit rates. Neither of those sources of information is based on an analysis of need in the context of contemporary living standards and social expectations. As noted in the Introduction and in Chapter 1, we need something which has the credibility of a proven link to broad contemporary public opinion, translated into income levels which can reasonably be expected to permit the ability to participate in mainstream society which we believe should be the right of every citizen.

Obviously, this is not a simple task. Sophisticated research is required to discover and periodically update our knowledge of contemporary public opinions and expectations regarding standards of living. Different family structures need to be taken into account, as do the effects of disabilities. Different sources of data need to be analysed, compared and – we would argue – 'triangulated' to see what they have to tell us about where minimum standards should lie.[3] But it will not do to argue that the task is too difficult and/or too subjective: the research discussed, especially in Chapters 1 and 2, shows that we have the methodology. Of course, it can and should be refined in the light of experience, but the obstacles to the development of such minimum income standards are political rather than technical. This is understandable: governments will worry that a clear picture of the income levels necessary, both in and out of work, to stay out of poverty, will expose existing provision to a harsh glare which would highlight deficiencies and could cause political embarrassment.

On the other hand, politicians might be persuaded to take the view that considerable political credibility could be derived from a willingness to grasp this nettle in an open and honest way. The establishment of clear targets, even if they are some way ahead of reality, need not be a stick with which to beat the Government if the latter is prepared to say that 'we cannot achieve this overnight, but we will make real and steady progress which will be measured and debated as we go along'. The present Government has agreed to targets and to monitoring, but the adoption of minimum income standards would help to achieve the necessary clarity and precision.

We should recognise that there are hazards in this approach: an excessively generous interpretation of needs could undermine the credibility of the process; while an excessively cautious approach could produce minimum standards which were too low and which would exaggerate progress or even achieve 'success' without actually eradicating poverty. The methodology used would need to be both transparent and as objective as possible.

CPAG has pursued these issues over the last few years in the context of its comments on the Government's anti-poverty programme and in particular in its lobbying around the proposed changes to children's benefits and tax credits.[4] If the tax credit strategy is to be, among other things, an instrument to tackle poverty, then the case for clear targets to inform the setting of their levels is surely compelling.

WORK AS A ROUTE OUT OF POVERTY

The Government has introduced an assortment of measures to get more people into paid work and has boosted in-work incomes through the establishment of the statutory minimum wage and its programme of tax credits. Overall, great emphasis has been laid on paid work as the main route out of poverty. It is indeed true that, if a person escapes poverty, finding a job is frequently the reason. But this does not mean that the Government's anti-poverty strategy can be based exclusively on 'welfare to work' policies. Economic fluctuations may mean that the jobs are not there, or they may not be in the right places. Moreover, paid employment is not a viable option for everybody. Aside from elderly people who have retired, there are others who cannot realistically be expected to seek or find work, including many with severe disabilities and others who have caring responsibilities for children or for people who are sick or disabled.

This is not to say that disabled people or carers who are able to and who wish to take up paid work should not be supported and helped to do so. Rather, it is to recognise that paid work cannot always be the answer and that government policy must not ignore those for whom that road is closed or inappropriate.

Caring responsibilities present particular difficulties. At what point does support for carers become undesirable pressure? It remains the case, for example, that lone parents of children under 16 are not required to seek or to be available for paid work as a condition of receiving income support. But compulsory 'work-focused' interviews are increasingly applied. CPAG believes that advice and support of this sort should be available but not imposed. There is also an issue around the age of the child at which jobseeking becomes a compulsory condition for the parent's benefit: some argue that 16 is too high, but some mothers on tough housing estates fear that their children would 'run wild' without a parent to keep an eye on them.[5] How far is it appropriate for the state – and commentators who live in much more comfortable circumstances – to disagree and to seek to enforce that opinion with financial punishment?

The extent to which disabled people and those who care for them will come under pressure of this sort remains to be seen.

We might add that, whether or not the claimant is required to seek work, the penalties for failure to comply with benefit conditions are in need of review, to render them less harsh and keep them to a minimum. Over the years, they have increased considerably both in extent and in severity. Moreover, there is the awkward question, which governments prefer to dodge, of the effects on children. Whatever the rights and wrongs of a given dispute between a parent and the benefit authorities, the child can hardly be held responsible – so the absurd pretence is maintained that children can be insulated from the effects on the family of cuts in their parents' benefits.

Wherever the boundaries are drawn as regards compulsory job-seeking, it will remain necessary to pay serious attention to the living standards of people who are not in paid work. In its early days, the Government seemed unable to see beyond its 'welfare to work' pro-gramme: but this changed as the commitment to tackle poverty among children and pensioners became more established. An even-handed approach must be sustained, tackling poverty both in and out of work.

MEANS-TESTING AND TAX CREDITS

The distinction between benefits and tax allowances always was rather dubious: the old family allowances were benefits and therefore public spending while child tax allowances were not, but when the two were amalgamated in the 1970s to form child benefit, the combined resources were a benefit; the recently defunct mortgage interest tax relief was not a benefit but a tax relief, although it eventually became a payment direct to the lender in most cases; working families' tax credit is accounted as public spending for some purposes and as revenue forgone for others; the projected integrated child credit will be made up partly of former benefits, partly of former tax credits and partly of a former tax allowance.

So the emergence of tax credits is not, as non-specialist commentators sometimes suppose, the creation of a new animal, but rather the re-branding of a very old one – the means-tested benefit. The latter has long been stigmatised and characterised as a symbol of 'dependency', hence the periodic name changes of individual benefits and the occasional invention of different terms for the genre in whole or in part ('income-related benefits' and more recently 'minimum income guarantees'). Tax credits are an attempt to create a non-stigmatised link with the world of work. The argument has sometimes been deployed that they are different because of payment through the wage packet, but couples receiving working families' tax credit have an option for payment to a non-employed main carer; and the integrated child credit will normally be paid to the main carer, regardless of employment status.

If such presentational devices improve take-up, then perhaps we should not carp – but there is a very real objection that means-tested benefits have considerable disadvantages, whatever they are called. It is far from clear that tax credits will be able to overcome the take-up problem. In one form or another (the detail is not yet decided) there will still be the problem of a high 'marginal tax rate' as income rises. Tax credits are still likely to be very complicated and difficult to understand, even after efforts at simplification. And it will be a pleasant surprise if they prove to be free of significant administrative problems.

Thus, while the tax credit strategy may well prove to be a vehicle for channelling greater resources towards families on low incomes, we have to be concerned that government policy is pulling so hard in that direction, especially given the general lack of policy attention paid to national insurance and other non-means-tested benefits. This problem is especially current in the development of the integrated child credit, which has its advantages but where there is a risk to the future of child benefit.[6] Similar concerns apply at the other end of the age range where, as noted in our Introduction, a reliance on private provision combined with means-tested benefits and credits has displaced government interest in the role and future of the basic retirement pension.

INEQUALITY, SOCIAL EXCLUSION AND THE WIDER DIMENSIONS OF POVERTY

We have discussed trends in and types of inequality; the place of income poverty within the wider context of social exclusion; and the other dimensions of poverty – the different deprivations which interact with income poverty and often afflict the same people, such as poor housing, poor health, exposure to crime and educational disadvantage.

CPAG, in addition to its concern with the future of children's benefits and credits, addressed many of these issues in its pre-general election publication, *An End in Sight?*[7] It would be useful to remind ourselves here of the conclusions which were reached there, if we are to focus consistently on the links between facts, analysis and the policies needed to tackle poverty. The contributors to that book were asked to be scrupulously fair in giving the Government credit where deserved and criticism where required. Their conclusions were highly consistent with the information presented in this edition of *Poverty: the facts*.

For example, efforts to tackle disadvantage in the labour market, through improvement and integration of employment services, were welcomed, although there was more to be done, particularly as regards older and/or disabled workers. A more adequate minimum wage, regularly uprated, was also required. The move towards greater compulsion was regretted, very much along the lines of the points made above. This was seen to undermine the good intentions of the Government's overall employment programme.[8]

The verdict regarding educational disadvantage was also mixed. There was an intention to commit greater resources, but too many of the previous Government's policies were still in place, there was a confusing plethora of initiatives requiring rationalisation and a continuing need to prioritise disadvantaged areas, schools and pupils.[9]

The relationship between poverty and ill-health was emphasised and certain groups identified whose health needs required particular attention, including disabled children and their families and young people who are looked after by local authorities or who are homeless. The restoration of benefit entitlements to 16- and 17-year-olds was called for. The ill-effects of educational disadvantage on health were also explored.[10]

The challenge facing the Government in relation to housing was one which had yet to be addressed effectively. There was a need for greater investment in social housing and more robust efforts to tackle homelessness and poor quality accommodation in the private rented sector. The continuing lack of progress in dealing with the problems surrounding the housing benefit scheme was also criticised.[11] The Government, in its second term, is showing signs of putting a lot more energy into housing issues, but there is a great deal to be done in addressing the consequences of decades of neglect.

Housing benefit reform is a question which could, over the next couple of years, become highly controversial in the context of poverty. There are many problems with both the structure and the administration of the scheme, but efforts to solve them are likely to be expensive or to cause significant losses to claimants. Especially in the private rented sector, the current scheme often fails woefully to meet the rents of even the poorest tenants. The Government does not seem to know what to do about this, merely flirting with an alternative system of restrictions, which could be little better.[12] The 'poverty lobby' must get involved in this debate and not be content to leave it to housing finance specialists: housing benefit shortfalls can lead to arrears and homelessness or alternatively cut into money for basic needs in a most cruel way. They should be much higher up the anti-poverty agenda.

An End in Sight? also explored the question of neighbourhood renewal, which was seen to raise important issues both of policy and of practice. There was an interdependence between local and national action which had to be recognised: neither would succeed without the other. Local action, moreover, had to challenge paternalism, avoid stigmatisation of the neighbourhoods concerned and genuinely seek to secure the participation of local people.[13]

The treatment of people from minority ethnic groups, whether members of long-established communities or newly arrived in this country, was seen as open to serious question. There was a need to institute a programme to tackle institutional racism in the delivery of public services, including those contracted out to the private sector. There was also an urgent need to address the scandal of the treatment of refugees and asylum seekers.[14] The Government has recognised the problem of institutional racism and has placed a duty on public bodies to promote equality of opportunity and good race relations.[15] It remains to be seen how successful this will be, but the move is obviously welcome. Less encouraging is the position regarding refugees and asylum seekers, where the announcement of a review of the voucher system represents only limited good news: shameful measures such as dispersal without adequate support and detention in prison-style conditions remain intact.

The policy questions raised in our pre-election work and the information brought together in this edition of *Poverty: the facts* therefore complement each other, painting a mixed picture of varying degrees of progress but enormous problems still to be overcome.

THE FUTURE

In the coming months and years, more research will be published and more information will appear in relation to financial poverty and associated deprivations. Existing findings and information will be updated. The debate will also move on, as concepts are questioned, disagreements aired and common ground identified. The growing internationalisation of the economy may also be accompanied by a more developed international perspective in the poverty debate. Considerable advances are being made in our understanding of the nature and consequences of poverty.

However, while information, analysis and debate can and should inform anti-poverty action, they should never be allowed to substitute for it.

Moreover, we need to anticipate possible setbacks. We currently have a Government which has declared itself committed to abolishing child poverty; a Chancellor of the Exchequer with a strong personal interest in the issue; and economic circumstances which are still relatively favourable. Any or all of these things could change. Again, as we said before the general election, the best way of ensuring the continuation of an anti-poverty agenda in government is to try to achieve a profile for this issue high enough to make it very difficult for any administration to get away with neglecting it. CPAG will be working to that end.

Writing in the previous (1996) edition of this book, CPAG's then Director, Sally Witcher, argued that: 'There is no reason – except an absence of political will – why, by the year 2000, we should not be able to report that both the numbers living in poverty and the depth of their poverty have decreased. But that would still not be enough. CPAG wants more for children than survival. They need access to opportunities – to education to reach their full potential, to proper health care and safe places to play. Most crucially, they and their families need sufficient income to allow them to participate in the normal, everyday activities that others take for granted.'[16]

The political will seems at last to be materialising – but there is still a long way to go. Let us hope that the next edition of *Poverty: the facts* is able to report on a markedly improved state of affairs. And through our lobbying and campaigning activity, locally as well as nationally, let us do our best to create and sustain the climate of public debate and opinion which will permit this to happen.

NOTES

1 See G Fimister (ed), *An End in Sight? Tackling child poverty in the UK*, CPAG, 2001

2 Lord Morris of Manchester, House of Lords, *Hansard*, 11 October 2000, cols 155-6

3 See J Veit-Wilson, 'Triangulation of Data from Existing Sources as a Basis for a Governmental Minimum Income Standard', memorandum published in *Integrated Child Credit*, Second Report of Session 2000-2001, House of Commons Social Security Committee, The Stationery Office, March 2001

4 See for example, M Barnes and G Fimister, 'Memorandum Submitted by the Child Poverty Action Group', in *Integrated Child Credit*, Second Report of Session 2000-2001, House of Commons Social Security Committee, The Stationery Office, March 2001

5 A point made forcefully to one of the authors of this book (G Fimister) at a meeting with mothers on low incomes in Newcastle upon Tyne, 1998.

6 See note 4, section 5

7 See note 1

8 See note 1, Chapter 3: R Exell, 'Employment and Poverty'

9 See note 1, Chapter 4: G Smith and T Smith, 'Excellence, Diversity and Inequality in Education'

10 See note 1, Chapter 5: M Shaw, D Dorling, D Gordon and G Davey Smith, 'Health and Poverty'

11 See note 1, Chapter 6: M Waters, 'Housing Under New Labour'

12 See G Fimister, 'Fimister's Focus' column, *Benefit*, vol. 7 no. 8, Institute of Revenues, Rating and Valuation, August 2001

13 See note 1, Chapter 7: P Alcock, 'Neighbourhood Renewal'

14 See note 1, Chapter 8: G Craig, 'Race and New Labour'

15 A Travis, 'Public Sector Forced to Tackle Racism', *Guardian*, 21 February 2001

16 S Witcher, Foreword, *Poverty: the facts*, CPAG, 1996, p viii

Index